Light to the Isles

A study of missionary theology
in Celtic and early Anglo-Saxon Britain

Douglas Dales

The Lutterworth Press

Cambridge

"Auditem insulae; et attendite, populi de longe. . . .
Ecce dedi te in lucem gentium, ut sis salus mea
usque ad extremum terrae"

Isaiah il, 1-6

British Library Cataloguing in Publication Data:
A catalogue record is available from the British Library.

Published by:
The Lutterworth Press
P.O. Box 60
Cambridge
CB1 2NT
England

ISBN 0 7188 2965 4

Printed in Great Britain by
St Edmundsbury Press Limited, Bury St Edmunds, Suffolk.

Contents

FOREWORD by Benedicta Ward, SLG

A people without history
Is not redeemed from time, for history is a pattern
Of timeless moments.   T.S.Eliot Four Quartets, 'East Coker'

The coming of Augustine from Italy to the English in Kent and that of
Aidan from Iona to the peoples north of the Humber must be counted
among the 'timeless moments' which form the pattern of the history of
these islands. Their work was recorded in the pages of the incomparable
historian, Bede, where their preaching 'by word and by example' was
presented as the new beginning of Christianity in the *alter orbis* of Britain.

The mission in the south of England was marked by the zeal of Gregory
the Great, whom Bede in his *Ecclesiastical History* affectionately called
'our apostle', the pope who earnestly longed to come to England himself,
and who eventually sent the monk Augustine with a band of forty companions. They were motivated not by force or ambition or even converting
fervour of a narrow kind but by the flame of charity which desires to
communicate the greatest of gifts to others:

They came . . . bearing as their standard a silver cross and the image of
our Lord and Saviour painted on a panel. They . . . uttered prayers to
the Lord . . . for the salvation of those for whom and to whom they
had come.

They spent the first weeks in prayer in the church of St Martin in Canterbury, thus linking themselves with Martin of Tours, the earlier monk-mis-
sionary of Gaul. The presence there of Bertha, the Christian queen, and
their contact with her pagan husband, Aethelbert, began the link between
church and state which was to prove so fruitful for both. A similar pattern
can be seen in the North, where Aidan preached and prayed and baptised in
close friendship with the kings and queens, and with the same loving care;
indeed, he had volunteered to go to the Northumbrians to replace a more
stern predecessor, and 'offer them the milk of simpler teaching'. (Bede,
Ecclesiastical History, iii, 5. p.229)

With such an example of the successful conversion of a nation by love, it
is no wonder that Boniface wrote to Jarrow to ask for copies of the works
of Bede, whom he called 'a lantern of the church', the inspired recorder of
the coming of Christianity to Anglo-Saxon England, to help in his preaching
in Germany.

Mr Dales has presented all this and more in his book, which comes most
aptly in this anniversary year, one thousand and four hundred years after
the coming of Augustine and his companions, setting their work in the
context of the earlier contacts with the barbarians by Martin, Patrick,

Samson, Gildas, Columba and Columbanus, and of the later work of Boniface and Theodore. It is a study based on careful and accurate scholarship, but presented as a voyage of discovery and a meeting with friends, most of all with Flecker's

> Monks of Rome from their home
> Where the blue seas break in foam,
> Augustine with his feet of snow.

It is also a book which by exploring the past discerns ways in which this inheritance can illuminate the present, surrounding it with 'a great cloud of witnesses'.

Benedicta Ward SLG
Oxford 1997

PREFACE

My sincere thanks are due to the Master of Marlborough College, my colleagues and my pupils for their interest and encouragement; also to Peregrine Horden and Sister Benedicta Ward SLG for their kindness and help on many occasions.

I should also like to pay tribute to Adrian Brink and Teresa Wheeler for invaluable help in preparing this book for publication; and to express appreciation to my dear wife, Geraldine, for her patience and support.

This book is dedicated to Christopher, Gwendoline and Basil, with hope and affection – *non angli sed angeli.*

Marlborough, Lent 1997
Douglas Dales

INTRODUCTION

The celebration in 1997 of the death of St Columba on Iona and the arrival of St Augustine at Canterbury in the summer of 597 draws attention to the remarkable ferment of monastic missionary activity that occurred in Britain at that time. In 1897, William Bright, then Regius Professor of Ecclesiastical History and Canon of Christ Church, Oxford, published the third and enlarged edition of his *Chapters of Early English Church History* to mark the thirteenth centenary of these events. In his preface he pays tribute to the work of Plummer in producing the first critical edition of Bede's historical works, upon which all subsequent research has rested. It is encouraging to reflect upon the wealth and breadth of writing that has since then shed so much light upon every aspect of English ecclesiastical and general history of the period A.D. 400-800.

These dates are significant for establishing the context of Columba's and Augustine's achievements. The end of Roman rule in Britain, and the first stirrings of missionary activity in Gaul, and from Britain to Ireland, took place in about 400, while 800 indicates the outer limit of the sustained missionary activity from England to Germany and the Low Countries, and its absorption into Carolingian church and society.

A cursory examination of the select bibliography at the end of this book, and more detailed reference to the very extensive bibliographies contained in many of the works mentioned there, will indicate the scope and quality of recent historiography. Discoveries in archaeology, palaeography, art, numismatics, and related fields have amplified, elucidated and corroborated the literary texts which remain. These are for the most part well-established in critical editions and competent translations. Their primacy remains undimmed.

The historical value of the literary texts has never been in doubt, and such ordered understanding of the history that there is rests upon them. They are almost entirely ecclesiastical in their origin, and for the most part comprise various forms of hagiography or related material. Since the time of Plummer and Bright there has emerged a much fuller and more sympathetic, if critical, appreciation of this particular genre of writing. There is therefore a fundamental affinity within the material remaining, whether its provenance be British, Irish or Anglo-Saxon. Taken as a whole throughout the period 400-800, it reflects faithfully the multifaceted activity of the Latin church in and around the British Isles, during a period of prolonged upheaval. As such these texts are a partial mirror also of the remarkable social and cultural developments which laid the foundations of England and its church.

It is important to emphasise and accept, however, that whatever the intrinsic historical value of the literature, it was in its original intent theological. This study attempts to give this inherent theology pre-eminence. It is thus an examination of particular people, and the beliefs they shared with those who remembered them, and who caused these texts to be written. The century since Bright wrote has seen the fundamental historical framework confirmed to a remarkable degree. The character and quality of the spiritual and theological vision that motivated the creation of this literature and the activities it describes can now be more securely appreciated.

Hagiographical literature is not, however, without its difficulties. It comes from a remote and singular period when the memory of the Roman era and of the church fathers was ever present. But the conditions that faced the church and its servants were often barbarous and insecure. The tenacity with which Latin Christian culture was maintained is remarkable. Yet this was the hidden stream which nurtured monastic education, missionary activity and the ascetic cultivation of sanctity.

How is sanctity to be described, let alone assessed? Hagiography conformed during this period to certain patterns crystallised in the classic lives of Antony, Benedict and Martin. In its written form it was consciously written within a tradition: it reflected a corporate spiritual expectation and perception. Yet within this corpus of literature, no hagiography simply mimics another. There is much incidental historical detail embedded within it, and it is possible to discern the lineaments of individual personalities. But hagiographies are not biographies: they are more like icons – true images rooted in history, but seen in the perspective of the eternal purpose of God in Christ.

The evidence of sanctity lay partly in teaching and example, partly in evangelism and miracles. Hence the remarkable and inextricable connection between education, mission and sanctity that persisted throughout this period. Whatever other social or political factors may have motivated or moulded the life of the church, and determined its impact upon society at that time, this troika is portrayed as the inner well-spring of the church's purpose and capacity to communicate the gospel effectively.

The prologue to this study examines the life and work of St Martin of Tours, captured by his faithful disciple, Sulpicius Severus. As a monastic and missionary bishop he was venerated as a role-model in Gaul and Britain throughout the period of this study. Part one comprises an appreciation of the conditions in the late Romano-British church which produced St Patrick. His writings, though brief, are missionary theology of the highest quality: he was a true disciple of St Paul. The vitality of the British church in Wales and elsewhere during the 'Dark Ages' of the fifth and sixth centuries emerges as a crucial link of education and mission, seen best in the *Life of St Samson* and the writings of Gildas. Through these channels monastic Christianity took root in Ireland, to exert a decisive influence in Britain and on the Continent in the sixth and seventh centuries.

Columba and Columbanus are the towering figures here, whose spiritual stature can be readily appreciated in their *Lives*, and in the writings associated with them and their followers.

Part two examines how Christianity came to the Anglo-Saxons, from Rome, Iona and Gaul. The theology and vision of St Gregory the great permeates the way Bede records the development of this mission in the seventh century. Despite the tensions between the Roman missionaries and some of the Irish Christians and their followers, each strand of mission saw itself as a faithful part of the one church of the West. Bede's essentially reconciling view is corroborated by the other remaining sources independent of him. These would have been the only window upon the work of the missionaries had Bede not written, and it is important that they are done full justice. During this period, dominant personalities like those of Aidan, Wilfrid, Theodore, and Cuthbert, whose careers shed much light on the growth of the English church and its intellectual and spiritual life, emerge.

Part three concludes by assessing the legacy of the mission to the English in terms first of Bede and his writings. His is the dominant mind whose *History* influences every approach to this period. Suffused throughout all his writings is a profound theology of the church and its mission. He was also a most effective teacher, and a percipient gauge of sanctity. His *De Templo* is the summation of his thought, and a master-key to understanding his *History*.

The second legacy of the mission to the English was the energetic missionary work of Willibrord and Boniface, and their English helpers and friends in the Low Countries and Germany in the eighth century. The long-term consequence of this activity and the learning it disseminated was immense for European culture. Of no less importance was the way it captured the united interest and support of the various regions of the English church. The memory of this chapter of English church life inspired the revival of mission by the Anglo-Saxons to Scandinavia in the tenth century.

When the forging of the English church is viewed 'sub specie aeternitatis', the death of a saint like Columba and the arrival of the Roman mission to Kent in the same year may not be just a coincidence. No less significant may be the creative co-operation and final reconciliation of the several strands of the mission: taken overall the distinctive features of Celtic and Roman pale before their united achievement. Equally the fundamental importance of the British and Welsh churches emerges from under the penumbra in which Bede unhappily placed them. The nexus between Christian education, effective evangelism, and the pursuit of sanctity is of abiding significance. So too is a positive receptivity towards and concern for Celtic and European neighbours. Finally the sense of urgency behind the mission sprang from a lively sense of the reality and nearness of the heavenly church. This was embodied in the person of the saint, who epitomised the true meaning of the church's life, and mediated the reality of the gospel and its saving power.

By listening to the spiritual testimony of these fathers of the English church, the words of T. S. Eliot may prove true:

the communication of the dead is tongued with fire beyond the language of the living.

PROLOGUE

I. MARTIN

The first missionary bishop to emerge in western Europe in the fourth century was St Martin of Tours. So powerful was the picture painted by his friend and contemporary, Sulpicius Severus, of his ministry and example that it coloured the whole pattern of literature arising from missionary activity in north-western Europe over the next four hundred year. Following Sulpicius' lead, the poet Venantius Fortunatus, and Martin's later successor Gregory of Tours publicised his fame in eloquent terms. In Gregory's words: 'he came to Gaul, converted a great number of pagans, and knocked down their temples and idols. He performed many miracles among the people'.[1] According to Gregory, Martin was only the third bishop of the see of Tours. His immediate predecessor had been bishop for 33 years, the first to be able to build a Christian church openly within the city. Gatianus, the first bishop of Tours, had been sent from Rome over 50 years before that to lead a persecuted flock in hiding. Martin was made bishop by popular acclaim as a protégé of his predecessor, Litorius, who had encouraged his monastic life and evangelistic activities. This was probably in the year 371:[2] Martin remained bishop until his death in 397.

Martin's life spans a crucial transition in the life of the western church. His parents were not Christian, and following his father's wishes he was destined for a military career. In this he was initially successful, until baptism into Christianity provoked a crisis of conscience and a deliberate withdrawal from the Roman army. Born perhaps in 336, he was still a young man in his early twenties when this decision was forced upon him. The famous story of his encounter with a beggar at the gates of Amiens, in which he gave him half his military cloak and so encountered Christ, was an early part of this process. Martin declared his resolve to become a 'soldier of God' – inspired it would seem by a childhood desire to become a hermit. Even as a soldier in the army his self-denial was such that he 'was regarded not so much as being a soldier as a monk'.[3] But to have served in any part of the Roman state 'militia' was a stigma in church circles: to the end of his life, even as a bishop, Martin was to endure criticism for his military service, not least from his successor as bishop of Tours.[4] Moreover, Martin never lost his terror of a pagan revival and renewal of persecution of Christianity. He received his early formation as a deacon and exorcist from St Hilary of Poitiers. Their ways parted for a while, during which Hilary went into exile in his struggle against the Arians, and Martin returned home to try and convert his parents. Upon returning to Italy, he attempted to live a monastic life in Milan till driven out as a partisan of Hilary's to an island off the coast where he remained for a time as a hermit. Finally, he caught up with Hilary in Poitiers,[5] probably in 360. With his help, Martin resumed a monastic life outside the city. There can be little doubt about the profound and sustained spiritual influence Hilary wrought upon Martin, and indirectly also upon Sulpicius Severus, Martin's hagiographer.[6] It was under Hilary's aegis that Martin began to become renowned for his healing 'powers', even to the extent of raising the dead.

The story of Martin's remarkable episcopate and spiritual life is told by his devoted friend and disciple, Sulpicius Severus, in whose own life Martin had played a decisive role as spiritual father. His *Life* of the saint was composed during, but at the very end, of Martin's lifetime. It is augmented by three letters written shortly after Martin's death; and by some discussion of affairs of ecclesiastical politics with which Martin was involved as bishop, towards the end of Sulpicius' *Sacred History*. By far the most lively and valuable supplementary material is found in the *Dialogues* he composed within a decade of Martin's death in defence of the saint's reputation as a miracle-worker.[7] Sulpicius himself was a noble landowner of Aquitaine who upon the death of his wife, and under the influence of his friend Paulinus of Nola, relinquished the bulk of his wealth to devote himself to the service of God with his household at Primuliacum. Crucial to this decision was the persuasion of St Martin, to whom Sulpicius made frequent visits and to whose example he became devoted: as Paulinus was to declare: 'Martin breathes right through you'.[8] As a result, the writings of Sulpicius are hardly unbiased: in several senses they are propaganda as will be demonstrated. But they are not uncritical, and are driven by certain theological concerns of an importance which transcends the particular career of Martin. In these they reflect and brilliantly articulate a mode of Christian witness within the structure of the existing church which was to exert an influence far beyond the confines of Gaul.

Both Sulpicius Severus and Gregory of Tours testify to the steady conflict with paganism in which the church at this time was engaged, in the towns and increasingly in the countryside also. In this endeavour, St Martin played a leading and singular role.[9] The broad picture given by Sulpicius can be confirmed by other literary and archaeological evidence, and Martin was by no means the only Gallic bishop so engaged. The most interesting devotee of Martin whom Gregory of Tours met was a hermit called Wulfolaic who copied both the ascetic and missionary feats of his hero.[10]

The call to be a missionary lay at the root of Martin's Christian ministry. His first attempt was towards his own family; this was in response to a dream and with the support of Hilary of Poitiers. On his journey across the mountains he narrowly escaped being murdered by robbers, one of whom was converted to Christianity by his own fearlessness. Shortly after this he had his first conscious confrontation with the devil who warned him: 'Wherever you go, or whatever you attempt, the devil will resist you'.[11] His visit home was a partial success: his example won many, including his own mother. Later as bishop he challenged both the classical religion of Roman culture, and also the paganism of the rural population. There is an amusing story of how he misconstrued a peasant funeral procession for a pagan rite, commanding it to be halted until he had verified its nature. Often rural shrines, such as the holy tree described in chapter XIII of the *Life*, provoked strong loyalty and local resistance. In this case the bystanders faced the loss of their temple with sullen equanimity, but challenged Martin as he attempted to cut down the tree 'because it had been dedicated to a demon'. As Elijah of old, this turned into a trial by ordeal as Martin was bound where the tree would fall. He deflected it by the sign of the cross to the amazement of all. It induced a wholesale conversion! Sulpicius concludes:

> Certainly, before the times of Martin, very few in those regions had received the name of Christ; but through his virtues and example that name has prevailed to such an extent that now there is no place thereabouts which is not filled with very crowded churches or monasteries. For wherever he destroyed heathen temples, there he used immediately to build either churches or monasteries.

Martin did not always get his way or escape unscathed. On one occasion a fire got out of hand as a temple was being destroyed and was only restrained by a miracle. At a major shrine called Leprosum, he was resisted with violence. After a three-day vigil of prayer, with 'angelic assistance', Martin succeeded in destroying the shrine and 'reduced all the altars and images to dust'. Lest they be found 'fighting against the bishop, . . . they began to cry out openly and to confess that the God of Martin ought to be worshipped, and that the idols should be despised, which were not able to help them'.[12] Twice Sulpicius relates how Martin was physically attacked while destroying temples, being delivered only by a miracle in each case. But perhaps more normal is the eirenic picture of dialogue with pagans as Martin tried to persuade them to relinquish their errors and ancient customs of their own volition. Sometimes this was a personal encounter, as between the bishop and a man of proconsular rank, called Tetradius. He had a slave whom he wished Martin to heal, promising to become a Christian if the cure occurred. After his baptism 'he always regarded Martin with extraordinary affection, as having been the author of his salvation'.[13] Martin was clearly a persuasive preacher and evangelist, and Sulpicius gives a vivid account, in the *Dialogues,* of Martin at work on a journey to Chartres. A great pagan crowd thronged round the bishop.

> Martin felt that some work was to be performed; and as the spirit within him was thus moving him, he was deeply excited. He at once began to preach to the heathen the word of God, . . . often groaning that so great a crowd should be ignorant of the Lord the Saviour.

The echoes of the gospels are clear.[14] Challenged by a distraught mother as 'a friend of God' to raise her dead son, he does so, 'perceiving, as he afterwards told us, that he could manifest power, in order to achieve the salvation of those waiting for its display'.

It is of singular interest that Martin perceived the devil in the guise of pagan deities. The belief that the gods of the Romans were initiated and empowered by demons had long been central to Christian polemic. But in the case of Martin, the devil 'presented himself to him changed into the person of Jupiter, often into that of Mercury and Minerva'.[15] Apparently, 'he found Mercury a cause of special annoyance, while he said that Jupiter was stupid and doltish!'[16] He saw his missionary feats as part of a deeper spiritual conflict, manipulating heavenly powers to destroy major pagan monuments.[17] The earliest miracle he performed was wrought by prayer until he 'perceived by means of the Spirit of God that power was present'.[18] The strength of his missionary activity had its roots in the ascetic nature of his life.

From the start Martin had intended if he could to lead an ascetic life, and the first occasion came immediately after leaving the army when he established 'a monastery for himself in Milan'. Thence he fled as an exile from the Arians to the island of Gallinaria where he narrowly escaped poisoning himself eating roots. Under Hilary's patronage he founded a monastic community or 'lavra' at Ligugé outside Poitiers, some of whose remains have been subject to archaeological investigation.[19] The significant feature of this development was its proximity to the episcopal see and its reliance upon Hilary's encouragement as bishop. This pattern was replicated by Martin upon his appointment as bishop of Tours: he soon created a monastic retreat for himself at Marmoutier just outside the city by the river Loire. In chapter X of the *Life*, Sulpicius Severus give a full if rather idealised description of the place. It was primarily a hermitage; but it soon attracted a colony of ascetics, disciples under Martin's personal direction. They shared a common economic life, and supported a scriptorium, and there are several references to the activities of Martin's monks throughout the corpus of Sulpicius' writings. Martin for his part felt continually the need for seclusion as a bishop, using also a cell by the cathedral. He remarked on more than one occasion that the life of a bishop undermined his spiritual life and its powers: for he was determined to retain the life of a monk. 'Full alike of dignity and courtesy, he kept up the position of a bishop properly, yet in such a way as not to lay aside the objects and virtues of a monk.' In due course his disciples were to fill churches and bishoprics throughout Gaul and so implant the rigour of their tradition on the Gallic church to a significant degree, as the writings of Gregory of Tours testify. Meanwhile his reputation as a spiritual father drew to him many, like Sulpicius himself, who to varying extents emulated his example.

However ambivalent Martin might have felt about the inroads made by his duties upon his spiritual life, and however much he might long for the privacy of a contemplative he did not shirk the vicissitudes of an active ministry. This is clearly what impressed Sulpicius, and later gave his writings about Martin their widespread practical appeal and effectiveness. The clue lies in the *Dialogues*. These commence with narratives about holy men of the East, mainly recluses: against these Martin is to be measured, and successfully contrasted. Even allowing for the rhetoric of polemic, a powerful case is being advanced:[20]

It is unfair that he (i.e. Martin) should be compared on the same terms with the recluses of the desert, or even with the anchorites. For they, at freedom from every hindrance, with heaven only and the angels as witnesses, were clearly instructed to perform admirable deeds; he, on the other hand, in the midst of crowds and intercourse with human beings – among quarrelsome clerics, and among furious bishops, while he was harassed with almost daily scandals on all sides, nevertheless stood firm absolutely with unconquerable virtue against all these things, and performed such wonders (i.e. miracles) as not even accomplished by those whom we have heard are, or at one time were, in the wilderness.

The foundation of Martin's active ministry was as an exorcist: to this he had first been ordained and trained by Hilary of Poitiers, and to the end of his life he maintained a running battle with the devil. Common to the many miracles of this kind recounted by Sulpicius is Martin's capacity to discern and expose the presence of evil in people and situations, like a sharp light beaming into murky corners. Within this field of ministry he showed great courage, for example on one occasion inserting his fingers into the mouth of a possessed and threatening person, saying: 'If you possess any power, devour these!'[21] His power extended also over nature, towards beasts and fire being manipulated he believed by evil. As bishop his mere entry into church would unhinge the possessed who might be present, and there is an extraordinary account of Martin's manner of ministry in the *Dialogues*.[22] 'He only had to set his foot outside the threshold of his cell and . . . the groanings of the demons announced the approach of the bishop to the clerics, who were not previously aware that he was coming.' This passage proceeds to describe various paranormal manifestations, such as levitation. But what is striking and surely authentic is the picture of how Martin dealt with such menacing turbulence:

If at any time Martin undertook the duty of exorcising the demons, he touched no one with his hands, and reproached no one in words, as a multitude of expressions is generally rolled forth by the clerics. Instead, the possessed being brought up to him he ordered all others to depart, and the doors being bolted, clothed in sackcloth and sprinkled with ashes, he stretched himself on the ground in the midst of the church and turned to prayer.

By this means he delivered some, but not it would seem by any means all.

His charism in this area was undergirded by a secure pastoral theology. His discernment clearly addressed the fear that stalked the lives of many; and the roots of this chronic fear might be manifold – personal, psychological or arising from illness, social, political, economic or in some undefined way cosmic. For example he stalled a flight of rumours about an impending barbarian invasion which were sweeping Trier.[23] The context of his activities sheds vivid light upon social conditions at that time. He for his part perceived them as skirmishes in a perpetual war, which had its own shape and character, and for him at least meaning too. Thus arose perhaps the most notable of his ripostes to the devil:

> If thou, thyself, wretched being, wouldst but desist from attacking mankind, and even at this period when the day of judgement is at hand, wouldst only repent of your deeds, I, with a true confidence in the Lord, would promise you the mercy of Christ![24]

Striking words which perhaps point to the eastern provenance of Martin's early monastic formation. For him, evil operated by intimidation and deception. Stories are told about exposure of spiritual impostors infiltrating his circle of disciples, and there is the splendid account of how the devil appeared to Martin at prayer apparently as Christ in regal glory: 'I am Christ; and being just about to descend to earth, I wished first to manifest myself to you'. To which Martin judiciously and shrewdly replied:

> The Lord Jesus did not predict that he would come clothed in purple, and with a glittering crown upon his head. I will not believe that Christ has come, unless he appears with that appearance and form in which he suffered, and openly displaying the marks of his wounds upon the cross.[25]

Whereupon the devil departed leaving only a disgusting smell! Yet this was just one rebuff, for according to Sulpicius' third letter, Martin saw the devil at hand as he was dying, to whom he directed this parting shot: 'Why do you stand there, you bloody monster? You shall find nothing in me, you deadly one'! He was a deliberate ascetic to the last, insisting on lying not on straw but on ashes, saying: 'It is not fitting that a Christian should die except among ashes; and I have sinned if I leave you a different example.'

If like Christ in St Mark's gospel, Martin was engaged in a formidable conflict with evil, his was also a ministry of healing and liberation like his Lord's. Indeed, like Francis for a later generation and social era, Martin's spiritual significance and greatness lay perhaps in the way his life and actions and the way they were remembered, gave a fresh and powerful expression to the gospel, appropriate to a changing relationship between church and society.

Martin's miracles of healing follow the gospel pattern closely.[26] His powers over nature have their roots in the Old Testament miracles of Elijah and Elisha, and also in the Acts of the Apostles. More immediate parallels may be found in the *Historia Monachorum* and the traditions already circulating about the desert fathers of the East. Some of the nature miracles were closely related to his missionary activities, and his overt challenges to pagan worship, as has been seen. After his death, his disciples liked to recall the way in which he commanded animals to obey him, recalling his rueful words: 'Serpents heed me, but men will not hear!'[27] Three further miracles recount his immunity to and control over fire, and three more over weather.

Finally there are four miracles which relate to the virtue contained in oil which Martin blessed and used as bishop. This fourfold pattern of miracles of command over nature became definitive for most later hagiography.

In his healing miracles, it is possible to discern clearly the direct influence of the gospels, and certain features of Martin's own personality and approach to this dimension of his ministry as bishop and holy man. Like his Lord, he took on successfully paralysis, dumbness from birth, chronic fever, leprosy, blindness, plague. On three occasions also he is recorded as having raised the dead. But how he handled these pastoral crises is most interesting and became exemplary. Mostly he eschewed public gaze and prayed in seclusion with or for the victim. Sometimes he acted in a practical and almost medical manner, pouring in oil or eye-salve and squeezing out poison. On more than one occasion his prayer and compassion healed people from whom he was distant, and some miracles were occasioned by things Martin had touched or used like his clothes or even a letter. In the cases of resuscitation of those who had recently died, he repeated the example of Elijah and Elisha and prostrated himself in prayer upon the corpse. In all cases prayer was his singular weapon.

Running through these stories is his manifest care for the poor. While entering Paris, he blessed and kissed a leper 'While all shuddered at seeing him do so': the kindness cured the man.[28] Such actions were the hall-mark of his life and witness as a Christian. It began with the famous encounter at the gates of Amiens when he cut in half his military cloak to clothe a 'poor man destitute of clothes'. 'During the following night he had a vision of Christ arrayed in that part of his cloak with which he had clothed the poor man.'[29] In the *Dialogues* there is a similar story of how Martin when bishop was approached by a poor man for some clothes. Because the archdeacon delayed in carrying out the bishop's orders, being too preoccupied by the gossip of the other clergy, the poor man collared Martin in private and in response the bishop secretly slipped off his own under-garment and gave it to him. Naked under his episcopal robes, Martin insisted that the archdeacon obtain the poor man's clothing. This he eventually did with an ill grace, and so the bishop went to celebrate mass in a 'rough garment out of the nearest shop, short and shaggy, and costing only five pieces of silver'. But a handful of his closest friends 'beheld a globe of fire dart from his head' while consecrating the altar.[30]

This story of the brush with his archdeacon is, however, part of a wider pattern of stories which Sulpicius delights in regaling. Martin's fellow-bishops found him hard to handle, and he did not suffer fools – especially clerical ones – gladly. Indeed he was intolerant of the ways of some bishops, specially at court or in synod, and appeared often an outsider and non-conformist. In his life was acted out the classic tension between prophet and priest, between charismatic and established functionary. But in this case the prophet and the charismatic was within the episcopal hierarchy, but as a monk and an active missionary very much on his own terms.

Martin therefore challenged the established notions of Gallic episcopacy; but at the same time his example and determination also helped to change and develop the nature and expectations of episcopacy in a way that was both versatile and abiding in its influence and example.[31]

But Martin was not in fact so isolated among the Gallic bishops of his day. Valentinus, bishop of Chartres, and Victricius of Rouen were clearly like-minded friends capable of persuading Martin to heal a sick girl.[32] Indeed, the career of Victricius affords a parallel with that of Martin, according to the letters of their mutual friend, Paulinus of Nola. Both had started off in the Roman army which they had left for conscientious reasons; both were missionaries and advocates of ascetic monasticism; both were charged with heresy, and to thwart his opponents in Gaul Victricius appealed to the pope in Rome.[33] To judge from the later perspective of Gregory of Tours, the labours of such bishops bore fruit in the fifth century, profoundly affecting the life of the Gallic church, especially in areas where Christian witness was contending with rural paganism.[34] Dissension between ascetic and more conventional bishops in Gaul remained a problem however. On the other hand, in the life and activities of a notable bishop of the next generation, Caesarius of Arles, it is possible to see how both traditions could be very creatively combined. The *Life of Caesarius* is modelled significantly upon that of Martin, though without its visionary and overtly missionary and polemical dimensions.[35]

The writings of Sulpicius Severus about St Martin arose in the midst of conflict and controversy within the Gallic church.[36] His own devotion to Martin's memory, and the claims he made for him, were challenged even as he was writing: this is evident at the end of his *Life*, in the letters which immediately followed its publication, and throughout the *Dialogues*. Martin himself had to endure criticism from within the ranks of his own clergy:

> He displayed indeed such marvellous patience in the endurance of injuries that even when he was bishop he allowed himself to be wronged by the lowest clergy with impunity. Nor did he either remove them from office for such conduct, or, as far as in him lay, repel them from a place in his affection.[37]

It was to rebut such detraction, especially from some of the bishops, that Sulpicius composed the *Life*. The rancour directed at the saint by the priest who was in fact to succeed him as bishop reveals the root of the quarrel. Martin had reproved Brictius, his protégé, for acquiring horses and slaves of both sexes. Brictius, overcome by anger and jealousy, (prompted, Martin perceived, by evil) assailed his patron for his early career as a soldier, accusing him of being 'entirely sunk into dotage by means of his baseless superstitions and ridiculous fancies about visions'.[38] Reconciliation eluded them, and according to Gregory of Tours Brictius remained a thorn in Martin's side thereafter, and an unruly successor to his see.[39]

Yet Brictius represented in a local way the antagonism felt by many of his fellow-bishops and clergy towards the spiritual challenge which Martin posed. The matter was set against the wider stage of the heresy of Priscillian of Avila, which posed a crisis within the Gallic church, and in the end involved the emperor in the active persecution of this ascetic group within the church. Sulpicius is a prime witness to the course of this controversy, both in his *Sacred History* and in the *Dialogues*. Martin stood out as a champion of ascetic life, and as a critic of the way in which certain of the Gallic bishops provoked the secular ruler to take violent steps against fellow-Christians. According to the very end of the *Sacred History*, Martin ran the risk of being himself accused of heresy for his fearless opposition to 'a secular ruler being judge in an ecclesiastical cause'.[40] In the *Dialogues* the personal cost of this position is revealed: Martin suspected the intentions of the persecutors of Priscillian towards the ascetic life in general, and wished to protect fellow-Christians, even heretics, from violent persecution. With great reluctance he went to the imperial court at Trier where he was manipulated into taking communion with his fellow-bishops in an attempt to prevent the execution in Spain of those accused of heresy. 'He judged it better to yield for the moment than to disregard the safety of those over whose heads a sword was hanging.' But he lived to regret this transgression of conscience and thereafter eschewed all future synods of bishops for the next sixteen years.

> When it happened that he cured some of the possessed more slowly and with less grace than usual, he at once confessed to us with tears that he felt a diminution of his power on account of the evil of that communion in which he had taken part for a moment through necessity, and not with a cordial spirit.[41]

Such was Martin's influence with the emperor Maximus that while he lived he was able to exert a brake upon the ferocity of the persecution. The testimony of Sulpicius is very interesting as to the way Martin coped with the often dictatorial mien of these secular rulers. In the *Life*, for example, the story is told of how Martin in complete contrast to the other bishops refused to flatter: 'in Martin alone, apostolic authority continued to assert itself'. He seldom came to court and when he did 'he commanded rather than entreated'. During a banquet the king offered him first a goblet of wine. Martin, instead of reciprocating by returning it to the king, gave it instead to his chaplain. It made a great impression: 'Martin had done what no bishop had dared to do. . . .' Meanwhile the saint cautioned the king against a planned campaign in Italy, predicting his certain death. Thus Martin safeguarded his independence and integrity as a bishop. It did not protect him from royal adulation, and in the *Dialogues* is told how the wife and queen of Maximus doted on him, and served him with personal devotion. But there was a sterner side to Martin's demeanour towards rulers. The way Martin protested at Valentinian's refusal to see him was to stage a sit-down strike in sackcloth and ashes for a week, enduring a hunger-strike as well. Finally Martin gained his access and shook the ruler's attitude. Nonetheless he refused all blandishments and gifts, 'jealously maintaining his own poverty'.[42] The positive moral value of such a consistent stance was demonstrated when as bishop of Tours, Martin had to deal with the rapacity of count Avitianus trying to intimidate the populace by some gruesome executions. Martin made his protest by sleeping on the threshold of this tyrant until, disturbed in his sleep, Avitianus admitted him. The aura of the bishop intimidated the count so that he caved in, released his victims and departed. Later Martin was able to exorcise him from the demon goading him to behave in this cruel manner.[43]

Such a resolute stand made him enemies, particularly among some of the bishops whom he rather showed up. On the other hand, it is quite evident that Martin received support from many highly placed people, upon whom he relied in fact for the conduct of his episcopate, both in his missionary activities and in his fostering of the monastic life. Mere example could not deliver in these controversial areas: capacity in terms of money, lands and political support, both local and at court, was indispensable. A quick review of Sulpicius's writing will reveal that this network was quite strong and responsive to Martin's aims. Even before he became bishop, Martin was familiar with the houses of the landed rich: he healed a slave of one – Lupicinus. A pagan proconsul called Tetradius begged Martin to heal his possessed slave in return for conversion to Christianity: 'he always regard- ed Martin with extraordinary affection, as having been the author of his salvation'.[44] An ex-prefect, Arborius, secured the cure of his sick daughter by a letter of Martin's and directly dedicated her as a virgin, insisting that Martin alone should receive her profession. Paulinus of Nola was healed by Martin of a cataract, and of course he gave great support to his friend Sulpicius, and was commended by Martin as an example of godly dis- position.[45] This appeal to the devout rich was evidenced in the 'noble youth' Clarus who was close to the heart of both Martin and Sulpicius, who founded a monastery nearby, and who died young.[46] Sulpicius himself derived stead- fast support from his mother-in-law, Bassula, as is clear from the tone of his letter to her describing the death of St Martin. In the *Dialogues* also, further well-placed sympathisers make an appearance: Evanthius, 'a highly Christian man, although occupied in the affairs of this world', was cured at a distance by Martin, to whom he then rushed a child dying of a snake's bite for a cure. A prefect, Auspicius, summoned Martin to pray for protection for his fields from hailstorms, which the saint secured while he yet lived according to the testimony of the man's son, Romulus. Finally, a wealthy soldier, Lycontius, begged Martin's prayers for his household stricken by plague. After a week of prayer and fasting, Martin averted it, and promptly used the thank-you gift of one hundred pounds to redeem captives, much to the chagrin of his monks.[47] The ability of Martin to command and sustain the loyalty and practical confidence of such Christian men of affairs was clearly crucial to the success of his ministry. Under his guidance and strict example, wealth became the servant of the church's mission.

The appeal of St Martin was however deeper, and it is possible in the writings of Sulpicius to discern the inner spiritual stature of the man which won the loyalty and devotion of such influential people.

Firstly, Martin embodied the principles of poverty and exile from one's native environment. This was a very fashionable preoccupation in the Latin-speaking church at this time, promoted notably by Jerome, but also by others. So in the *Life*, Martin' childhood ambition to serve God is emphasised, despite his pagan family, so that by the age of twelve 'he desired to enter the life of hermit'. This his father naturally withstood, forcing Martin into a military career, which proved an exile of different kind, so that by his demeanour he came to be regarded more as a monk than a soldier by his peers. Upon leaving the army, Martin found in Hilary a spiritual father and patron. But both father and son are portrayed as exiles, separated for a while when Martin returns to his own 'patria' to try and convert his parents, and Hilary is driven into exile for the sake of orthodox belief. In this persecution Martin shares when driven from his small monastery in Milan into eremitic seclusion on the island of Gallinaria. Like a pilgrim he seeks again his mentor, Hilary, first in Rome but in vain, so crossing the Alps and reaching him at last in Poitiers, where far from his native land he settles down to the monastic life. The theme recurs throughout the traditions surrounding him: for example, his reluctance to become a bishop, his attitude towards property, and the final manner of his dying among ashes; 'for here we have no continuing city'.[48]

At the heart of Martin's own spirituality lay a profound belief in the spiritual potency of virginity. This was the hidden presupposition upon which his entire life and ministry rested, and he called his disciples to no less a commitment. Looking at a field full of flowers, untrampled by pigs or ungrazed by cattle, he could acclaim it as a mirror of virginity: 'decked with flowers to the very extreme of beauty, it shines as if adorned with glittering gems. Blessed is such beauty and worthy of God; for nothing is to be compared with virginity!' To a man who had separated from his wife so that both might pursue the monastic life, but who now wished to resume relations with her, Martin used the analogy of the incongruity of women fighting with men in a line of battle to shore up his vocation and resolve. When a holy female recluse refused to receive him, he was not at all offended but rather rejoiced and accepted a gift at her hand, which was rare indeed. Finally Sulpicius himself overheard a visionary conversation of Martin, which the saint confided had been with the holy virgins, Mary, Thecla and Agnes.[49] The significance of virginity lay not simply in its renunciation of sexual and familial relations or of possessions; but as a sign of dedication to God, an inner martyrdom of love and preparation for the eternal reality of heaven which might even now be apprehended in time. Poverty, exile and the espousal of virginity constituted a total self-offering by a person to God in response to the divine self-giving of the Spirit.

This hidden charism was the wellspring of the occasional miracle. Its aura and attraction was communicated by Martin to his supporters and followers by the power of friendship, expressed either as spiritual direction and formation, or as intercession. The labours of Sulpicius Severus are clearly a monument to a decisive friendship. This is suffused throughout his writings, and ensures that although he selects and writes as a partisan, his encomium is not uncritical nor mere propaganda: the truth about his friend's personality and belief leaves its own indelible and determining hallmark. Towards the end of the *Life*, Sulpicius inserts a personal testimony to the impact Martin initially made upon him as a spiritual father, and throughout his writings he is concerned to defend his reputation fairly. The *Dialogues* take place between friends and sympathisers of the saint, and the attractive power of such reminiscence is explicitly attested at several points. This saint had a human context without which his memory would have become stylised as it appears later in the writings of Gregory of Tours: he was a man in dialogue with friends who were both congenial and faithful, and receptive to his teaching and charisma. On many occasions Martin is portrayed as a man who acted out of sympathy and compassion to those who sought his friendship and help, by letter, gift, and above all by intercession. His prayer was powerful, and, it was believed, unquenched by death. Thus in the second letter of Sulpicius, Martin appears in glory to his friend. It is a moving picture:

> He appeared to me with that aspect and form of body which I had known so well, but he could not be steadfastly beheld, though he could be clearly recognised. . . . I felt his hand placed on my head with the sweetest touch, while amid the solemn words of benediction, he repeated again and again the name of the cross so familiar to his lips.

This occurrence cut Sulpicius to the quick, being almost indescribable. Yet he concludes to his friend Aurelius the deacon to whom he writes:

> So I now desire you to be comforted, although I am unable to console myself. He will not be absent from us; believe me, he will never, never forsake us, but will be present with us as we discourse regarding him, and will be near us as we pray . . . and he will protect us, as he did but a little time ago, with his unceasing benediction.

It was certainly this fervour of love and devotion, as well as any miracle wrought posthumously that initiated the cult of Martin as the saint of Tours, to which development Gregory of Tours gives the detail in his *History*.

The broad themes of Martin's life and ministry, as portrayed by his friend Sulpicius, were to provide a template for measuring the role and achievements of holy men and women over the succeeding centuries. They were rooted in the Bible and in the emerging traditions of the monks. Yet they addressed directly the precise range of conditions which pertained in northwestern Europe as the power of the Roman Empire waned. Within this framework of understanding the gospel of Christ engaged the mixed and sometimes turbulent conditions of the barbarian west, mediating to it the values of late Christian antiquity, and conjoining evangelism with sound organisation of church life in the pursuit of holiness. Always the inner life and character of a saint is elusive, and hard to communicate to another generation. Although hagiography may appear at first glance stereotyped, deeper examination reveals the way in which, using this established mode of expression and association like a filter, the true and distinctive pattern of divine life in a particular individual may be discerned. The *Life* of St Martin proved therefore successful beyond the expectations of Sulpicius Severus and the narrow confines of the saint's friends. It became the language for expressing and penetrating the authentic witness of the gospel in the lives of many for several centuries thereafter. It proved of decisive importance in the region of most active mission – the conversion of the various peoples of the British Isles.

Wherein lay, therefore, the 'Apostolic' character of Martin's authority and witness to which Sulpicius pays repeated testimony and insistence? Firstly as a champion of orthodoxy, a mantle he received from St Hilary of Poitiers. The influence of St Hilary upon both Martin and Sulpicius is significant and the orthodoxy of Martin's stand is not mitigated by his pastoral sympathy for the hapless followers of Priscillian.[50] This conviction was vouched for by Martin's visions of the saints of the New Testament, notably Peter and Paul. Furthermore, there was a decidedly apocalyptic strain to Martin's private teaching, bred in part out of a profound fear of renewal of pagan persecution of Christianity.[51] 'He added that this persecution would have for its object to compel men *to deny Christ as God* . . . ordering all men to be circumcised according to the Law.' There would be conflict between Antichrist ruling the eastern empire, and Nero redivivus ruling in the west. Martin expected this catastrophe to occur imminently, as did his circle of disciples. The most sturdy expression of this championship of orthodox belief lay, however, in the way in which Martin asserted and maintained the integrity and relative independence of the church in the face of secular rulers and episcopal corruption. His moral stance rested upon a traditional doctrine, dating from the years of persecution and beyond; his notion of episcopacy thus straddled two eras – before and after the Constantinian establishment of the church. His attitude was perforce ambivalent: without the sympathy or acquiescence of the secular power, his overt missionary activity could hardly proceed as it did; but his suspicion of the ease with which the bishops of Gaul could become adjuncts of the imperial court and conformed to the mores of the secular aristocracy never abated.

Of decisive importance were his miracles as expression of the powerful charisma with which as a holy man and bishop he was endowed. These conformed to the pattern of the gospels, and also echoed those of Old Testament saints, and of the apostles in the Acts. His whole teaching and example brought new life to the ancient examples of prophets and seers. He exercised Christ's power to exorcise and heal. Like St Paul he was engaged in a running conflict with the devil and had visions of heaven in the midst of it. His sanctity etched the force of these upon the experience and memory of his people and friends in a way that outlasted his immediate generation. As Sulpicius concludes his account of Martin's funeral in his third letter: 'Martin, poor and insignificant on earth, has a rich entrance granted him in heaven'. His was truly a ministry apostolic in its nature and impact.

Seen more widely Sulpicius' picture of St Martin gives a fascinating glimpse into the state of the church in Gaul as it emerged from the nightmare of persecution to become the uneasy partner of Roman secular rule. The fundamental ambivalence of this changed situation is pervasive, and accounts for not a few of the divisions and conflicts within the church. It is a period when the tide of monastic fervour was invading Gaul from the East, attracting and distracting many inside and outside the fledgling monastic communities. The new social position of the bishops, and the enthusiasm of asceticism gave prominence to the holy man, the spiritual father, who might wield an authority by virtue of his charism, disconcerting to established ecclesiastical authorities who still did not feel really secure in their new freedom. The eruption of heresy in the form of Spanish Priscillianism signalled the dangers of this flux of authority, and lured some to invoke the secular power to enforce, if not orthodoxy, at least control.

Then there was the question of mission, of active evangelism among the rural pagans, and of challenge to the privileged status of major Greco-Roman cults in the cities and villas. Here Martin's work and that of his monks showed what could be done; and as bishop he was able to follow up initiatives with the founding of new parishes, churches and monasteries. While fulfilling the traditional pastoral role of bishop in concert with his peers, he went further; and so created a new role-model of episcopacy which broke out of the settled order of Gallic city bishoprics and responded instead to a 'frontier' situation of mission and social upheaval. If his word could stem panic and rumours of barbarian aggression in Trier, it meant that the charismatic bishop could wield an authority, reinforced by teaching and miracle, which could bring confidence and a new focus of loyalty and purpose in at times a fluid social scene. Martin's example was remembered as an example of how in a new situation a bishop might retain independence and initiative, with the support of his monastic followers and their sympathetic lay patrons. This role-model proved remarkably versatile and enduring for the next four hundred years, as will be seen in the unfolding picture of missionary activity to and within the British Isles.

PART 1

II. PATRICK

Christianity came to Roman Britain by ways unknown; yet in the early third century Tertullian and Origen were both able to talk in vague and rhetorical terms about the spread of the faith to these islands. By the fourth century, the existence of an ordered British church is confirmed by the principal church historians, Sozomen and Eusebius.[1] The most likely initial route was probably Jewish traders in London, Lincoln and other trading centres. For example among the three martyrs mentioned by Bede, one of those at Caerleon was called Aaron.[2] A similar Jewish trading presence in the south-west in the context of the export of valuable minerals from Britain may account for the early tradition associated with Glastonbury, just across the Severn sea from Caerleon. Here, according to an early text, was an ancient wooden church already holy and revered when the first settled Christian population came across it at some date unknown.[3] The martyrdom of St Alban was remembered by Fortunatus in the Gallic church, and his shrine at Verulamium was visited by Germanus of Auxerre in the fifth century. But the occasion described of Alban's conversion by a fleeing priest does not necessarily indicate a church existing in his day at Verulamium. Bede's testimony rests upon an early *Passio Albani*, used also by Gildas who concluded that Alban died under the persecution of Diocletian. But this is unlikely as Christians in Britain appear to have been shielded by Constantius I. So he and his companions died either in the middle of the third century, or just possibly at its beginning under Severus.[4]

There is very little archaeological evidence for Christianity in Britain before 400. The Water Newton hoard, and more recently the cross found in an industrial town near Shepton Mallett on the Fosse Way are the most significant indicators of Christians among the artisan population.[5] But in the years after Constantine's endorsement of the Christian church, bishops from Britain appear regularly at church councils: three bishops, a priest and a deacon attest the decrees of the council of Arles in 314, confirming the existence of sees in York, London and possibly Colchester. British bishops went also to Nicea in 325, perhaps to Sardica and certainly to Arminium in 359.[6] The pattern of church government appears to have followed the Gallic model being based in the towns. But in the later fourth century as these began to decline, support for the church rested more upon certain circles of the landed gentry living in their villas. Certainly archaeological evidence would seem to support this: the private chapel at Lullingstone in Kent, the mosaics at Hinton St Mary in Dorset, and the lavish treasure unearthed at Mildenhall in Suffolk to mention the most striking examples. Firm archaeological evidence for churches from this last century of Roman rule is lacking; possible sites have been mooted at Caerwent, Canterbury, Silchester and Richborough in Kent. More impressive is the considerable burial ground at Poundbury near Dorchester in Dorset with its distinctive Christian enclave. The martyrdom shrine of St Alban lay outside the city walls of Verulamium, possibly in the midst of an existing cemetery, as in Gaul. Similar mausoleum sites have been indicated at Faversham in Kent and at Wells in Somerset. The impression gained by the end of the fourth century is of a church not numerically strong, and still challenged by paganism, both Roman and Celtic. Its influential support lay among certain groups of the landed classes, though its presence in the towns was no longer negligible. In its development it marched in step with the Gallic church but rather as a junior partner. How it survived the end of Roman rule in 410 and transformed itself successfully during the various upheavals in Britain in the second half of the fifth century, however, remains shrouded in mystery.

At certain points in the fourth and fifth centuries, the documentary evidence for the vitality of the British church is fuller than the archaeological. In the minds of the early Christian fathers Britain represented the end of the known world, a wild zone whose conversion represented a triumph for the gospel. In the words of Chrysostom: 'Before this time those in Britain fed on human flesh, but now they refresh their souls by fasting.' Or Jerome: 'If Satan does indeed possess the whole earth, how is it that the spoils of the Cross are gathered from the very corners of the world? (i.e. Britain and India)' – 'The heavenly palace rests equally in Jerusalem and in Britain, for the kingdom of God is within you.' Augustine asserts: 'For the word of God is preached not only on the continent but also in the islands in the midst of the sea where there are plenty of Christians and servants of God.' Or Porphyry writing to Jerome: 'The fertile province of Britain and the Irish people and indeed all the barbarian peoples as far as the great ocean came to know Moses and the prophets.'[7] Palladius and Theodoret report pilgrims from Britain to the Holy Land at the beginning of the fifth century. The steady belief that the advance of the gospel into the British Isles confirmed the inexorable strength and spread of Christian truth became, in the wake of the sack of Rome in 410, an expectation that it portended the end of the world and the fulfilment of the prophecies of Christ. There is no evidence that it inspired any general missionary impulse in the Gallic or even the British church. On the other hand the Gallic and Roman churches clearly regarded the British church as of some importance in the fight against heresy, first Arianism and later Pelagianism. Hilary of Poitiers, for example, claims the solid support of the British bishops for the orthodox Nicene faith in the prologue to his De Synodis,[8] a position maintained also by Athanasius. Certainly there is little evidence of Arianism in Britain, despite the stern judgements later of Gildas and, following him, Bede.[9]

Pelagianism, however, had a strong tap-root in Britain. It asserted the role of free-will in assisting human salvation, and its protagonist, Pelagius, was himself from Britain. He was vigorously opposed by St Augustine of Hippo among others, and his views were condemned early in the fifth century. However, his support in Britain seems to have been considerable among certain of the landed Christian aristocrats in the period before and after the formal end of Roman rule. The emphasis upon the essential co-operation between divine grace and the human will appealed to the growing monastic movement and its lay supporters. Augustine's ally, Prosper of Aquitaine, tells how a certain Agricola introduced Pelagian teaching into the British church, and Gennadius mentions a British bishop, Fastidius, who wrote tracts on living the Christian life to a wealthy widow called Fatalis in the spirit of this teaching.[10] Despite the strictures of the Latin church, Britain remained a safe backwater for those with Pelagian tendencies. As early as 380, the Scilly Isles had been used as a place of exile for Priscillianist bishops, according to Sulpicius Severus.[11] The state of the British church therefore remained of concern to the Gallic bishops, and indirectly to Rome also.

Before the year 396, Victricius bishop of Rouen, friend of St Martin of Tours, visited Britain at the request of his fellow-bishops in Gaul and northern Italy to bring peace in some unknown dispute there.[12] The most fully reported case of Gallic episcopal intervention was the visit of bishop Germanus of Auxerre in 429.[13] Bede's account rests upon the *Life of St Germanus* by Constantius, written around 475. Germanus was perhaps accompanied by a fellow-bishop, Lupus of Troyes; they came at the behest of the British church to deal with a revival of Pelagianism. They embarked on an active preaching mission in both towns and countryside, working miracles on occasion. In due course they were met by representatives of the Pelagian party, 'ostentatiously displaying their wealth in their gorgeous robes, and surrounded by a multitude of their supporters'. Open public debate was resolved when the heretics proved unable to cure the child of one of the rulers. Germanus did so using a little bag with relics of saints inside it. Later Germanus proceeded to venerate the shrine of St Alban, leaving there relics of other saints he had brought with him. Like St Martin of Tours, Germanus narrowly escaped being killed in a house fire; ill himself, he nonetheless cured many of their diseases. Finally he showed his versatility by organising and baptising an army of British to see off a Pictish attack. This occurred at Easter, and for the occasion the bishops built a small field church of wattle. Then Germanus turned general, lured the enemy into a narrow valley, and intimidated them into flight by leading the British in the shout, 'Alleluia!' So, without any bloodshed, 'they won a victory by faith and not by might'. This was in no way an evangelistic mission to the British; it was an assault on heresy with a view to re-establishing the catholic faith. Towards the end of his life, perhaps in 437, Germanus returned to Britain, with Severus later bishop of Trier, to displace again heretical teachers. But there is no mention of any British bishops acting in collaboration with Germanus, possibly because Constantius is really writing an encomium of the saint. Equally such representatives of the post-Roman government that appear in the story seem indifferent to the issue. The whole drama seems to take place in and around London, at Verulamium, and the battle in northern Kent.

The most reliable source for this precise period is the chronicler, Prosper of Aquitaine. According to him, Germanus was sent by pope Celestine to counter heresy and to restore the British church to orthodox belief. This was done upon the advice of the deacon, Palladius, who was active in the polemic against Pelagianism. Celestine was a vigorous pope, urgent in his opposition to any form of heresy or division in the church. Two years later, according to Prosper who was in Rome at the time, the pope ordained Palladius as bishop to the Christian believers in Ireland.[14] Once again this was not an overt missionary enterprise; it was provision for existing Christians in Ireland, whether British or Irish in origin is unclear. This may have been a precaution against the spread of Pelagian exiles to Ireland. It may also have been in some way an assertion of Roman authority and interest in an area now lost to the Empire. To this time would seem to date the odd story, included by Bede, of how pope Eleutherius responded to an appeal by a legendary British king, Lucius, in the second century and sent Christian missionaries to Britain.[15] This fable was inserted into the *Liber Pontificalis* around the time of Prosper's *Chronicle* and there Bede found it. What is of more interest is that Prosper composed a pamphlet urging the new pope Sixtus to carry on the battle against Pelagianism in 434, in which he reports the success of the papal mission in Ireland led by Palladius: referring to pope Celestine's intentions he says, 'by ordaining a bishop for the Irish, while he was eager to keep the Roman island (i.e. Britain) catholic, he also made the barbarian Island (i.e. Ireland) Christian.'[16] In another document, called *The Call of the Nations*, Prosper becomes the first Christian writer actually to discuss missionary strategy, a thing which hitherto had been the preserve of Arian missionaries among the Germanic peoples on the Continent.

> Christian grace was not content to have the same frontiers as Rome, and Christianity has now subjugated many people to the sceptre of Christ's cross whom Rome did not conquer with her arms. Rome became greater under the lead of the apostolic bishopric by means of the citadel of religion than the force of power.

It would, however, be wrong to deduce that such vitality as there was in the British church in the fifth century was seduced into Pelagianism. The evidence is scanty, but there is a tradition of St Ninian who sometime before the middle of the fifth century was sent as a bishop to Christians in Galloway, perhaps from the church at Carlisle.[17] According to Bede, Ninian was a 'reverend and holy Briton who had received orthodox instruction at Rome in the faith and mysteries of the truth.' His church at Whithorn was called Candida Casa 'because Ninian built a church of stone there, using a method unusual among Britons.' From a very early date this church was dedicated to St Martin of Tours. All this is confirmed in an eighth-century poem about the saint. Nearby the Kirkmadrine stones commemorate in Gallic style two bishops later than Ninian, while the Lativus stone at Whithorn indicates a Christian presence by around 450. Archaeological investigation has revealed remains of a stone building daubed with cream plaster, and traces of an early cemetery disturbing possible Roman cremations.[18] Whithorn later became an Anglian bishopric at around the time Bede was writing.

The second half of the fifth century saw the first substantial migrations of Britons to Brittany in response to the Saxon invasions. In 461 is recorded the presence of a British bishop in the diocese of Tours, Mansuetus; in 465 at the council of Vannes a Briton Padarn was ordained as a suffragan bishop. In a letter of Sidonius Apollinaris to the British bishop, Faustus of Riez, he refers to another British priest and monk, Riochatus, as an emissary bringing copies of Faustus' books entitled *De Gratia*.[19] These were written around the year 470 and were approved at the council of Arles in 472-3, and were intended to oppose the predestinarian theology of a critic called Lucidus. Like his master Cassian, Faustus insists on the important role of the human will in co-operating with the work of divine grace in a person. He was prepared also to assert the corporeal nature of the human soul because although invisible it was confined in the frame of the physical body.[20] He had been for twenty-six years abbot of the monastery at Lérins, before becoming bishop of Riez in 459, suffering exile for a time because of his opposition to the Arianising policy of the Visigothic king, Euric. He was an able spokesman for the ascendant monastic party in the Gallic church at this time.

Taken together these fragments provide some credible context for the ministry and teaching of the most remarkable and well-documented representative of the British church – St Patrick.

All that can be known about St Patrick for certain has to be deduced from the two writings of his that have been preserved, his *Confession* and his *Letter to Coroticus*. It is reasonably sure that he lived in the first half of the fifth century, having been brought up in Roman Britain during the closing years of Roman imperial rule.[21] His writing gives the closest glimpse of the Roman British church, placing it firmly in the wider context of the Gallic church with which it clearly enjoyed reasonable contact.

Patrick was born to a prosperous landowning family: his father was a deacon in the church and also a 'decurion' responsible for the collection of taxes; his grandfather was a priest. In his own words, 'I was a free man in worldly position'.[22] At the age of sixteen he was captured by Irish pirates and carried off into slavery in Ireland, interrupting his formal Latin education. This handicap rankled with him for the rest of his life, becoming a symptom of the trauma he had experienced.[23] His enforced isolation as a shepherd taught him however to pray, 'so that in one day I would say as many as a hundred prayers and nearly as many at night.'[24] Finally he escaped, traversed Ireland and fled by sea, either to Gaul or more probably to Britain, by means of some Irish traders or raiders from whom he had eventually to escape. After a period in Britain with his family, he felt a divine call to return to Ireland as a missionary. In this enterprise he did not enjoy the full support of his fellow-clergy, some of whom remained ambivalent towards his aspirations as a missionary among such a dangerous people, and later towards his being a bishop at all. In part at least, his *Confession* is an answer to his critics, written probably towards the end of his life. The scepticism and gossip of those who should have supported him pained Patrick deeply and exposed his inner sense of insecurity. His whole treatise is a riposte to the mocking comment: 'Why is this fellow exposing himself to danger among enemies who do not know God?'[25] Yet his *Letter to Coroticus* reveals Patrick's moral strength as a missionary bishop. It is a sharp rebuke to a local gangster who had abducted some newly baptised Irish Christians into slavery. His verdict is clear: 'One who betrays Christians into the hands of Irish and Picts is far from the love of God.'[26]

It is as works of theology in the context of mission that Patrick's writings stand out with an unique character and authority. In many ways he was a true disciple of St Paul, producing the first genuinely autobiographical writing about Christian missionary activity. In its form, the *Confession* may be influenced by Augustine's famous work of the same name; more probably it is redolent of the deposition of Christian confessors facing persecution. It rests heavily upon the Old Latin version of the Bible which antedated the Vulgate, and the language of scripture has become for Patrick a supreme means of expression, more than compensating for the deficiencies of his formal education in Latin rhetoric.[27] In style his writing is of a piece with Christian Latin literature in Gaul at this time, and there is reason to suppose that Patrick had been for a brief while at least in Gaul.[28] A number of significant themes emerge which give insight into his theology and psychology as a missionary bishop.

In his *Letter to Coroticus*, Patrick asserts that he is a bishop living among 'barbarian tribes as an exile and refugee for the love of God.' He claims a 'part with those called by God and predestined to proclaim the gospel among no inconsiderable persecutions even to the end of the earth.'[29] No-one compelled him to pursue this path, bound as he is 'in the Spirit' never to revisit any of his own kinsfolk. Only divine grace enabled 'this holy compassion' which he has been exercising towards his former captors, for whom he bargained away his aristocratic status. 'In short I am a slave of Christ to an outlandish nation because of the unspeakable glory of eternal life which is Christ Jesus our Lord.'[30] Everywhere Patrick's sense of God's call to him to be a missionary is evident, as is his debt to his great mentor St Paul, the spirit of whose writings he so deeply imbued. It ran counter to his youthful expectations, yet gave meaning and purpose to all that subsequently happened to him.[31]

He describes this call in moving and graphic terms. He actually names the messenger from God who delivered the summons as Victoricus. Perhaps this indicates familiarity with the writings of Paulinus of Nola whose emissary to Sulpicius Severus was of this name. More plausibly it alludes to Victricius of Rouen, the friend of Martin of Tours, who came to Britain as bishop at the end of the fourth century; or perhaps it has its root in the missionary initiative of Palladius from Rome to Ireland and its impact upon the British church during Patrick's youth. Victoricus came in a dream to Patrick bearing numerous letters from Ireland, and the heading of the one glimpsed by Patrick was 'The Cry of the Irish'. He continues:

and while I was reading aloud . . . I heard the voice of those who were by the wood of Voclut which is near the western sea, and this is what they cried, as with one voice, 'Holy boy, we are asking you to come and walk among us again,' and I was struck deeply to the heart and was not able to read any further, and at that I woke up.[32]

The echo of St Paul's vision of the Macedonian in Acts 16.9 is clear; but the personal authenticity of this testimony is beyond doubt. Patrick's conviction sustained him to the end: 'I have never had any motive apart from the gospel, and the promise to return to that nation from which I had only just been able to escape.'[33] Patrick's sense of divine providence was very strong:

I made the journey to Ireland against my will, to the point where I was near collapse, but this was rather for my good, because I was reformed by God through the experience, and he moulded me so that I should be today what was once far from me; so that I should take trouble and labour for the salvation of others, whereas then I used to take no thought even for my own.[34]

For despite his nominally Christian upbringing, it was only in captivity that he became 'a believer in the living God', and only in the weakness of affliction did he begin to experience the nature of God's power.

So he composed his *Confession* in part at least as a tribute to God for the way he had sustained Patrick in his calling in the midst of many dangers, 'who kept me faithful in the day of my trial so that today I can offer him confidently the sacrifice of my life as a living victim to Christ my Lord.'[35] Despite opposition at home, Patrick persevered until he was able, 'to come and preach the gospel to Irish tribes and endure insults from unbelievers, to bear the reproach of my pilgrimage and many persecutions, . . . and to sacrifice my free status for the good of others,' willing even to face martyrdom for the gospel.[36] He has taken to heart the evangelistic texts of the New Testament, seeing himself as a 'fisher of men' fulfilling the predictions of Christ.[37] He interprets opposition and suffering in spiritual terms, having 'thrown himself into the hands of Almighty God who reigns everywhere', confident of deliverance even in the midst of death.[38] Patrick sees his mission as bringing the gospel to the ends of the earth, beyond the reach of other missionaries of whom he seems aware: 'you can see that we are witnesses that the gospel has been preached as far as the point where there is no beyond.'[39]

Patrick was a person of orthodox Christian belief, determined to build up the life of the church in a lasting way. His *Letter to Coroticus* is quite revealing of this. Like St Paul, he regards those whom he has helped convert as spiritual children, 'begotten in large numbers for God and confirmed in Christ.' For them in part he writes his *Confession* as a kind of legacy.[40] His emissary to this tyrant is one of his own priests whom he 'taught from his childhood up'. Elsewhere in the *Confession* he is adamant that he never took fees either for baptisms or for ordination: 'when the Lord ordained clergy everywhere through me ... I gave this ministry to them without charge.'[41] Part of his horror at the pillage of Coroticus is that he has defiled the sacred rites of baptism and confirmation by his ruthlessness: his victims were still 'bearing the chrism, still in their white dress' when they were killed. His only consolation is that their passage to Paradise has been secured.[42] He challenges Coroticus on moral grounds, appealing to some familiarity with Christianity, reminding him of the formidable spiritual powers with which bishops are endowed.[43] Coroticus seems to have despised their position because they were Irish; Patrick reminds him that Christian baptism transcends racial distinctions and imparts equal value to all who believe.[44] This lofty view of the church, and of the role of bishops within it, is what sustains and gives shape to his mission. But it also accounts for the degree of pain endured by Patrick when he was subject to criticism from some of his fellow-bishops in Britain and perhaps in Ireland also. This seems to have arisen out of jealousy and misunderstanding, and a feeling of threat also because of his activities among a people whom many in western Britain especially feared as Roman power declined and disappeared. Patrick for his part may have magnified his reactions because of his relative isolation as a missionary. Certainly a significant part of the *Confession* is taken up with rebutting charges and insinuations against him, some of them going back to his youth. It makes depressing reading. As is too often the case in the history of the church, the impulse towards evangelism and mission induces ambivalence and even resentment among more established parts of church life. Patrick appears as a man thrown back upon his own resources, and hence his reliance upon scripture, and especially upon the testimony of St Paul.

His theology is expressed in the language of Nicene orthodoxy as mediated to the British church from Gaul. There is striking evidence of this in the *Confession* where he cites 'in extenso' a credal 'Rule of Faith' to which he later refers. In his *Letter to Coroticus* he refers to 'Christ my God',[45] and this 'Rule of Faith' has obviously been coloured by reaction to the Arian controversy of the fourth century. The root of some of its language lies in a commentary on the Apocalypse by Victorinus of Pettau, who died as a martyr under Diocletian. But the strong Trinitarian emphasis and the clauses against Arianism are the work of later hands, perhaps Gallic Christians supporting Hilary of Poitiers.[46] This 'Rule' asserts the uniqueness of God,

and his Son Jesus Christ whom we profess to have always existed with the Father, begotten spiritually before the origin of the world in an inexpressible way by the Father before all beginning, and through him were made things both visible and invisible.

The Lordship of Christ is affirmed in Pauline terms, as is the gift of the Holy Spirit – 'the gift and pledge of immortality, who makes those who believe and obey to be sons of God and coheirs with Christ, and we confess and adore Him, one God in Trinity of sacred name.' It is this precise belief that informs the more spiritual aspects of Patrick's theology.

Patrick's spiritual outlook was penitential and ascetic in temper. At the start of his *Confession* he regarded his fate as a punishment for his sins, both his personal failures and also those of his church: 'we had not been obedient to our bishops who used to warn us about our salvation.' So his people were enduring the fate of Israel in the Old Testament, and being scattered among hostile nations, a view later espoused by Gildas and transmitted by him to Bede. In his own afflictions he saw the hand of a loving God, however, disciplining and reforming him to his purpose. So he could regard himself as a stone lifted out of deep mud to be placed on the very top of the wall, called by God in a remarkable and personal manner.[47] At several crucial moments in his life, Patrick detected the providence of God, often intimated to him by a dream: the opportunity for escape from slavery, the change of heart of the sailors with whom he wished to escape, the provision of food on their journey, and his final liberation from their hands. On a grander scale, he clearly regarded his whole mission as a miracle of divine grace, overcoming many obstacles.[48]

Patrick was a man of deep prayer: this was the wellspring of his whole life, which he learned young during the hardships of his slavery. By it he penetrated the inner language of scripture, and his testimony is best heard in his own words: immediately after the account of his call to be a missionary, he writes:

And on another night – I do not know, God knows whether it was in me or beside me – someone was speaking in the most elegant language which I listened to but could not understand; except that at the end of the speech he spoke these words, 'He who gave his life for you, he it is who speaks in you,' and at that I woke up full of joy. And another time I saw him praying in me, and I was as it were within my body and heard him above me, that is above my inner man, and there he was praying earnestly with groans. While this was going on I was in amazement, wondering and considering who it could be who was praying in me, but at the end of the prayer he spoke to the effect that it was the Spirit, and at that I woke and recalled the words of the Apostle (i.e. Paul in Romans 8.26).[49]

Such a depth of prayer provoked spiritual conflict, and this Patrick graphically describes on two occasions. Once while he was escaping and was clearly in physical or moral danger from his captors; the other during the rancour surrounding the beginnings of his mission and the initial rejection of him as a bishop.[50] He never felt secure against such assaults, but it drove him deeper into prayer, and reliance upon divine aid for his ministry.

There is no evidence that Patrick's ascetic vocation led him formally to become a monk. But it is clear from his writings where his sympathy lay as this new movement began to infiltrate the British and Irish churches. Indeed his attitude may have further antagonised bishops unsympathetic to the claims of the monks, and so his writings may capture a time of flux in the life of the British church in the fifth century, as was certainly the case in Gaul. In his *Letter to Coroticus* he mentions the disruptive impact of this raid upon the growth of the church in Ireland where 'the sons of the Irish and the daughters of sub-kings were becoming monks and virgins of Christ.' Now he fears for their violation.[51] In the *Confession* he actually describes the conversion of a noble Irish woman who received a message from an angel to become a dedicated virgin of Christ. He then mentions that these devotees seldom enjoyed the approval of their fathers, indicating especially the hardships endured by Christian slaves, Irish and British, who wished to pursue this path. Yet despite such social pressures, Patrick points to a steady and significant growth in numbers of ascetics in Ireland. This does not mean necessarily that organised monasteries were being established during his time. But it was a movement of the Spirit which he encouraged and for which he felt a direct responsibility, refusing to consider a visit to Britain or to Gaul which might leave them, and especially the women, unprotected. Patrick may have known about and even had brief experience of monastic life as it was developing in Gaul, and seems to make reference to it when he expresses a long-held desire to 'see the face of the holy ones of my Lord' in Gaul.[52] Instead duty holds him in Ireland, even though its dictates weaken his capacity as he imagines to lead a truly holy life 'of perfection'. So instead he commends his disciples 'to follow the way of imitation better and to do more.'[53] Espousing the poverty of Christ, he demonstrates his own 'imitation' by wisely and firmly refusing any gifts from such devotees.[54]

Such conduct sprang also from certain well-considered attitudes towards how Christian mission might be conducted with complete integrity. Following the example of St Paul, Patrick consistently refused payment for divine services, financing instead much of his activity from his own resources. His ministry of evangelism was his personal gift to his hearers whose salvation he sought. He often had to make gifts to local rulers, and employ their sons as escorts for his movements and activities. These escorts did not always protect him from robbery and arrest, but such purchase of influence at court was indispensable for a peripatetic bishop in a potentially hostile tribal society. In a similar manner Patrick had to bribe and favour the legal advisers of the local rulers: 'I reckon that I spent among them not less than the price of fifteen men!'[55] There is no doubt that despite these efforts at local diplomacy to advance his mission, Patrick went often in fear for his life. The rhetoric of faith does not mitigate this reality: 'I daily expect either assassination or trickery or reduction to slavery or some accident or other.' He might anticipate martyrdom, but his lurid description of such a fate leaves little to the imagination.[56]

His attitude towards Coroticus and his followers reveals another and more risky side to Patrick's diplomacy as a missionary bishop. He directly challenges the outlawry and cruelty of their action, citing the words of prophets in the Old Testament to support his indictment. His verdict is summed up in the words 'a murderer cannot be with Christ'.[57] For this reason he regards them as excommunicate, in the grip of evil, and under divine judgement in which Patrick had a strong belief.[58] By this action he placed himself in the midst of a long and honourable tradition which continued to find full expression in the later life of the Celtic church, notably in the writings of Gildas. The courage and candour of Patrick's stance is striking.

In general his attitude towards Irish paganism was pretty unsympathetic, as summed up in this description: 'those in Ireland who never had knowledge of God but up to now always only worshipped idols and filthy things.' During his escape, Patrick was careful to avoid taking an oath which had pagan connotations, or eating honey that had been offered to the gods. Towards the end of his *Confession* he repudiates sun-worship: 'all who worship it will come to a bad end in wretched punishment as well.' Instead Christ is the true sun, to be worshipped and adored and in whose radiance Christians will rise to eternal life. In this case Patrick reveals the way in which aspects of pagan worship might be assimilated to Christian belief. His dream during his escape, in which he clearly felt the force of pagan religion pressing upon him, was broken by the sunrise and his calling upon Elijah, possibly a subconscious confusion with the Greek word for the sun 'helios'. The sun's radiance brought him deliverance which he associated with the presence of Christ and of the Holy Spirit.[59]

The striking thing about Patrick's writing is its sense of personal directness which transcends the attempts at formal rhetorical style in which he knows he is inadept. His use of the Bible is singular: a cursory analysis reveals more than 224 citations, roughly evenly divided between the Old Testament, the New Testament, and the writings of St Paul by whose testimony Patrick is deeply influenced at all points. His writings stand apart as a deeply spiritual account of the impact of missionary activity upon a person not wholly representative of his own church and generation. It was probably the inherent quality of these texts that ensured their copying and transmission during the next two hundred years when all memory of the historical St Patrick appears to have been lost in Ireland.

III. SAMSON AND GILDAS

The decline of Roman imperial power in north-western Europe, and the movements of Anglo-Saxon raiders and immigrants across the North Sea and the Channel inevitably disrupted to some extent the trade across those seas. In Britain, after the middle of the fifth century, the eastern and most fertile part of the land was subject to sporadic wars and invasion, and the established society of the post-Roman era began to break down, being replaced by war-lords anxious to defend their own areas of influence, not only against the incomers but also at times against each other. The fate of the church in these areas during this time remains largely obscure.

In the western part of Britain, however, a very different picture may be discerned, albeit dimly in places. Significant contacts with Gaul, Spain and the Mediterranean were maintained and in some ways enhanced, and by the end of the fifth century monasticism was making its mark all along the western seaboard of the British isles. Both in legend and in reality this was 'the age of the saints' in what is now described as the Celtic church. Why this was so emerges against the background of a fascinating pattern of other historical evidence remaining from this period.

The western seaways became an important bond of communication and cultural exchange during this turbulent period. Evidence of trade emerges in some of the early literature, for example in the *Confession* of St Patrick or the *Life of St Columbanus*, and has been confirmed by archaeological finds of material from north Africa and the eastern Mediterranean as well as from Gaul, imported during the fifth and sixth centuries, at Tintagel in Cornwall and at Dinas Powys near Cardiff in south Wales.[1] In Wales and in Cornwall, patterns of inscribed stones reveal immigration from Christian Gaul and more dominantly from Ireland. The movement of peoples was often complex and intermittent and is not always now easy to track down precisely. Many British fled to Brittany and to northern Spain where they created a distinctive and lasting cultural presence. Others fled into Wales and from there to Ireland; there is evidence too of Gallic presence and influence in southern Ireland early in the fifth century. Irish settlement in Wales penetrated the country using the existing Roman roads, and by the middle of the fifth century an important sub-kingdom was established in Brecon in addition to significant settlement in south-west Wales. From there the Irish migrated to north-eastern Cornwall, while others moved directly from Ireland itself to southern Cornwall and through there to the Continent. Clearly the topography of these coasts assisted such movement, settlement and trade during troubled times: islands, deep and often hidden havens, peninsulas capable of local defence were of benefit to these persistent, if small-scale activities. There is some evidence too that in south-eastern Wales, refugees from eastern Britain helped develop a strong focus of Christian culture and land-holding in the middle of the fifth century.[2] A possible church at Caerwent, use of a villa at Llantwit Major, the emergence of the discrete area called 'Ercing' on the borders of Herefordshire, and some evidence from the Llandaff charters would seem to support such a phenomenon.[3] It is against this background that the missions from Wales and perhaps Gaul to south-eastern Ireland, of Patrick to north-eastern Ireland, and later in the fifth century of Kentigern to south-western Scotland have to be seen.

Before passing to consider the literary evidence, notice must be taken of the evidence of the inscribed stones in Wales of this period. The earliest group comprise three groups of interesting and significant features. One group carry Latin inscriptions using Roman capital letters with phrases similar to Gallic and even North African Christian usage: 'hic iacit', 'in pace', 'in hoc tumulo', 'memoria'. Lying as they do in least Romanised parts of Wales, in from the western coasts and around Brecon, they seem to indicate contact with and even immigration from Gaul in the fifth century. Closely parallel to them are stones which carry inscriptions in the Irish 'Ogham' script, a series of linear marks representing the Roman alphabet and developed in Ireland in the third and fourth centuries. These are found also in southern and south-western Ireland and in Cornwall from this period. They would seem to confirm later traditions in Wales of Irish rule in areas of settlement in these parts. Sometimes these Ogham inscriptions rerender a parallel Latin text on the same stone. Examination of these inscribed stones reveals how the two Christian symbols of 'chi-rho' and of the cross became customary and intertwined during the fifth and sixth centuries.[4]

The decisive development of the fifth century was the arrival of widespread monastic life in western Britain. Sympathy for the teaching of Pelagius may well have been strong in Britain in certain aristocratic circles in the early part of the century. Certainly the missions of both Germanus and Palladius were concerned in part to rebut this heretical influence, and there is some reason to suppose that one of the followers of Pelagius, a Briton called Fastidius, may have been the author of some ascetical tracts – *De Vita Christiana*, *De Viduitate servanda*, and others of similar spirit.[5] Gennadius describes him as a British bishop. The British monk, Faustus, became for a time abbot of the monastery of Lérins in 433. Here in 410, St Honoratus had founded one of the first monasteries in Gaul on an island off Cannes. From it came a succession of distinguished monastic churchmen who were to influence the life of the Gallic church during the fifth century, notably Hilary of Arles, Vincent, Lupus of Troyes, and Caesarius of Arles. In their different ways these men shaped the early medieval church north of the Alps in a decisive and lasting manner, integrating the waxing monastic life into the wider structure of the church. This did not occur without controversy however. The issue revolved around the role of human effort in conjunction with divine grace in achieving salvation. St Augustine and his followers, anxious to worst the teaching of Pelagius which elevated human effort to an inordinate degree, challenged the teaching of the monks, influenced by teaching from the East mediated by Cassian, that ascribed crucial significance to ascetic endeavour in enabling divine grace to act within a person. Prosper of Aquitaine was a principal protagonist of this position, seeking and obtaining the support of Rome in the matter. In 431 pope Celestine sent the decree 'Apostolici verba' to the bishops of Gaul, cautioning them against innovative teaching and expressing disquiet at monastic bishops being intruded. Faustus, abbot of Lérins, was an able spokesman for what is called the 'semi-Pelagian' position, the theology of the monks, and this in reality came to determine the monastic influence upon the church, both in Gaul and in Britain too.[6]

The style of monasticism that began to take root in western Britain by the year 500 had its origins in the eastern Mediterranean, in Syria, Palestine and Egypt. It comprised quite small communities, mainly of men, living in 'sketes' where they shared certain elements of a common life while preserving the solitary life of hermits, to which the earliest monks in Britain were devoted. Both archaeology and the literature testify to the paramount importance of the eremitic life in Britain at this time, though there is no tangible evidence of any monastic site as such before the year 500. But the ascetic way of life, both for men and women is indicated as well-established and growing in the writings of St Patrick, and is part of the background to the earliest traditions surviving from Wales at this time. Once again the topography of the western coastal areas lent itself to this development, being in a way a kind of 'desert' with its headlands and coves, but also well-connected by means of sea transport. The influence of St Basil and of Cassian, both eloquent fathers of eastern monastic life now permeating the west, may be detected throughout the remaining literature of the Celtic church.

The archaeological pattern of early monastic remains provides important evidence for the distribution and ethos of this development. Islands and old or existing strongholds are the most common sites, as are also headlands and peninsulas: safety and seclusion were equally desirable. The principle of enclosure was established by the raising of a 'vallum' or earthen bank around the congeries of huts and small chapel which constituted such an early monastery. Very often within and around such enclosures there grew up cemeteries, with places of devotion near the graves of holy men, or the sanctuaries where their relics were venerated. The most striking indicators and remains from this age of the monastic saints are the many place-names throughout Wales, Ireland, Cornwall and Brittany. These afford elusive and tantalising evidence for the movement and influence of obscure holy men and women throughout these parts, often the same name occurring in several locations within a region, or else far apart across the seas. In Wales, the prefix 'Llan' signifies a holy place or enclosure of, or dedicated to a saint, the word 'merthyr' (from Latin 'martyrium') a place where a saint's relic was venerated. Often, as in Cornwall, it is only by a place-name that a saint is commemorated at all, and around such shadowy figures legends and folk-traditions sprang up in later medieval times to fill the vacuum of history. But there remain places still steeped in the spiritual memory of those times, often replete with some archaeological remains to be seen: the cell of St Seiriol upon Anglesey, the baptistery of St Cybi on the Lleyn peninsula, the peninsula of St David's, to name three of the most notable in Wales. The island of Bardsey, 'isle of twenty thousand saints', remains a goal of pilgrimage and a place of eremitic prayer to this day.[7]

The most likely source for this monastic influx was from the eastern Mediterranean, through Spain and Aquitaine. The growth of the eremitic or anchoretic life in Ireland certainly, and probably in Wales also, was nurtured by the transmission of books as well as the testimony of travellers and perhaps refugees. Certainly the earliest Irish Christian art owed much to Coptic and Syrian influences, and there is clear evidence of contact with Mozarabic Spain as well. Lismore in southern Ireland became during the fifth to seventh centuries an important centre of contact and so of the whole eremitic movement in Ireland. There was correspondingly an important centre of British ecclesiastical life and influence in Galicia in north-west Spain. Many of the customs of the Celtic church, which the later Roman missionaries to England challenged, in fact owed their origin to this formative period of close contact with the continental church – the calculation of Easter and certain distinctive liturgical practices to which the Celtic Christians clung with varying degrees of conservatism. This separate channel of influence independent from Rome remained a constant feature of church life in Ireland throughout the early middle ages.[8]

It is with great difficulty that any reliable picture is built of the activity of these Welsh and Irish saints who have left their mark on the landscape in place-names and fragmentary archaeological remains. For example the most famous Welsh saint and founding-father, St David, who probably died at the very end of the fifth century and whose impress may still be sensed in the place of his burial and its environs, is known only through a *Life* written late in the eleventh century as a piece of propaganda against the claims of the see of Canterbury under the Normans. Most of the lives of the Welsh saints date from this period. From such fragmentary traditions that remain embedded in these later writings, certain common features however emerge. The first is the dominant monastic ethos, exerting its sway over families of churches and lesser religious communities owing allegiance to the founding saint. Then there are the strong family connections, often with royal associations, which determined and sustained the landed roots of these foundations. Finally there is the propensity for learning and travel, by which the memory of the saint was sown both in the neighbouring area and much more widely, including overseas in Cornwall, Brittany and to a lesser extent in Ireland.[9]

The most reliable window into the activity of the Welsh church in the fifth and sixth centuries is provided by the *Life of St Samson*, written perhaps as early as the seventh century. Its centre of interest is in south-eastern Wales where perhaps Christianity persisted unbroken from the time of Roman rule. Three founding fathers emerge: Dubricius (or Dyfrig) who was a monk and bishop in the borderland of Hereford and Gwent where there are ancient church dedications to him. According to the *Life of St Samson* his influence spread abroad, and there is a church dedication to him in Somerset. He probably died around the year 550 perhaps as a recluse on Bardsey island, and there remains an uncompleted inscription referring to him on Caldey island also. Iltud also plays an important role, dying perhaps earlier in the sixth century before Dubricius, having created the monastery of Llaniltud Fawr where Samson trained as a monk. According to the *Life of St Samson*, Iltud was a person of great learning, and a disciple of Germanus of Auxerre, having been ordained priest by him. He was an astute spiritual father, endowed with prophetic gifts as well as formidable wisdom culled from much study. His foundation became the most notable centre of education in the Welsh church at this time.

A more shadowy figure is Cadoc, who about this time founded the monastic church at Llancarfan not far from Llaniltud Fawr. He may have been a contemporary of David, and also of Teilo, who created a centre of monastic life and active evangelism in and around Llandeilo Fawr in Dyfed. These three bishops represent the second main generation of Christian mission in Wales. Their work was paralleled by the missionary asceticism of St Samson himself, first in Wales and then in Brittany where he died as bishop of Dol around the year 565. His work abroad was part of a wider penetration of Brittany at this time by immigrants from Britain and Wales, notable among whom in the later life of the church was Paul Aurelian, better known as Paul de Léon who came thither as a missionary bishop in the sixth century. Finally the long-term influence of Llaniltud Fawr is confirmed in the memory of Finnian, abbot of Clonard in Ireland, who it is said received his spiritual formation there. He founded at Clonard the most important and influential house of Irish monasticism, compiling the earliest of the penitentials. He died in 549. No less significant as a disciple and then a master of Welsh and Irish monasticism in the sixth century was Gildas who probably died around the year 570.[10]

The *Life of St Samson* rests upon as secure a line of transmission as any hagiography of this early period. It was commissioned by a bishop, Tigernomalus, who perhaps lived in Cornwall, but was written primarily for the monks at Dol where the saint lay buried in the foundation he had created there: it ends with a sermon upon his cult and its celebration.[11] The author was a Breton monk of that house, but the line of information stretches back across the sea to Llaniltud Fawr in Wales. His authority was an old Welsh monk, a deacon and kinsman of St Samson's, who himself had received material from his uncle, another deacon and contemporary of

Samson's mother to whom he was related. This deacon's name was Henoc, and clearly there were written accounts of the 'acta' of the saint upon which this author relied, possibly in part from memory.[12] His work assumes a classic hagiographical structure and pattern, being much influenced by the *Life of St Martin of Tours*. But this is never explicitly referred to, perhaps because of the conflict between the Breton church and the see of Tours from which it was claiming independence at this time.[13] The style of the work is coloured by scripture but he uses a version earlier than the Vulgate. His frame of literary reference is typical of the monastic church at this date – Sulpicius Severus, Jerome, Rufinus, Fortunatus, Cassian and Evagrius, and explicitly Gregory the great. But there is no work cited or alluded to later than the end of the sixth century.[14] In which case the date of composition might be as early as 610-615, assuming Samson died around the year 565.

Through the hagiographic frame, however, a credible and distinctive picture may be discerned with quite a high biographical flavour. It is anchored in the strong family tradition running throughout, and which lends its own authority to the traditions being remembered and collected. It was from Samson's mother that some of the early material was received by the deacon Henoc. His parents were later commemorated in the diptychs which were read out at mass in the monastery; they were members of the Welsh aristocracy.[15] His conception like that of Samuel was a miracle against natural infertility, mediated by a holy man, Librarius, in response to prayer and the manufacture of a silver rod as a votive offering. The holiness of the child's future vocation and ministry was also predicted by visions.[16] Family pressure almost prevented Samson's education for the monastic life and the priesthood, they 'regarding the office of a cleric as unworthy of his family'.[17] Throughout his career as a monk in Wales, Samson was in touch and interacted with his immediate kin. Yet he had to be commanded to visit his father who was dying. Upon making his confession to his son he recovered, whereupon both he and his wife took religious vows, using their wealth to endow monasteries and as alms for the poor.[18] They were joined by his father's brother and his family, and returned with Samson to his monastery. To his uncle he later gave a monastery in Ireland, though only after much heart-searching on account of the kinship ties.[19] His father accompanied him in his search for a 'desert' near the Severn, and before his departure abroad he visited his mother and aunt to consecrate their churches as bishop. In Cornwall he entrusted his father with the rule of a monastery he founded there, taking his cousin the deacon Henoc with him to Brittany. There is a disarming candour about the way in which the demands and religious aspirations of his family intruded upon his own path, indicating the immense difficulty with which a person might uproot himself from his social situation, and the way in which religious devotion could quickly become another means of strengthening kinship ties within the monastic 'familia'.

The *Life* falls into several discrete parts: Samson's monastic life and formation at Llaniltud Fawr; his ascetic vocation upon Caldey island concluding with a visit to Ireland; his consecration as bishop and 'peregrinus' as the 'Elect of God' – a favourite appellation in this work; his sojourn in Cornwall, and finally his arrival in Brittany and the founding of Dol.

Llaniltud Fawr was clearly regarded as a well-established centre of Christian education and monastic formation by Samson's parents, early in the sixth century. Iltud its founder was a 'famous master of the Britons', a 'disciple of St Germanus' who had ordained him priest as a young man. Later in the *Life* there is an oblique reference to a monastery founded by Germanus over which Samson was prevailed upon to rule briefly as abbot.[20] It may be therefore that Germanus' visits in the middle of the fifth century had been to promote catholic monastic life in Britain, and in an area secure from the Saxon incursions in the Severn valley. If so, his labour was not in vain, and this *Life* describes Iltud as 'of all the Britons the most accomplished in all the Scriptures . . . and in Philosophy of every kind'. He was also a man of psychic powers, 'a most wise magician, having knowledge of the future'.[21] Over the proper use of such gifts within Christianity he was to clash with his protégé, Samson: 'of a truth it is not meet to practise worldly magic along with heavenly wisdom'. This occurred when Samson offered to go and cure a monk bitten by a snake.[22] Iltud was venerated as a seer and an 'elder' of singular spiritual influence and power.

Iltud welcomed Samson, apparently predicting his future priesthood and missionary career. He flourished under his hand, receiving both learning and spiritual formation from him, Iltud having to check at times Samson's zeal for the ascetic life. He was ordained deacon by bishop Dubricius, who appears as a frequent visitor to the monastery, and who like Iltud saw great promise in Samson's devotion and holiness. Inevitably this provoked envy and opposition from some of his fellows, led by Iltud's own nephews, who feared lest Samson should take over the monastery upon Iltud's death. Their vendetta is recounted in some detail, reaching a climax in an attempt to poison him, whereupon the prime mover's evil possession was revealed when he received the eucharist at Samson's hand. Samson in due course cured him, but tension remained, especially as Samson pursued an even more ascetic path and began to feel himself out of step with the more relaxed regime of Iltud's monastery.

So after much heart-searching and with Iltud's support, Samson migrated to Caldey island to lead the life of a hermit under the direction of the holy man, Piro. His conduct there is thus described: 'leading with untiring patience a wonderful, isolated and above all a heavenly life, he ceased not, day or night, from prayer and communion with God. Spending the whole day in working with his hands and in prayer, and the whole night in the mystical interpretation of Holy Scripture, he used to carry the lamp to his own dwelling in order that bent upon reading, he might either write something or exercise himself in spiritual contemplation'.[23] This mingling of biblical study with contemplative prayer was the foundation of his spiritual life and learning. He maintained this way of life even when upon Piro's accidental death he became abbot in his stead.[24] It was at this time that Samson entertained some Irishmen returning from a pilgrimage to Rome, and went with them for a while to Ireland. There he delivered an abbot possessed by evil who became his disciple, travelling with Samson to Brittany and dying at Penetal, the monastery he later founded in Normandy.[25] After his return to Caldey, Samson sought again 'to find a suitable desert', and with his father and the two monks he had rescued from evil, migrated to a disused fortress and cave near the Severn where he lived an enclosed life, emerging only to sing mass in the little oratory they created there.[26] 'He was ever desiring to tread that evangelical and narrow path which leads to heaven.'[27]

Samson was not long left in peace to pursue his chosen path for at a synod of the British church nearby he was summoned to become a bishop, to be consecrated on the feast of the Apostle Peter's Chair – 22 February, probably in the year 521.[28] Instead Samson in a vision felt himself consecrated by the apostles, Peter, James and John themselves. This was in turn intimated to bishop Dubricius and through him to the synod where it swayed opinion finally in Samson's favour, there evidently having been reservations in certain quarters. During the consecration, Dubricius and others witnessed the presence of the Holy Spirit, as a dove hovering over Samson as at his earlier ordinations, and as a fire proceeding from his mouth and nostrils during mass. Here there is an obvious parallel to St Martin of Tours.

> And what is greater than all these things, . . . when he sang mass, the angels of God ever became holy ministers of the altar and of sacrifice along with him, and often broke the oblation with their hands, though he alone saw it.[29]

It was in the context of preparation for the Paschal mass, during a night vigil, that Samson received the angelic call to work abroad as a 'peregrinus' and missionary bishop. The whole episode reveals an active episcopate, fidelity to catholic liturgical traditions, and a deep devotion to the eucharist in the British church at this time.

He migrated to Brittany via Cornwall, as did many other such pilgrim saints during these years. He went first to the monastery at St Kew near the Camel estuary where it is presumed he landed from Wales. Here he consulted a seer called Juniavus (possibly Winniau) who advised him to proceed immediately with his journey to the continent.[30] But according to other traditions, Samson remained for some time in Cornwall, where his memory was venerated at Padstow, St Kew, Southill, Golant, and in the Scilly isles where there is an island named after him. His companions Mewan and Austell were also thus remembered who later followed him to Brittany.[31] The *Life* recounts how Samson brought with him his holy vessels and books, and also his chariot from Ireland! These accompanied him as he finally progressed to the south coast of Cornwall for the journey overseas. It is in this context that the story is told of Samson's encounter with pagan worship of an image in the area of Trigg. He proceeded silently and began to persuade the people gently to leave off their idolatry. A timely miracle clinched the debate, as in the *Life of St Martin of Tours*, and later the writer was able himself to 'trace the sign of the cross which St Samson with his own hand carved by means of an iron instrument on a standing stone' in that place.[32]

But lurking behind this reversal of paganism was an altogether more searching deliverance. The chief confessed to the saint that his folk were ruled by a great fear and 'anxiety of mind'. It took the form of a predatory serpent whom all dreaded. Samson made the journey into the wild, located the cave in which it dwelt and destroyed it by noosing it with his girdle, 'flung it from a certain height and charged it in the name of the Lord Jesus not to live any longer.'[33] He made the cave a cell for eremitic prayer, and founded a small monastery nearby, causing a spring to arise by a miracle, and entrusting the new community to his own father to rule. It is a strange tale, matched in this *Life* by two other similar miracles: a parallel exorcism in Brittany, and a serpent he and his family encountered on his return with them from the healing of his father. Significantly this is described as 'the serpent of which we have heard from our parents', which Samson spots 'as if he saw merely a little snake'. He charms and binds it by the recital of psalms, confining it within a circle in which he placed his cross. Here there is an interesting association with the circle cross-forms of inscribed stones in Wales from this period. Also in connection with his visit home to his sick father is the hair-raising account of an encounter with a sorceress, 'a very old woman with shaggy grey hair, with her garments of red and holding in her hand a bloody trident'. With this she assaulted and nearly killed Samson's terrified companion, and was only halted by the invocation of the name of Christ. Steeped in evil, she refuses to help the stricken man, so the saint condemns her to die, and she does. Instead like Elijah of old, Samson resuscitates the dying man by prayer and the breath of life. There is, therefore, in Samson's example a fusion of pastoral sense, recalled in his persuasion of the people of the Channel isles to abandon pagan rites by gentle means and amiable appeals to their children,[34] with a robust challenge and belligerence towards pagan superstition, particularly when it took the form of fear of evil. It seems that he was able by his own faith and charismatic authority to exorcise from the minds of whole communities that which exercised paranoic fear over them, or which had become the symbol of their dread. Hard as it is to form an accurate assessment at this remove of such phenomena, the possibility of irrational and crippling psychoses developing in primitive and vulnerable communities must not be underrated. Samson, like his biblical namesake, was revered and remembered as a spiritual warrior, not afraid to 'play the man', a frequent rejoinder in the *Life*, as the 'Elect of God', armed with prayer and the power of the holy Name of Christ.

The *Life* concludes with the account of how St Samson arrived in Brittany, and was immediately recognised as a healer by a man with a leprous wife and a possessed daughter, both of whom he cured by prayer. The actual foundation of the monastery at Dol is simply referred to with brevity, and the writer turns his attention to how Samson, like St Martin, challenged successfully the Frankish King Childebert who was holding the rightful ruler, Judwal, captive. Upon arrival at court he cured a possessed chieftain by the use of episcopal oil, tried to persuade the king to meet him, and when refused threatened divine retribution. The queen remained violently opposed, and tried to poison him, a trick Samson exposed by the sign of the Cross. Twice more she tried to kill him before the royal couple relented and agreed to release their captive. After liberating them from fear of a predatory serpent, Samson created a monastery in the place of its den with active support of the king, now overawed by the saint's power. After a sea journey home via the Channel Isles, Judwal regained his kingdom with Samson's support. The whole account is coloured by the example of St Martin, revealing the relative independence and fearlessness of Samson as a missionary bishop, whose challenge to tyranny on moral grounds was no less fierce than his conflict with evil itself.

There is evidence in the Life that Samson antagonised some of his fellow-clergy and monks by his rigour: he apparently, like Martin, endured 'much envy and evil-speaking at the hands of perverse priests'.[35] Moments of conflict emerge throughout the Life, even in the encomium at the end when the story is told of how Samson and Dubricius disagreed in their estimate of a young deacon who turned out to be entrammelled in sorcery. In the end the truth came out, the boy died, and Samson for three days and nights interceded with fasting for his deliverance while the body lay outside the monastery unburied. Finally, the requiem mass was said and the tragic victim buried by Samson in peace. The moral drawn by the writer was that 'it is not in the least possible to hide anything at any time, good or evil, from the saints'.[36] But the tale may also touch on the tensions within a close monastic community induced by so powerful a charismatic figure as St Samson. It is in this last section, which is an exhortation to the community at Dol suitably to venerate their founder, that the teaching of St Gregory the great is cited several times in support of the point that 'to honour the festivals of the saints is nothing else than to adjust lovingly our minds to their good qualities'.[37] Indeed this whole sermon affords a glimpse into how saints were perceived at this time. The saint is the instrument of divine activity still among his faithful disciples, so his commemoration is also a celebration of the many miracles wrought by him during and after his earthly life. 'We firmly believe him to be engaged there in another, better and unending life among the saints of God, whom we perceive shining forth among us who are alive, strong and mighty in the work of God.'[38] But moral actions must be consistent with professions of veneration if Christians are to benefit from the care of the saints. In words cited from St Gregory: 'It profits nothing to take part in the feasts of men if it chance that one is absent from the feasts of Angels.'[39] Instead, men should follow diligently, and if need be in hardship, the paths blazed by the saints, and 'know perfectly well that Almighty God is the clearest discerner not of words but of deeds'.[40] He concludes with a fitting pen-portrait of St Samson the ascetic: recalling his lengthy fasts and all-night vigils in prayer and communion with God, he remembers being told how the saint spent Lent,

> withdrawn from human habitations to some rather remote spot, carrying with him only three loaves to suffice him until the joy of Paschal celebration, God supporting him in all things. Having zeal for God and for His church burning in his heart . . . filled, so to speak, with God, he was courteous and dear to all.[41]

Samson's self-imposed exile and mission to Brittany was only part of a wider and formative movement within the British church towards its emigré cousins in the former Roman province of Armorica. This area, now called Brittany, had been persistently invaded and settled by Britons migrating from Saxon advances in Britain on and off throughout the fifth century. By the middle of the sixth century they had transformed the whole area into several Celtic tribal kingdoms in which were successfully planted monastic bishoprics largely independent of the Gallic church. In 461, a British bishop, Mansuetus, is recorded signing as a suffragan of Tours. Shortly after, in 465, the bishop of Tours presided over a synod at Vannes to appoint Paternus bishop. The significance of Faustus of Riez, abbot of Lérins and probably a Breton, has already been discussed. In 511 a Breton bishop, Modestus, appears at a synod in Orleans. But the invasions of the Franks and the scale of British immigration in the early part of the sixth century drove a wedge between the Gallic church at Tours and the bishops in Brittany, and it appears that Samson himself might have been one of the last to collaborate with the church in the lands now under Frankish rule, signing himself in 555 or 557 at a synod in Paris, while under the patronage of king Childebert, as 'Samson, bishop and sinner'.[42]

Gildas remains the most prominent figure from the British church in the sixth century. He seems to have lived between 500 and 570, being a younger contemporary of St Samson of Dol. The Breton monk who compiled his *Life* in the eleventh century claimed that he was a northerner who came to south Wales where he received education at the hands of Iltud, presumably at Llaniltud Fawr. Later he went to Ireland, before retiring to Brittany where he founded the monastery at Rhuys which became the centre of his cult in those parts. But this *Life* so obviously shadows that of St Samson that these facts cannot be regarded as certain. However, the rulers whom he castigates in his principal work *De Excidio* lived in south Wales, and he may have been venerated there.[43] What is clear is that he was well-versed in Latin, being trained in grammar and rhetoric in the late Roman manner. Like other contemporaries in Gaul, he may well have trained for a secular career before relinquishing it to become a monk and priest. This would imply access to a reasonable level of education in Britain in the centuries after the Roman departure, for Gildas' audience must have been able to understand his message in all the rich pattern of its Latin allusions and style. Gildas, indeed, refers to this as he upbraids one of the petty tyrants who had as teacher 'the refined master of almost all Britain', possibly a reference to St Iltud.[44] His writing is full of allusions to Virgil, as well as use of several versions of the Bible. The *De Excidio* is a prophetic diatribe against degeneracy among the British rulers and church, and as such it was taken up by Bede, and so popularised among the Anglo-Saxons from Alcuin to Wulfstan of York in the early 11th century.

It was, however, as a monastic father that Gildas was most revered among his own people in his lifetime and immediately thereafter.[45] He appears to have been the first formally to collate authoritative extracts from the Bible and the fathers to form the basis for penitential teaching about the keeping of the monastic rule. Some of this is encapsulated in fragments of his work which passed into penitential codes in Ireland, and thence to Brittany and the Continental church in the seventh and eighth centuries. The significance of this development, which became a distinctive contribution by the Celtic church to wider Christendom, is corroborated by two important testimonies from the early sixth century. The first is contained within a letter of the Irish missionary St Columbanus to pope Gregory the great, in which he refers to the authority of Gildas as a spiritual teacher, whom another venerated Father Vennianus had consulted on the vexed issue of whether a monk might leave the place and abbot of his first profession in pursuit of a more strict life elsewhere.[46] The identification of Vennianus is not wholly resolved, but it is quite probable that he was Finnian, the notable spiritual father whose authority lay behind the earliest Irish penitentials, and who was associated with Moville and Clonard. He may well have been a British missionary to the Irish church.[47] By some distant and confused memory, he may also be identified with the person St Samson consulted in Cornwall on the way to Brittany. Both Finnian and Gildas were held up to the pope as fathers of the 'western church' – of Britain, Ireland and Brittany, by Columbanus, whose own missionary activities and monastic foundations did so much to disseminate elements of Celtic monastic ethos to the continental church. Finnian appears also in Adomnan's *Life of St Columba* as the spiritual father of that saint as well.[48]

The second corroborating testimony to the spirit of Gildas' monastic teaching is found in the *Life of St Samson*, written probably shortly after the letter of Columbanus: 'much of Samson's career could be seen as illustrating the trend advocated by Gildas.'[49] Both this *Life* and the 'fragmenta' of Gildas are concerned to incorporate a renewed monastic life within the existing episcopal and monastic structure of the British church, and to temper extremes of asceticism by due obedience and consistent charity. There was to be no antagonism between ordained ministry and the vocation of the holy man in his community, and this conjunction was indeed a feature of the Celtic church at this time.[50] This was in a sense the spiritual legacy of Gildas and his generation, later to be enshrined in the Irish canons of the eighth century, and their penitential discipline. Certainly the comparison between the 'fragmenta' of Gildas addressed to the monastic life within the church, and the unfolding of the *Life of St Samson* is a close and fruitful one, the saint embodying and enabling the pattern of virtues and attitudes being commended. As with Columba at Iona, so with Samson: the life bore a fruit that took institutional expression, while the living memory of the saint remained as a luminous exemplar.

Examination of the remaining 'fragmenta' provides important insight into the spirit of Gildas' teaching and monastic life at that time, and this is echoed in the penitential also ascribed to him.[51] Using biblical examples, he moderates the desire to excommunicate those not observing a strict rule within the life of the church, condemning those who through pride look down from their own asceticism upon others, reminding them that 'abstinence from bodily food is useless without charity.' In one fragment there is a summary of the message of the *De Excidio*, in which condemnation of moral degeneracy is set against an eschatological perspective and expectation. This coupled with false asceticism is seen as the rule of pride, and therefore of the devil. Instead,

the Lord calls blessed not those who despise their brothers, but the poor, . . . those who hunger and thirst not for water, in order to despise others, but for righteousness; . . . not men who cause war, but men who endure persecution for the sake of righteousness.

The fourth fragment is probably the answer secured by Finnian to which Columbanus makes reference in his letter to the pope. It cautions against restless monks leaving their communities for specious and judgmental reasons, and is in spirit not far removed from the *Rule of St Benedict* with which it is roughly contemporary. However, 'a laxer abbot should not hold back a monk of his if he is inclined to stricter ways', and how this should occur is exemplified in some detail in the *Life of St Samson*, where there is due emphasis placed upon obedience and consideration towards the first abbot, in this case Iltud. Likewise, Gildas is firm in upholding the authority of bishops and of abbots as spiritual fathers and judges of men. 'The chief should not be changed except at the choice of his subjects, nor the subject obtain the place of his superior without the advice of an elder.' Thus the hermit or spiritual father played a crucial role in offering guidance within the life of the Celtic church at this time. But such judgement exercised by superiors is placed within a divine perspective: 'The judgement about the uncertain end to life comes home to us all when we read in the scriptures that an apostle was destroyed by greed, and that a thief confessed and was carried to heaven.' So the exercise of judgement within the church and the monastic community must be a work of clemency, gentleness and patience. Only major sins, not mere suspicion, should exclude a person from communion and table-fellowship: 'they may not deserve to be communicants;

yet at the same time we may perhaps, thanks to evil thoughts, be in communion with devils.' In the *Life of St Samson* there is a graphic illustration of just such a tangle within the life of the monastery which came to a head at the eucharist. Instead a more generous attitude is commended: 'a wise man recognises the gleam of truth whoever utters it.' However, in the face of corruption in the church which is incorrigible – 'when the ship is holed, let the man who can swim – swim!'

This last shrill note of despair colours the *De Excidio* – the *Ruin of Britain* which Gildas wrote towards the middle of the sixth century. It is a tragic monument to a society about to be engulfed and divided by pagan invasion from the east. In it he proves himself heir to the prophetic tradition of Samson, Patrick and Martin of Tours. He models his diatribe on those of the 'celibate prophet' Jeremiah, regarding the prophets of the Bible as 'favouring the good and forbidding men the bad; they were in a sense the mouth of God and the instrument of the Holy Spirit.'[52] His judgement is the harbinger of storm, warning of corruption, violence and internal weakness in both church and state, which if not checked swiftly will render the British prey to their adversaries like Israel of old. Indeed, it is to the theodicy of the Old Testament that he turns to make sense of the catastrophe that he feels will soon befall his people: it is for their sins that they are about to be punished again. His attitude towards the Anglo-Saxon invaders is one of deep hatred: they are 'the old enemy, bent on total destruction, and (as was their wont) on settlement from one end of the country to another.' 'Hated by man and God', they are 'like wolves in the fold.'[53] This is the theological perspective which determines his presentation of the history and fate of the British in the years after the Roman departure as the tide of Anglo-Saxon advance ebbed and flowed. As he writes, the long peace secured by the British at the battle of Badon (c.500) was coming to an end. Already the land was partitioned so that, for example, the holy shrines of the martyrs Alban, and of Aaron and Julius at Caerleon, were denied to many of the Christian British.[54] Within a generation of his writing, the resistance of the southern British would be broken forever at the battle of Dyrham in 577, by which the west Saxons gained access to the Severn sea, and so split the British in Wales from those in the south-west peninsula.

In pursuit of this theological vision, Gildas turns a severe judgement towards his own people in their plight. He writes out of deep pain and gloom. He imposes upon the history of the British under Roman rule and since that time the paradigm of rebellious and apostate Israel in the Old Testament. They are truly a 'latter-day Israel' to be tried by battle and scourged by plagues.[55] They are berated for cowardice and duplicity in a way that condemns them as a race. Unwittingly Gildas gave a great weapon to his enemies the Anglo-Saxons; for, in the hands of Bede, this self-condemnation was turned into justification for the 'ethnic cleansing' of the perfidious British by God's new chosen race.[56]

Gildas emerges from the pages of the *De Excidio* as a great master of the

Bible, especially of the Old Testament. The book is an extensive commentary upon a major tradition within the Bible which he is attempting to relate
to the needs of his countrymen. He states his theological approach thus: 'I
gazed on these things and many others in the Old Testament as though in a
mirror reflecting our own life; then I turned to the New Testament also and
read there more clearly what had previously been dark to me.'[57] Against the
careless demoralisation of his society he raises the standard of biblical teaching
and truth. Because the appointed 'watch-men' – the bishops and clergy of
the British – 'are bowed under the pressure of their great burdens, and
have no time to take breath', Gildas as teacher will arise with his clarion
call.[58] At his hands, the Old Testament becomes a 'mirror for princes' and
a rebuke for bishops also. At great length he cites passage after passage to
reinforce his message, before turning to the New Testament for guidance
as to how things should be. By name he assails the rulers of his people,
known princes in south Wales in the first half of the sixth century, for their
sins, before caricaturing the failings of the clergy in lurid terms.[59]

Over against this perceived decay in church life, Gildas appears to set the
faithfulness of the new 'remnant' – the monks. Towards the end of his
historical prologue, he says: 'the rest are counted so small a number that,
as they lie in her lap, the holy mother church in a sense does not see them,
though they are the only true sons she has left. By their holy prayers they
support my weakness from total collapse, like posts and columns of salvation.'[60] Later in his critique of corrupt rulers, he recalls one of them to
his own monastic formation while a young prince: 'you first pondered a
great deal at that time day and night on the godly life and the Rule of the
monks; then . . . you vowed to be a monk for ever.'[61] From this tradition of
faithfulness, Gildas erects the positive side to his teaching, using the New
Testament particularly as a yardstick for righteous living for both princes
and clerics. His appeal rests upon the 'authority of law and the saints', and
he cites St Ignatius of Antioch from his own letters, and also St Basil and
the martyr Polycarp as role-models for his hearers. His treatment of scripture is very much in the spirit of the later penitentials, and he appeals to the
memory of the readings at ordination to reinforce his point.[62] Over all this
there is a spirit of urgency and eschatological expectation as the day of
divine judgement draws near for the British church. His closing words are
a prayer for the faithful few in the face of calamity:

> May the almighty God of all consolation and pity preserve the very few
> good shepherds from all harm, and, conquering the common enemy,
> make them citizens of the heavenly Jerusalem, that is of the congrega-
> tion of all the saints: the Father, the Son, and the Holy Spirit, to whom
> be honour and glory for ever and ever, Amen.[63]

The *De Excidio* of Gildas is a tragic 'cri de coeur' from someone well-
equipped intellectually and spiritually to address the common dangers, but
apparently powerless in the face of a combination of forces beyond his or
anyone else's control. It conveys the sense of a 'last-ditch stand' in the

face of impending loss of cultural identity and racial security. Its poignancy is the more extreme as it is the last voice of the British church, a church not without vitality but which was about to be placed on the defensive for ever. Yet the picture of that church which may be glimpsed in the pages of Bede, a hostile witness, is one stamped still by the spiritual ethos of the generation of Gildas: monastic and episcopal, obstinate in its own well-tried traditions, and deferential to the counsel of the holy man.[64] Insofar as the teaching of Gildas and others from the sixth century became enshrined in the penitentials and spiritual tradition of the Irish church, it remained indirectly formative of the life of the English church in the course of the seventh century. The memory of Gildas was cherished most among the monks, probably in Brittany and certainly in Ireland: for them he was 'Gildas Sapiens' – Gildas the Wise. In an age of migration and cruel flight, the monastic ideal he and his generation adumbrated became for many a lifeboat away from a sinking ship. The voice of the exile, whether Old Testament prophet or monastic father, made its own impression upon the spiritual consciousness of the western church with its singular blend of urgency, grief and consolation. To pursue this path was to make a virtue out of necessity and to bring purpose to uprootedness: the call to become a 'peregrinus' or pilgrim for the sake of the Kingdom of God became central in the life of that church most moulded by British influence – the monastic world of the Irish.

IV. COLUMBA AND COLUMBANUS

The figure who towers over the history of Irish Christianity during the sixth century is St Columba, who died in 597, the year in which St Augustine came from Rome to Canterbury. His life is told by Adomnan, a successor as abbot of Iona, who wrote a century later, but who utilized to the full the rich traditions and memories of the saint in his own monastic community. Columba was born around 520 and was related to the Ui Neill rulers in the northern part of Ireland. He was fostered by a priest, Cruithnechan, and as a young deacon by Gemman at a school in Leinster where, like his younger contemporary, Columbanus, he was educated. Adomnan also mentions bishop Finnian as another mentor, perhaps the same British teacher and monastic father mentioned in the life of St Samson.[1] Of particular interest is the tradition cited in the second preface:

> A certain pilgrim from Britain, named Mochta, a holy disciple of the holy bishop Patrick, made this prophecy about our patron, which has been passed down by those who learnt it of old and held to be genuine:
>
> In the last days of the world, a son will be born whose name Columba will become famous through all the provinces of the ocean's islands, and he will be a bright light in the last days of the world. . . . A man very dear to God and of great merit in his sight.

If Mochta's memory was commemorated at Iona and so his obituary found its way into the earliest annals compiled there, this might indicate some conscious continuation of the memory of St Patrick's mission in the sixth and seventh centuries.

Little otherwise is known for certain of Columba's early life and religious formation in Ireland. In 563, however, he left his home as a 'pilgrim for Christ' to Britain. The impetus for such a move may have been partly political, and later tradition regarded it as a consequence of some involvement by Columba as a partisan during the battle of Cul Drebene two years earlier. Certainly around this time, according to Adomnan, Columba was temporarily excommunicated by an Irish synod.[3] But here there may be a parallel with some of the difficulties experienced by St Patrick with his own church, or by St Samson in disentangling himself from his kin and their claims. Columba may well have been related also to the ruling families among the Dal Riata, the Irish settlers in western Scotland at that time, one of whom, the ruler Comgall, gave him the island of Iona in which to found a monastery. He did not come alone but with twelve companions,[4] who are recorded in an early tradition appended to one version of Adomnan's *Life*. From Iona, the saint founded a network of related monastic communities – upon an unknown island called Hinba, in Tiree and in due course at Durrow in Ireland itself. Hinba was a retreat for penitents and hermits, while each house was ruled by a prior appointed by Columba. There are intermittent references to pastoral and evangelistic contact by the saint and his followers in neighbouring parts, and also with the local rulers, both Irish and Pictish. Adomnan emphasises Columba's political influence: on one occasion being summoned in a vision to ordain Aedan as king of Dal Riata against his own personal inclinations; and on another occasion presiding over a conference in 575 between Aedan and the northern Ui Neill overlord at Druim Cett near Derry.[5] Bede remembered Columba as a missionary to the Picts in the far north of Scotland: 'he converted that people to the faith of Christ by his preaching and example'.[6] This memory is corroborated by the very early poem from Iona, the 'Amra Choluimb Chille' which recalls how the saint 'preached to the tribes of the Tay'; and there is mention in Adomnan's *Life* of several visits, one of which was to the Pictish king Bridei, when Columba worsted the pagan magician, and like Martin and Samson before him thus commanded the king's respect and attention.[7] Within a hundred years of Columba's death the influence of Iona was paramount among the Pictish churches. In the saint's lifetime the ramification of this influence is best summed up perhaps in the charming story of how a book of hymns written out by St Columba himself fell into a stream in Ireland and was returned to its owner, a Pictish priest called Eigenan, and found to be intact and undamaged.[8] It is important too as testimony to Columba's reputation as a scholar and copier of books. There is a whole cluster of stories from the monastery in Adomnan's *Life* which indicate the prevalence of this activity in the saint's life and circle of disciples, and of the veneration of books made by him as virtual relics. One claimed to be so, the *Cathach of St Columba* – a psalter from the end of the sixth century, remains to this day.[9]

By the time Columba died in 597, Iona had become an important centre of monastic life and culture, a 'familia' bound together by a common discipleship to so charismatic and formidable a father, for whom travel by sea to and fro maintained steady communication. Gradually the influence of Iona and the cult of St Columba spread up the western coast of Scotland and into the Pictish kingdoms, while Durrow remained the centre of growing Ionan influence in Ireland.[10] Of central importance to the strength of this tradition in the seventh century were the successors of St Columba as abbots of Iona. His immediate heir was his close friend and disciple Baithene, followed by a kinsman Lasren. These were colleagues of the saint who appear in stories in the *Life*. Fergnae, the fourth abbot was of the next generation although himself a witness while young to Columba's sanctity: he died in 623.[11] The next abbot, Segene, played an important role in the controversy over the date of Easter concerning which an Irish cleric, Cummian, and later two popes addressed letters to him. Segene was also responsible for sending Aidan as a missionary bishop to Lindisfarne at the request of the Northumbrian king, Oswald, who had sheltered under his protection while in exile in Iona. It also appears that Segene took the initiative in beginning to collect and confirm stories about St Columba.[13] His nephew, Cummene, who later became abbot after him, compiled a book on the miraculous powers of the saint to which Adomnan refers indirectly; a fragment from this work was inserted into one of the versions of the *Life*.[14] It is likely that during Cummene's abbacy the famous book of Durrow, a richly illuminated gospel-book, was produced. This, the earliest of such Irish books, was unlikely to have been the only example of this sophisticated craftsmanship, emulated later in the Lindisfarne gospels in Northumbria, and in the book of Kells. According to the annals, Cummene and his immediate successor, Failbe, visited Ireland on a regular basis to supervise the Columban foundations there. Cummene died in 669, and Failbe in 679, to be succeeded by Adomnan, the hagiographer of St Columba.

The poetry remaining from Iona during the seventh century constitutes an eloquent testimony to the memory of the saint, to the resources gathered at the monastery, and to the rich theology which emerged there to underpin Adomnan's own achievements. The most important poem is the 'Amra Choluimb Chille', an elegy upon the saint's life and death probably composed shortly after 597 by a poet called Dallan Fogaill. It is one of the earliest Gaelic poems, and in it Columba himself is recalled and celebrated as a poet: 'he went with two songs to heaven after his cross'.[15] Two ancient poems remain which are by tradition attributed to the saint: a Latin work 'Altus prosator', heavily influenced by the Bible in both the old Latin and Vulgate versions, and the 'Adiutor laborantium', like the 'Altus prosator' an alphabetical Latin poem, which sets forth a theological vision of dependency upon Christ for protection and rescue, which might well serve as a commentary upon the picture of Columba himself painted by Adomnan in his *Life*.[16]

The 'Amra Choluimb Chille' is the most important testimony to the memory of St Columba remaining apart from Adomnan's *Life*. Dallan its author was clearly educated in a monastery, well-acquainted with the Bible and the church fathers. His is a formal paean of praise for a Christian hero. It may have been commissioned with both an aristocratic audience and monastic 'familia' in mind, so his picture of Columba is slightly different from that of Adomnan. It was authorized by Aed, king of the Cenel Conaill and of Tara, a kinsman of the saint's, who died in 598, so there is strong emphasis on Columba's noble ancestry in the poem. He appears as an active protagonist in political as well as religious affairs, and as a missionary among the Picts. From the spiritual authority of his ascetic life he was able to act as a spiritual warrior on behalf of his people, especially the poor. It makes explicit Columba's reputation and energy as a scholar and teacher: 'he fixed the psalms, he made known the books of Law'. His interests extended also to the computation of dates and seasons, like Bede. For him Basil and Cassian were pillars of monastic theology. His authority as a spiritual figure was confirmed by angelic visions, proof of his heavenly nobility.

The poem laments the passing of one who was a 'sage', 'the leader of nations who guarded the living', 'our chief of the needy', 'our messenger of the Lord – the seer who used to keep fears from us ... who would explain the true Word'. 'The whole work, it was his: it is now a harp without a key, it is a church without an abbot.'

He suffered briefly until he triumphed:

He was a terror to the devil,

to whom mass was a noose.

By his mighty skill, he kept law firm.

Rome was known, order was known,

knowledge of the Godhead was granted to him.

Truly blessed when he died,

he was wise about apostles, about angels.[17]

The drama of his life and its meaning mirrored that of Christ himself:

He climbs to the depth for the sake of the God of humanity. By longings he is stretched, he sold his eye's desire. ... He was full of light ... a shelter to the naked and a teat to the poor. Fresh was each bitter blast he suffered. ... From the dark journeys of man he sat down with God.[18]

Midway between Dallan at the moment of Columba's death and Adomnan a century later stands the poet Beccan, who was possibly the hermit to whom Cummian also addressed his letter to Segene, commemorated in the annals of Ulster compiled on Iona as having died on the island of Rum in 677.[19] His poem reflects the growing cult of the saint among his own community to whom he stands in deepening intimacy; it may be in places influenced by Dallan's earlier encomium. Its ethos is summed up in this stanza:

Though it was known near and far who Colum was, he was unique:

His name glistened like the sun; he was a light before all.

The poet commends himself to the heavenly intercession of such a patron. His other work, 'Tiugraind Beccain' is similar in tone and reinforces the impression created by Adomnan:

Beloved of God, he lived against a stringent rock,

a rough struggle, the place one could find Colum's bed.

He crucified his body, left behind sleek sides;

he chose learning, embraced stone slabs, gave up bedding.

He possessed books, renounced fully claims of kinship:

for love of learning he gave up wars, gave up strongholds.

Colum Cille, Colum who was, Colum who will be,

constant Colum, not he the protection to be lamented.

Colum, we sing, until death's tryst, after, before,

by poetry's rules, which gives welcome to him we serve.[20]

A poem seeking Columba's protection attributed to Adomnan, another piece by one of his contemporaries in devotion to the Virgin Mary, and an *Alphabet of Devotion* by a younger contemporary of St Columba called Colman communicate something of the rich seam of monastic piety which developed during this period.[21] It is a theological tradition in which heavenly vision and earthly ethics mingle seamlessly: the emphasis is upon an eternal life to be discovered in the midst of daily faith and obedience, to which the example and memory of St Columba bore abiding witness.

From these poems as well as from the works of Adomnan himself, Iona emerges as a formidable centre of Christian learning in the seventh century, though as Bede indicates not the only one in the Irish church. Remote physically, the island monastery was far from cut off from the wider world of Christian learning. In addition to both Latin versions of the Bible, there is evidence of some Greek learning in the work of Columba and his disciples, and knowledge of apocryphal literature like the gospel of Nicodemus and the book of Enoch. The tradition of church fathers used is solidly monastic in emphasis: the *Life of St Antony* by Athanasius in Latin translation by Evagrius; the *Actus Sylvestri* which purported to report the dealing of a fourth century pope with the Christian emperor, Constantine. The biblical works of Jerome and of his pupil, Philip the presbyter, and Augustine's *City of God* appear to lie behind some of the theology of the poetry. The writings of Sulpicius Severus, the hagiographer of St Martin, and the *Conferences* of Cassian, and the *Dialogues* of Gregory the great form the fundamental frame for the formulation of Adomnan's own theology.[22]

Adomnan stands as a figure of considerable stature – as a scholar and theologian, and also as an abbot with political influence beyond Iona. He was of Irish origin, born around 628 and dying in 704. In many ways he is of comparable intellectual calibre to Bede, and the weight of his learning is reflected in the range of works attributed to him. In addition to his most famous work, the *Life* of St Columba, Adomnan also composed earlier a book called *De locis sanctis*. How this arose is told by Bede.[23] A Gallic bishop called Arculf, who had made an extensive pilgrimage to the Holy Land and neighbouring parts, was wrecked upon the west coast of Britain on his way home. He found his way to Iona where Adomnan interviewed him and recorded his traveller's impressions. The book came into the possession of Bede as a result of one of Adomnan's visits to Northumbria, and he cites parts of his own abridgement of it in his *History*. In 697, Adomnan went back to Ireland where he instituted by agreement a body of laws, designed to protect women, children and clergy from injury. Compensation was due to Iona for any infringement, and it was guaranteed by the rulers in Ireland, Scotland and among the Picts.[24] It became known as the 'Cain Adomnan' or the 'Law of the Innocents'. To Adomnan are attributed also some 'Canons' ruling monastic discipline and diet.[25] Even if these are not his direct work, they fit within a tendency of Irish monasticism towards the codification of moral theology and law which took form in the *Collectio Canonum Hibernensis*, part of which was compiled on Iona in the first part of the eighth century. At about the same time, and probably somewhat earlier in the seventh century, annals were compiled by the monastery which later came to underlie the *Annals of Ulster*.[26]

Bede's view of Adomnan was deeply respectful and sympathetic: 'he was a good and wise man with an excellent knowledge of the scriptures'.[27] He came first to Northumbria in 686 as he himself reports in the *Life* (in the aftermath of the disastrous battle of Nechtansmere in 685 in which the Northumbrian king, Ecgfrith, had been killed) to bring back captives taken by the English.[28] He returned because the new king Aldfrith was a friend who may well have studied under Adomnan in Iona, as he certainly did with the English scholar, Aldhelm in the south.[29] During their second visit two years later, Adomnan spent time at Bede's own monastery with its abbot Ceolfrith, during which the vexed issue of the date of Easter was raised. In a letter cited by Bede and attributed by him to Ceolfrith, Adomnan's visit is mentioned, and the fact that he was persuaded to adopt the catholic observances and return commending them to his brethren.[30] Bede asserts that at Iona Adomnan's change of heart was long resisted, although he made headway in Ireland, probably in the north. In Bede's words – 'he was a man who greatly loved unity and peace' and eschewed controversy,[31] a view borne out also by Ceolfrith upon whose authority Bede's own view must rest: 'he showed wonderful prudence, humility and devotion, in word and deed'. He brought for his friend king Aldfrith a copy of his own book *De Locis Sanctis*, who had it transcribed. But his *Life of St Columba* did not find its way to Northumbria, although Bede may have known of it by repute, for he says: 'Some written records of his life and teachings are said to have been preserved by his disciples. Whatever he was himself, we know this for certain about him, that he left successors distinguished for their great abstinence, their love of God, and their observance of the Rule.'[32]

Adomnan's *Life of St Columba* is the most sophisticated piece of hagiography remaining from this period. In quality it is on a par with Bede's own *Life of St Cuthbert*, and while it does not have the range of his *History* it matches it in the depth of theology enshrined within it. For it is not simply a systematic gathering together of well-attested traditions within the Ionan monastic 'familia'; it is also a rigorous and profound exposition of what constitutes a saint – how a saint emerges and is perceived.

Adomnan probably wrote his *Life of St Columba* to commemorate the centenary of the saint's death in 697. But in many ways his work was the culmination of a collaborative effort by the Ionan community over many years. Adomnan says in his second preface:

No one should think that I would write anything false about this remarkable man, nor even anything doubtful or uncertain. Let it be understood that I shall tell only what I learnt from the account handed down by our elders, men both reliable and informed, and that I shall write without equivocation what I have learnt by diligent enquiry, either from what I could find already in writing or from what I heard recounted without a trace of doubt by informed and reliable old men.

On nearly a dozen occasions Adomnan indicates precisely the authority or line of transmission that brought the story to his attention. Mention has already been made of the earlier collation of traditions by Adomnan's predecessor, Cummene the White, part of which found its way into one of the manuscripts of the *Life*. Adomnan's picture is also corroborated by the drift of the Ionan poetry from the seventh century, and by Bede's testimony which probably came from Pictish sources.

The *Life* is consciously moulded on the classics of hagiography with which the Irish monks were familiar. From Athanasius' *Life of St Antony*, Adomnan, like Sulpicius Severus before him, adopted the strange device of the double preface. Adomnan quotes directly from both sources at various points to enhance the meaning of his text. Like Sulpicius he divides his material into three books, though with a rather different theological import. He also alludes to the *Dialogues* of St Gregory the great, drawing a parallel with the contemplative spirituality and visions of St Benedict there described. Like all such writing, the style and presentation of content are influenced by the Bible to an overwhelming degree, and there is an obvious and contemporary parallel with the emergence of hagiography in Northumbria, at the colony of Iona upon Lindisfarne, commemorating St Cuthbert. Like Bede, Adomnan has to handle stories from outside the monastic 'familia' of a more popular nature; and in doing so he reveals a restraint and critical spirit comparable to Bede's. Like Bede also, Adomnan's mind is an ordered one, exhaustive but selective in its approach, both writers being influenced by the writer of St Luke's gospel and the Acts of the Apostles.

What is striking about Adomnan's *Life* is its profound theological character. In many ways it is an extended meditation upon the working of the Holy Spirit, as he makes clear in his second preface. The name 'Columba' signifies 'dove' in Latin, a mystical symbol of the Holy Spirit in the Bible. It also indicates a 'simple and innocent' life as commended by Christ in the gospels. So Adomnan divides his material threefold, 'of which the first will contain prophetic revelations; the second, divine miracles effected through him; the third, appearances of angels, and certain manifestations of heavenly brightness above the man of God'.[33] To some extent, therefore, the tripartite structure of the book mirrors the threefold 'economy' of divine action in human history: the Old Testament – a time of prophetic work and action; the gospel – the miraculous communication of the Word of God in Jesus; the time of the church, stretching from the New Testament through the fathers and hastening towards the End, confirmed by miraculous indications and visions of heaven and eternal life. In another way there may even be a Trinitarian vision behind Adomnan's approach: the Holy Spirit is the Spirit of the Father and of the Son, the communicator of divine meaning to man; and a saint embodies the presence of the Holy Spirit. So Columba is the voice of the Father in prophecy, the hand of Christ in miracles, and the mirror of the fire of the Spirit's presence, effulgent with divine light. It is the last book concerning angelic visitations, heavenly visions, and glimpses of divine light in Columba which lifts this work on to a new plane of hagiography. Elements present in the *Life of St Martin*, implicit in the mysterious incarnational theology of the *Life of St Antony*, and meditated upon by St Gregory in his *Life of Benedict*, now receive a thoroughgoing and almost systematic presentation, as manifestations of a profound theology of transfiguration which anticipates in many ways the later 'hesychast' traditions of the Eastern church.

On the other hand the figure of Columba which emerges from the pages of Adomnan's *Life* is one rooted very much in a precise historical context. His lineage is described, and the moment of his departure as 'a pilgrim for Christ' from Ireland to Britain is dated exactly in relation to the battle of Cul Drebene, when the saint was aged forty-two. Although Adomnan uses passages from the *Actus Sylvestri* and the closing part of the *Life of St Martin* to sum up his verdict upon the saint's life-style, he inserts his own characteristic and historically rooted details: Columba was 'an island soldier for thirty-four years', a scholar committed to reading and writing. Like St Antony, 'his holy face ever showed gladness' because he 'was happy in his inmost heart with the joy of the Holy Spirit'.

There is a powerful political emphasis evident from the start of the *Life*, in that Adomnan portrays Columba as a potent arbiter in the fate of kings. 'In the terrible clashings of battles, by virtue of prayer he obtained from God that some kings were conquered, and other rulers were conquerors.' This was not only a memory of a past role in history:

> This special favour was bestowed by God, who honours all saints, on
> him, not only while he continued in this present life, but also after his
> departure from the flesh, as on a triumphant and powerful champion.[34]

Whereupon Adomnan recounts the story he received from his predecessor, Failbe, who had heard king Oswald tell it to abbot Segene, how Columba had appeared to the young king on the eve of his momentous battle against the British ruler, Cadwalla. Victory was promised by the saint in a memorable vision, and the English army agreed to accept baptism if it were secured. Thus Bede's account is corroborated, and both writers regarded it as a turning-point crucial to the advance of the Christian mission in Northumbria. Both also saw Oswald as 'ordained by God as emperor of the whole of Britain'.[35]

Elsewhere in the *Life*, Adomnan describes Diormit, as ruler of all Ireland, 'ordained by God's will', in the context of a prophecy by Columba against Findchan who had assisted in the ordination to the priesthood of the murderer of the king.[36] As in the Bible, the king is the 'Lord's anointed' and his murder is sacrilege. This is dramatically indicated later in the *Life* when Columba is bidden three times by an angel to ordain Aedan as king of Dal Riata. Columba resists the command because of a preference for Aedan's brother, but is stricken by the angel leaving a scar for life. The angel held 'a book of glass' in his hand 'of the ordination of kings' – a strange detail. In the end Columba obeyed. But it is here that there is the insertion from the book of Cummene the White which contains a prophecy by the saint to the new king and his heirs of prosperity provided they do not play false with

him or his successors 'or my kindred who are in Ireland'. Clearly Columba
is being modelled upon Samuel in the Old Testament, and this language of
royal anointing, used already by Gildas metaphorically in *De Excidio*, passed
into the *Canonum Hibernensis*, and so lay behind the Frankish anointing of
Pippin in 751.[37] A similar theology of kingship permeates the *History* of
Bede.

Columba's sanctity is set amidst a network of relationships with other
holy men and monastic founders. There is a charming story of how Finten
and his mentor Colum Crag received news of Columba's death just as the
young Finten had obtained his elder's blessing to go to Iona. He was
welcomed instead by the saint's successor, Baithene, to whom Columba
had delivered a prophecy prior to his death, predicting that Finten would
become 'an abbot of monks and a leader of souls to the heavenly kingdom'.[38] This is matched by a whole chain of similar stories of monastic
and spiritual friendship and visitations to Columba in Iona. Mostly they
were remembered because the holy man made some prediction either to or
about the arrival of the visitor. Often his predictions had a distinct ethical
twist to them, not least in relation to various kings and their heirs. In this
the saint proved to be the mouthpiece of divine judgement. Sometimes his
prophetic charisma revealed telepathic powers, imparting knowledge of far
off battles, or in one case a volcanic eruption in Italy.[39] On other occasions
it confirmed the strong bonds of monastic confraternity and prayer which
could communicate needs and risks in an almost psychic manner. What is
quite clear is that the saint possessed formidable powers to read the hearts
and minds of others, and on occasion to expose hidden sins. There is also
the moving story of how the aegis of the saint went out to monks labouring
in the fields of Iona: 'a fragrant smell of marvellous sweetness, as of all
flowers combined into one; and also a heat as of fire, not painful, but in
some manner pleasant; and in addition a kind of inspired joyousness of
heart, strange and incomparable, which in a moment miraculously revives
me, and so greatly gladdens me that all grief and all labour are forgotten'.[40]
Naturally many of these stories spring from and shed much light upon life
in the monastery on Iona. Some have their focus in the context of divine
worship, as in the story of the unworthy priest exposed by Columba on a
visit to Ireland – 'the clean rite of the sacred offering administered by an
unclean man'.[41] A bishop, Cronan, who came to Iona in disguise was revealed by Columba as they were about to consecrate the eucharist together as
priests: ' "Christ bless you, brother; break this bread alone, according to
the episcopal rite!" . . . Hearing the saint say this, the humble pilgrim was
much astonished, and reverenced Christ in the saint.'[42]

Underlying this formidable but many-sided tradition about St Columba as
a prophet is a clear theology, which Adomnan adumbrates by reference to
St Paul, and using words drawn from St Gregory's *Dialogues* in which he
describes the contemplative vision of St Benedict. To his disciple Lugbe's
enquiry he vouchsafed in return for an oath of silence during his lifetime

this response: 'There are some, although few indeed, on whom divine favour has bestowed the gift of contemplation, clearly and very distinctly, with scope of mind miraculously enlarged, in one and the same moment, as though under one ray of the sun, even the whole circle of the whole earth, with the ocean and sky about it'.[43]

In Book II, Adomnan clearly models his presentation of the miracles of Columba upon the gospels. He opens with a 'miracle of power' in which the saint while a deacon in Ireland changed water into wine for the eucharist, where the parallel with Christ's first miracle at Cana in Galilee is drawn. Likewise at Durrow he blessed a tree so that its fruit became sweet instead of bitter. Like the apostles of old he healed in the name of Christ:

by the extending of his holy hand, or when they were sprinkled with water blessed by him, or even by touching the hem of his cloak, or by receiving a blessing of any thing, such as salt, or bread, and dipping it in water, very many sick people, believing, regained full health.[44]

There follow a sequence of stories of miracles to do with nature, some of which adopt a folkloric character: drawing water from a rock for baptism, stilling storms and challenging to conflict pagan magicians among the Picts by cleansing a polluted well, and later exposing a sorcerer drawing milk from a bull![45] Some of the miracles reveal the pastoral and evangelistic side to Columba's ministry. The cure of a holy virgin who had broken her hip, of a monk's bleeding nose, the rescue of his friend and constant companion, Diormit, from imminent death, – these occurred within the 'familia' of his monastic circle. Others helped lay men and women, such as when his intuition bade him pray for a mother in childbirth in Ireland, or when he intervened with a married couple where the wife had a sexual aversion to her husband: after prolonged prayer, and refusal by the saint to countenance divorce, her heart was changed – 'For him whom I loathed yesterday I love today. In this past night (how, I do not know) my heart has been changed in me from hate to love'.[46] There are several stories also of where Columba's blessing or intercession protected the monastery at Iona from plague and infertility, or from assaults of evil.

What is striking is the marked ethical dimension to many of the miracles, emphasising many of the features of Adomnan's *Law of the Innocents*. Hospitable laymen are blessed by the saint, while a rich man 'who spurned Christ in pilgrim guests' is condemned to beggary.[47] There is a clutch of stories in which evildoers and oppressors are cursed by Columba and on one occasion at least he narrowly missed being murdered by such an antagonist.[48] There is the sad account of how while a young deacon in Ireland with his master, Gemman, they tried to protect a young girl being chased by a criminal, who 'killed the girl with a spear, under their robes, leaving her dead at their feet'. Columba's doom consigns the murderer to immediate death.[49] While among the Picts, he challenged a magician at court to release an Irish slave 'as an act of human kindness'. For refusing to do so the magician fell sick and only then relented. Finally in his capacity to raise a dead child on the same visit, he showed himself 'a man prophetic and apostolic'.[50]

Adomnan obviously took great pains in the collation of Book III concerning the visions of St Columba. The section begins with a cluster of stories to do with his birth: a vision by his mother during her pregnancy, by his foster-father, the priest Cruithnechan, of the descent of the Holy Spirit upon the child in a ball of fire, and St Brendan's vision of an angel accompanying the saint after he had been excommunicated by an Irish synod.[51] Some of his visions entailed glimpses into the heavenly destinies of others and the conflict with evil which surrounded their souls' passage, both of ordinary people as well as of other holy men.[52] Some of his visions appeared telepathic, to do with events far away or imminent, mostly within the circle of the extended monastic 'familia'. On Iona he was remembered as having converse with angels who assisted him in protecting the monastery: a particular small hill became his place of such heavenly prayer.[53] In this as on another occasion he was spied upon by another monk who was sworn to silence while the saint lived. Central to these manifestations is the descent of a heavenly light, visible to some: as in the *Life of St Martin*, on one occasion four holy men present while Columba celebrated the eucharist saw

a kind of fiery ball, radiant and very bright, that continued to glow from the head of St Columba as he stood before the altar and consecrated the holy oblation, and to rise upwards like a column, until those holiest mysteries were completed.[54]

On another occasion while on the island of Hinba in retreat, for three days Columba remained in ecstasy confined to a hut which became filled with a divine light and spiritual songs.

As he afterwards admitted in the presence of very few men, he saw openly revealed many of the secret things that have been hidden since the world began. Also everything that in the sacred scriptures is dark and difficult became plain, and was shown more clearly that day to the eyes of his purest heart.[55]

A young monk who later became abbot witnessed Columba at prayer in church surrounded by an overwhelming light; his nephew a priest told Adomnan directly about this.[56]

Columba's death also was surrounded by such manifestations: angels were restrained from taking him from this world by the intercession of other churches. At mass shortly before his death he saw the angel who a week later would take him home.[57] Even the horse which drew the milk knew of his master's imminent demise. The closing words which he wrote in the psalter he was copying were – 'But they that seek the Lord shall not want for anything which is good'. It was his close companion, Diormit, who witnessed his end, praying in a church filled with light. Others far away also saw his passing in a pillar of fire.

The intensity of devotion felt by the disciples of St Columba to his memory and authority sustained them in their work of spreading Christianity among the Picts during the seventh century, and in fostering monastic foundations in Scotland, Ireland and Northumbria. More contentiously it accounts for the tenacity with which the Ionan monks insisted upon maintaining a date for Easter which had become out of step with the rest of the Latin church. The matter was resolved among the southern Irish and on the Continent by the middle of the seventh century. But in England it divided the missionary enterprise among the Anglo-Saxons tragically as Bede records in some detail. He was of, course, a partisan for the Roman position, and a skilled practitioner and assiduous propagandist of it in his writings. Nonetheless his personal sympathy with the Ionan church whose missionaries had so effectively sown the gospel across northern and midland England enabled him to register the reasons for the dispute which came to a head at the Synod of Whitby in 663.[58] The outline of the debate is recorded rather tersely by Eddius in his *Life of St Wilfrid*, one of the protagonists for the Roman position. The case for the Ionan custom was put by bishop Colman of Lindisfarne who appealed to tradition and to the sanctity of St Columba and his followers 'plainly inspired by the Holy Spirit'. To the ironic smile of the Northumbrian king, Oswy, who asked, 'Tell me which is greater in the kingdom of heaven, Columba or the apostle Peter?', the 'whole synod' began to chant the Petrine text from St Matthew's gospel. The king, fearing to offend 'the porter who keeps the keys', imposed the Roman line upon the reluctant Irish clergy, and Colman retired from Lindisfarne a humiliated figure.[59]

Bede's account is fuller because of his obsessive interest in the details of the case, but also fairer and more circumspect. In the end, Colman appealed to tradition as the Irish had received it a century earlier when in fact the method of calculating Easter at Rome was still unreformed. But he also with more feeling appealed to the holy memory of St Columba: surely so great a saint could not have been wrong, nor should his spiritual authority be thus repudiated?

> Or must we believe that our most revered father Columba and his successors, men beloved of God, who celebrated Easter in this same way, judged and acted contrary to the holy scriptures, seeing that there were many of them to whose holiness the heavenly signs and the miracles they performed bore witness. And as I have no doubt that they were saints, I shall never cease from following their way of life, their customs and their teaching.

Bede portrays Wilfrid as directly and scornfully impugning this memory and tradition, insinuating that on the day of judgement the disciples of Columba and even the saint himself might be shown up as false. He mocks their 'rude simplicity' and 'pious intent', sincere but in ignorance, concluding with the inflammatory words; 'And even if that Columba of yours – yes, and ours too, if he belonged to Christ – was a holy man of mighty works, is he to be preferred to the most blessed chief of the apostles?'

Whereupon king Oswy put his finger on the nub of the issue; 'Have you anything to show that an equal authority was given to your Columba?' By this argument Colman was felled.[60]

Bede implies that the debate was badly handled and its outcome a matter for regret. On the other hand he knew that the issue of uniformity over Easter was a question of authority crucial to the unity and effectiveness of the Roman church and its mission, of which the Irish monasteries linked to Iona had never claimed not to be a part. The division troubled him greatly and its resolution is an important theme to his *History*. In the context of the development of Anglo-Saxon missions to Germany and Frisia, he recounts how Egbert, a holy man and 'peregrinus' among the Irish, wished himself to go, but was prevented, being charged by a vision 'to go to Columba's monasteries, for they are cutting a crooked furrow, and he must call them back to the true line'. Before going on to recount his final success at Iona, Bede tells how Adomnan abbot of Iona on a visit to Northumbria was personally persuaded to change his mind on the issue by the arguments of Bede's abbot Ceolfrith. Although he was unable to persuade the community in Iona, he prevailed among the Ionan houses in the northern part of Ireland. It fell to Egbert 'a most gracious teacher and devout doer of all that he taught' to bring them round to the catholic observance in a spirit of charity. In this way, Bede believed, the mission of St Aidan was reciprocated by an English emissary who stayed on Iona for thirteen years, having converted in 715 the followers of St Columba to 'the grace of unity', and finally dying on Easter day 729.[61] This resolution forms the climax of Bede's *History*. His own verdict upon St Columba is clear enough: he was 'the first teacher of the faith to the Picts . . . and the first founder of the monastery of Iona, . . a true monk in life no less than habit', a spiritual father measured by the distinction and devotion of his successors, to whom the Northumbrian church owed both its existence and its character.[62]

The career and influence of St Columba is mirrored and amplified in that of his younger contemporary, St Columbanus, who died in 615. Fortunately his *Life* was authorized and written by an Italian monk, Jonas, who joined the saint's foundation at Bobbio three years after his death. The work was published in 643 after extensive research among the Columbanian communities in France. In addition several significant writings of Columbanus remain: six letters; thirteen sermons; a composite Rule and penitential; and several poems also. Other writings referred to among these have however been lost.

Jonas emphasises the quality of Columbanus' education in Ireland before he became a monk – 'grammar, rhetoric, geometry and the Holy Scriptures'. This he obtained in Leinster where he was born. It was the word of a holy woman who directed him away from the romances of noble youth to- wards the ascetic ideal, despite his mother's opposition: 'she would never see him again in this life, but wherever the way of salvation led him, there he would go'.[63] His first monastic formation was at the hands of Sinell, where he became learned in scripture and a specialist on the Psalter. From here he went to join Columba's friend, Comgall, founder and abbot of Bangor in northern Ireland. He became established there in the ascetic life and as a teacher, until around the year 590. Then, summoned he believed personally by the divine call to Abraham to leave his country and kindred, and overcoming Comgall's profound reluctance, he finally departed with twelve companions from Ireland. Travelling perhaps by way of Cornwall, they arrived first in Brittany to plan a monastic mission to parts of Gaul where they believed the Christian faith hung by a thread. This they began to achieve by the fervour and example of their common life. Their evangelism had a strongly penitential note about it. In a land where 'the Creed alone remained, the saving grace of penance and the longing to root out the lusts of the flesh were to be found only in a few'.[64] For reasons which Jonas fails to indicate, Columbanus finally obtained the patronage of Childebert II of Austrasia. This took concrete form in the creation of his first monastery at Annegray, in a disused Roman fort in the Vosges mountains. Here they lived in great isolation and poverty, rescued at times by the bounty of local sympathisers. In time Columbanus gained a reputation as a healer, and to escape public attention he adopted the life of a recluse in a cave 'crucifying his own will'.[65]

'As the number of monks increased greatly, he sought in the same wilderness a better location for a monastery.' This he found amidst the ruined Roman baths at Luxeuil. His leadership generated a large popular following, not least among the children of the nobility, and soon he had to found a second house nearby. For the direction of these houses he composed his Rules. A cycle of stories remain from this period concerning Columbanus' monastic leadership and spiritual discernment. The core of his community were of Irish or British extraction, including his most famous disciple St Gall. His relations with the local nobility are indicated in two stories in which a duke receives sons at the prayer of the saint who become monastic founders in the Columbanian connection. Clearly his capability as a spiritual leader was considerable, vouched for by a sequence of stories of how he directed and remedied the economic needs of his monks, his favourite text being: 'the Lord is able to furnish a table for his servants in the wilderness'.[66] He was remembered also for a remarkable rapport with animals, and a hold over his followers as ruler and intercessor which appears to have been formidable. It is from this period that his *Penitential* dates.

The success of St Columbanus proved his downfall however. The ethos of his Irish monasticism, with its separate date for Easter and strong penitential emphasis brought him into collision with some of the Frankish bishops, outside whose control he claimed to be. After the death of Childebert in 596, he gradually fell foul of the court also, refusing to bless the illegitimate sons of king Theoderic. This antagonised the queen-grandmother, Brunhilda, who launched a campaign against the new monasteries, seeking to undermine

Columbanus' influence. The saint challenged the king but in vain. His enemies exploited the breach with the bishops: 'Brunhilda began again to incite the king against Columbanus in every way, urged all the nobles and others at court to do the same, and influenced the bishops to attack Columbanus' faith and to abolish his monastic rule'.[67] The issue came to a head over the inviolability of monastic enclosure. For his intransigence, Columbanus was exiled from his monastery by force. While under arrest at Besançon he liberated captives in the prison who took refuge in a church, while he himself escaped, and returned to Luxeuil, where another attempt to arrest him failed. Finally he was obliged to relent, to face return to Ireland and to bid his brethren farewell. So some twenty years after his arrival, in 610, he made his way via Tours to Nantes to seek an Irish ship. Weather prevented his voyage, miraculously it was believed. Columbanus instead made his way to Chlotar of Neustria, and with his protection to the court of king Theodebert via Paris, gathering support on the way.

Theodebert welcomed the saint and offered him opportunities to found monasteries and to engage in missionary work with the help of brethren who joined him from Luxeuil. They rowed up the Rhine to Bregenz, and the song Columbanus composed for the rowers remains! His aim was to evangelise the Swabians,[68] and Jonas tells a story of how the saint challenged a beer festival in honour of Woden. But they experienced great hardship while at Bregenz. During this time, Columbanus toyed with the idea of going further east to evangelise the Wends – a Slav tribe. 'When he purposed to make his vows, the angel of the Lord appeared to him in a vision, and showed him in a little circle the structure of the world, just as the circle of the universe is usually drawn with a pen in a book.'[69] This the saint took as a sign to wait until another door of opportunity should open. Which it soon did, as he had to flee the victory of Theoderic his old enemy over his protector Theodebert, who was cruelly murdered by his grandmother Brunhilda. Columbanus crossed the Alps into Italy, where he was welcomed by Agilulf, king of the Lombards. This ruler gave him the old church at Bobbio in the Apennines, a shrine dedicated like the church at Luxeuil to St Peter. The monastery was founded in 613, and despite the entreaties of the new Frankish ruler, the saint's old friend Chlotar, he would not return thence to Luxeuil, with which however he maintained a close contact through its abbot Eustasius who enjoyed the king's favours. Columbanus died at Bobbio on 23 November 615, and was buried there.

The remaining writings of Columbanus corroborate and illuminate further the *Life* by Jonas, and the earliest life of St Gall amplifies the picture of missionary activity around Bregenz by the Irish hermits, where Gall remained until his death having refused to accompany Columbanus to Italy.[70] There are three letters Columbanus wrote to various popes. The second written, during the vacancy after the death of Gregory the great, appealed for respect for Irish customs by the Frankish church. Its context is established by an epistle directed to a Frankish synod of bishops at Chalons in 603 to which the saint was summoned by the archbishop of Lyons. He refused, criticising instead the moral laxity and lack of evangelistic zeal of the bishops – like his hero St Martin before him. His fourth and sixth letters are directed to his monks, the earlier being written while waiting in Nantes to the community at Luxeuil, appealing for peace and unity. His fifth letter is a lengthy if misguided attempt to resolve the complicated quarrel within the catholic church in northern Italy over the 'Three Chapters'. It is a direct appeal to pope Boniface IV in which he declares that 'by all men everywhere freedom should be given to the truth' and that popes are subject to the 'sensus fidelium' expressed in Councils and determined by Scripture. To this orthodoxy the Irish church also bears witness: 'For we Irish, inhabitants of the world's edge, are disciples of saints Peter and Paul and of all the disciples who wrote the sacred canon by the Holy Spirit, and we accept nothing outside the evangelical and apostolic teaching . . . the catholic faith as it was delivered by you first, who are successors of the holy apostles, and is now maintained by us unbroken.'[71] This being affirmed, he is not averse to challenging what he perceived to be papal obstinacy: 'you perhaps in this matter claim for yourself before all other some proud measure of greater authority and power in things divine'. The Irish position was, therefore, already the same blend of orthodoxy and independence which was to be challenged half a century later at the English synod of Whitby.

While in Italy at the Lombard court in Milan, Columbanus apparently composed 'an excellent and learned work' against the Arians who had the ear of the king. This is now lost, but the remaining sermons date from this time. They are treatises of orthodox moral theology, culled from Jerome, Augustine, Caesarius of Arles and Gregory the great, in their doctrine strongly influenced by St Hilary's *De Trinitate*. They are close too to the spirit of his Penitential. This was the first of its kind to be promulgated on the continent, and it relied heavily upon the earlier work of Finnian and Gildas. The pastoral theology of Gregory the great which Columbanus knew also left its mark. The rather fragmentary remains of his original monastic rule combine the severity of Comgall with the sagacity of Cassian and Basil. Renunciation of the world is a theme also of his poems which are in Latin of a high quality, and which reflect amply the rich tradition of classical Latin available in the Ireland of his youth. 'Of Latin literature his knowledge was both deep and wide': his last poem, 'Fidelio', composed in Milan in 613, is strongly influenced by Horace, pure in its rhythm and mythology – 'from the literary point of view it forms the crown of Columbanus' achievement'[72] It reflects the importance of that blend of rhetorical and biblical Latin education sustained by the British, Irish and Gallic churches during the fifth and sixth centuries.

It is fortunate that in the existing writings of St Columbanus it is possible to discern a clear and deep spiritual teaching which helps to interpret and mitigate the apparent severity of his monastic rule and example.[73] He was clearly an effective communicator, both to his monks and to a wider public.

Love of God is the true goal of human life: 'If you suppress that liberty, you suppress his dignity.'[74] Reliance on the stability of this world and its values is an illusion, broken by scrutiny of conscience, prayer and unfailing charity towards others: 'to sigh impatiently for heaven is the way not to be attached to earth.'[75] The way of the Cross is the path of true discipleship, while 'love of God renews his image in us. . . . Happy therefore is that soul . . . whom love wounds'.[76] It is in the last of his two extant sermons that his mystical teaching reaches its full flower. He prays to be 'kindled with that fire of divine love, that the flame of His love, the longing of His so great charity, would mount above the stars, and the divine fire would ever burn within' him. The light within the hidden sanctuary of the heart becomes a lantern from which light shines for the benefit of others. It is the fire of love for Christ – 'that we may know no other love apart from you who are eternal.'[77] In the final sermon, Columbanus speaks of Christ as the fountain of living water. 'He who loves drinks of Him . . . he drinks who burns with the love of wisdom.' To this end all monastic life and penitential discipline tends, for 'the affliction of the body bears no fruit without moderation of the soul'.[78] It was the particular genius of St Columbanus and his disciples to make this way more widely accessible to Christian laity outside the monasteries which nonetheless embodied the challenge of this spiritual path. The widest legacy of this monastic missionary movement was indeed to popularise the use of private penance and spiritual direction in the Gallic church in an irreversible way. Thus 'the saving grace of penance and the longing to root out the lusts of the flesh' were no longer to be confined to 'the few'.[79] Following the example of Columbanus himself, the prayer from the psalms already emphasised by Cassian and commended by Benedict began to become more universal: 'O, God, come to my aid! O, Lord, hasten to aid me!' [80]

St Columbanus' first remaining letter was to pope Gregory the great in 600 when he was being assailed by the Gallic bishops for the customs of his monastic foundations. Its sequel is the fourth letter written immediately after Gregory's death to his unknown successor. It is obvious that these are fragments of a more sustained correspondence. In the first letter, the saint mentions the papal commissary, Candidus, who administered the papal estates in Gaul, and requests from the pope his homilies on Ezekiel about which he has heard. Certainly Columbanus knew Gregory's *Pastoral Rule* and he may have received it soon after it was written: it permeates his own moral theology and writing. In return he makes mention of three tomes of theology he has written and sent to Rome, which are now lost. The alacrity with which the Columbanian houses took up the example and teaching of St Benedict is also evidence of an early affinity between their founder and the pope who commended Benedict in his *Dialogues*. [81] In response to the first letter, in which Columbanus made a spirited defence of the Irish calculation of Easter, the pope placed him under the protection and guidance of the abbot of Lérins. As in his later letter to Boniface IV the orthodoxy and antiquity of tradition received by the Irish are asserted unequivocally. Clearly Columbanus regarded the pope as a potential ally who would understand the nature of his monastic and missionary vocation.

There is no evidence that Columbanus was privy to Gregory's plans to send a mission to England in 597, though it is perhaps unlikely that he was altogether ignorant of its progress. Certainly the Roman missionaries knew about him and about the tensions which existed between the Gallic bishops and the followers of Columbanus over matters such as the date of Easter and other aspects of ecclesiastical discipline. Gregory died in 604, and his first archbishop of Canterbury, Augustine died shortly after. It fell to the new archbishop, Laurence, to try to address the divergence between the Roman mission church and the existing British and Irish churches over Easter and other matters, before advancing the mission to the English further: 'He also endeavoured to bestow his pastoral care upon the other inhabitants of Britain as well as upon those Irish who live in Ireland.' [82] This overture occurred at the very height of Columbanus' quarrel with the archbishop of Lyons and his colleagues, and this probably accounts for the hostile behaviour to which Laurence refers.

Thus the tone and content of Bede's account and the source it cites only make full sense against the background of tension and conflict within the Gallic church upon which the English mission crucially depended for its success. Laurence wrote a letter subscribed by his suffragans at Rochester and London to the clergy of both British and Irish churches: the text to the Irish remains; like Gregory, Laurence describes himself and his colleagues as 'servants of the servants of God'. He begs and warns them 'to keep the unity of peace and of catholic observance with the church of Christ which is scattered over the whole world'. He refers to the papal mandate for his mission and the reputation for holiness of both the British and Irish churches. The divergence discovered has been disillusioning and painful:

> We have learned from bishop Dagan when he came to this island, and from abbot Columbanus when he came to Gaul that the Irish do not differ from the Britons in their way of life. For when bishop Dagan came to us he refused to take food, not only with us but even in the very house where we took our meals.

This appeal fell on deaf British ears, for as late as 705, Aldhelm was complaining about similar conduct to Geraint king of Devon and Cornwall.

As if to emphasise what was at stake and the papal desire for unity, Bede immediately recounts how Mellitus, bishop of London, returned to Rome to a synod summoned by pope Boniface IV 'to draw up regulations concerning the monastic life and harmony'. While there he consulted also 'about the needs of the English church' and returned with the decrees of the synod and letters of direction. Even allowing for Bede's fervour in the matter of Easter observance, it is clear that the papal mission to England took place against a background of potential conflict and actual division between and within the Irish and Gallic churches. It is also evident from the care that Gregory took with diplomatic preparations for his mission in 597 that he had not only to steer his missionaries through the shoals of Merovingian court politics, but also to secure the support, active or tacit of the Gallic bishops. How far Laurence's bid to bring the Irish as well as the British church under his jurisdiction was serious, or rhetorical and moral, is hard now to judge. But the context for the English mission was not quite as simple perhaps as Bede portrays or perhaps even knew.

The influence of St Columbanus persisted long after his death, determining the missionary and monastic labours of his disciples both Irish and Frankish. In fact their persistence and spirit account significantly for the relative success of the Roman mission in southern England after the death of its initial founders.

The quest for 'peregrinatio', voluntary exile abroad for the love of Christ and the conversion of souls continued to inspire men like the Anglo-Saxon Egbert who sojourned in Ireland and finally secured peace with Iona over Easter. It motivated continued missionary activity in and around Gaul throughout the seventh century, much of the initiative being taken by monks from Luxeuil, or those trained and influenced by them. For example Eustasius, Columbanus' successor as abbot of Luxeuil, evangelised the Bavarians; St Amand led an important mission to the pagan Franks on the north-east borders of Gaul, assisted for a time around 640 by Columbanus' biographer, Jonas. Amand's reputation as a missionary was considerable, and he sought the support of the papacy in his labours.[83]

The contribution of the Gallic church to the evangelisation of the Anglo-Saxons is an important part of the story upon which Bede lays little direct emphasis. Clearly the dynastic marriage between the king of Kent and the Merovingian royal house indicates a close link, corroborated by evidence of trade and archaeology. Equally there were significant Saxon populations along the coast of Gaul – near Boulogne, at Bayeux and near Nantes, where in the middle of the sixth century Bishop Felix's successful mission was commemorated by Venantius Fortunatus. Three Gallic bishops held sees in England in the middle of the seventh centuries: Felix of East Anglia; Agilbert and his nephew Leutherius of Wessex. Wini, bishop of Wessex and later of London was consecrated in Gaul; as was Wilfrid, and later Berhtwald as Archbishop of Canterbury: both these two English bishops had close links with Lyons. Justus, bishop of Rochester, one of the first missionaries, and Peter abbot of the monastery at Canterbury attended a synod at Paris in 614, and Peter's death near Boulogne while on a 'mission to Gaul' is recorded by Bede. [84]

Both southern England and north-eastern Gaul were swept throughout this century by a wave of monastic missionary ventures, resulting in the creation of many monasteries. The ethos of these houses owed much to the spirit and teaching of Columbanus and Luxeuil, in their asceticism, their devotion to the see and cult of St Peter, and in their gradual dissemination of the Rule of St Benedict. In 628, Bobbio was placed under the direct jurisdiction of the pope – a significant precedent. In the north-east, the labours of St Amand were not isolated: in 641 Ouen became bishop of Rouen and initiated missionary activity in the farther reaches of his diocese. Omer and Bertin, both monks of Luxeuil evangelised the Pas-de-Calais in the middle of the century, founding and ruling the monastery at Sithieu. Meanwhile Eligius bishop of Noyon, like Ouen a courtier and also a skilled craftsman, became an apostle to Flanders; and Wandrille who had been a monk at Bobbio founded the important monastic centre at Fontenelle in 657. This field of active mission was hardly far removed from that in Kent in England, and must be considered as part of the context of support for the English mission after its initial setbacks.

The patronage of the royal family and nobility was critical for the success of these missions and the establishment of so many monasteries in north-eastern Gaul. In 660, the monastery at Corbie was founded by monks from Luxeuil at the behest of Bathild, an English slave who had become consort to Clovis II and in due time regent. She also founded a convent at Chelles to which in the end she was forced to retire. [85] It was constituted by nuns from Jouarre which was part of the Columbanian connection, and its first abbess had close links with Agilbert who became bishop in Wessex. [86] That England was perceived as an attractive missionary area is intimated in the early lives of Amand and also Riquier, a Frankish protégé of Irish missionaries and the ascetic founder of Chelles, both of whom wished to preach across the channel, and in the case of Riquier actually did so in the 640s.[87] Felix's mission to East Anglia around 630, and the eremitic career of the Irish Fursey there and also his foundation at Lagny and cult at Peronne are part of this picture. [88] Finally Bede himself indicates how powerful the lure of monastic life had become to certain nobility in Kent by the middle of the century when he tells how daughters of the royal family in East Anglia and Kent went across to Gaul to this end.

At that time, because there were not yet many monasteries founded in England, numbers of people from Britain used to enter the monasteries of the Franks or Gauls to practise the monastic life; they also sent their daughters to be taught in them and to be wedded to the heavenly bridegroom. They mostly went to the monasteries at Brie, Chelles, and Andelys-sur-Seine.[89]

He proceeds then to speak of the holiness of one of them, Eorcengota, daughter of the king of Kent, who went to Faremoutier, a house founded in 617 under the aegis of St Columbanus, later endowed by Bathild, whose first abbess had a reputation for miracles recorded by Jonas of Bobbio.

PART TWO

V. AUGUSTINE AND PAULINUS

There was, therefore, a much wider context for the mission sent by pope Gregory the great in 597 to Kent. His was probably, in part at least, a response to the ferment of evangelism occurring within and around the Gallic church, a significant papal contribution whose importance may not have seemed so great at the time however to those Gallic bishops upon whose support it so crucially rested. There was also a much wider context in the pope's mind which may be discerned throughout his pontificate.[1] He believed deeply in Christian mission to correct heretics and win pagans, urging secular rulers to support the church in its task. This expectation is evident in his letter to the newly converted king of Kent, Ethelbert, written in 601, in which the ruler is enjoined to act as a second Constantine in favour of Christianity and to the detriment of paganism.[2] Yet from the remaining correspondence to do with the English mission a certain development and unfolding of his missionary theology may be discerned. Moreover, the picture that emerges may be confirmed by the two major witnesses to the character of the Gregorian mission: Bede of course; but also more immediately the earliest life of St Gregory written at Whitby by an unknown monk early in the eighth century.[3]

This striking text affords a fascinating window into how the tradition of the mission to Kent was remembered in the north of England, and at many points it is independently corroborated by Bede to whom this *Life* was unknown. The line of transmission and authority is clear: it was written during the lifetime of Aelfflaed abbess of Whitby, the daughter of Eanflaed, who as daughter of king Edwin had had to flee to Kent for safety after her father's death, under the protection of bishop Paulinus, one of Gregory's missionaries.[4] Eanflaed imbued the spirit of the Roman mission, and later as queen of Northumbria gave its protagonists active support. The *Life* clearly represents Canterbury tradition mediated to Whitby by this route. It also contains the fullest articulation of the theology of that mission, indebted as that was to Gregory's own spiritual teaching and vision. It is singular too in that it is not at all moulded by the classical hagiographical style evident in other contemporary lives of saints.[5] The theology of mission it adumbrates is certainly corroborated by Bede and by the remaining letters of the pope. It is a book well versed in the Bible, and in a wide selection of Gregory's own works.

It is, of course, remarkable that the first life of this saint was composed in England, well ahead of any more formal biography; and the impulse so to

venerate the 'apostle of the English' is evident also in the substantial obituary composed by Bede in the opening chapter of book II of his *History*.
Both works cull material from the *Liber Pontificalis* and from the
autobiographical testimonies of Gregory at the beginning of the *Moralia*
and elsewhere. For the newly converted English, Gregory was their saint,
their father-in-God, as is borne out for example also in the writings of
Aldhelm.[6] His assessment, written in the south of England shortly before
the composition of the Whitby *Life*, gives a typical frame: the pope was
endowed with a prophetic vision in sending his mission, by which the
English were rescued from the errors of paganism, taught the gospel and
given the sacraments of grace. His was a truly pastoral action which
continued to function by means of his writings. This also is the estimate of
the Whitby monk:

> It is said that, as a sign of holiness, he attained to the grace of prophecy,
> shown in his unique gift that enabled him to understand our needs. So
> we must not pass over in silence how, through the Spirit of God and
> with incomparable discernment of his inward eye, he foresaw and made
> provision for our conversion to God.[7]

This was the true miracle of his life and pontificate, and it is in this
context that the writer tells the already traditional story, also in Bede, of the
saint's encounter with the English slave-boys in the market in Rome. The
force of this story for both writers is that it impelled Gregory to consider
embarking on the mission to England himself with the blessing of pope
Benedict I, saying 'It would be a wretched thing for hell to be filled with
such lovely vessels.' In this intention he was prevented by public opinion in
Rome. The echo of St Paul's words in Romans 9.23 is clear; the writings
of the apostle inevitably moulded his theology of mission in all its aspects
as they unfolded. There is contingent evidence of the saint's premeditation
of this mission, even though he was not able to put it in hand until after he
had been pope for seven years. In a letter to his agent in Gaul, Candidus,
written in 595, he urges him to use income from the papal estates there to
assist the poor and to purchase English slave-boys 'who are seventeen or
eighteen years old, that they may be given to God and educated in the
monasteries.' Even while these transactions are under way, such candi-
dates are to be attended by a priest with a view to their conversion 'lest any
sort of sickness befall on the way, so that he may baptize those whom he
perceives to be dying.' Like Aidan and Willibrord later this may well have
been a ploy preparatory to mission, to secure converts fluent in the language
and customs of the English population.[8]

Like Bede, the Whitby monk emphasises the way in which Gregory's
monastic vocation underlay his spiritual vision and so proved to be the
foundation to the mission. Both writers give great prominence to the pref-
atory letter to Leander in the *Moralia* in which he sets out his preference
for the contemplative life, seeking the 'haven of the monastery', and cling-
ing to his monastic rule of life while in the midst of ecclesiastical duties.[9]

Like Columbanus, Gregory could command complete obedience from his monks, as he had to do when Augustine's companions lost heart and sent their leader back to Rome. It was as abbot that he returned, his master's plenipotentiary as this mobile monastery made its way across Gaul to the Channel and beyond.[10] The pope's letter is indicative: it is a call to duty unwavering, carrying out the Lord's work with 'constancy and fervour', knowing that Gregory himself would have accompanied them in person if he could. In spirit he was with them, and the importance of this monastic bond is evident in two contemporary letters of the pope's, not in Bede. In a letter to the Frankish kings, Theoderic and Theodebert, commending Augustine, Gregory seems to regard the ruler of Kent and his subjects as in some way under the sway of the Merovingian kings. He asserts that the English in fact have sought conversion, but that 'priests in the vicinity' – perhaps in northern France, or in Britain itself – have neglected to respond. Now they are to be pressed into service as intermediaries in assistance of Augustine in dealing with the English – the 'interpreters' mentioned in Bede's account most probably. In this task, Augustine is the 'servant of God whose zeal and steadfastness are well known to us'. It is the kings' duty to protect and help him 'for the sake of souls' and in fulfilment of their vocation as Christian rulers. Similarly in a letter to the bishop of Alexandria, Eulogius, Gregory rejoices to share news of the success of Augustine's mission, describing him as a 'monk of my monastery', now made bishop by 'the bishops of the Germans' who have enabled his mission to proceed.[11]

Part of the reason why the Whitby monk composed his encomium was to explain Gregory's greatness as a saint even though 'we have heard of few miracles' accomplished by him. These he says are not the only measure of a saint, however. Instead he gives a definition of miracles and their purpose which accurately distils what is known of Gregory's own teaching on the matter:

Miracles are granted for the destruction of the idols of the unbelieving pagans, or sometimes to confirm the weak faith of believers; most of all, they are granted to those who instruct the pagans, and so, the more gloriously and frequently they are manifested in those lands, the more convincing they become as teachers.[12]

Thus the conversion and healing of souls is the truest miracle of grace; in the words of the saint from his *Homilies on the gospels*: 'Miracles are the greater, the more spiritual they are. . . . If they are spiritual they are so much more the surer.' This writer also believes that the continuing miracle of Gregory's life is the communication of divine truth through his writings. In a striking assertion, he claims: 'Christ therefore avails us more as He speaks through St Gregory than when He made the apostle Peter walk on the waves.'[13] Instead, patience and humility are the true signs of Christ-like virtue. This moral caution towards miracles is mirrored in the pope's letters concerning the mission. In his letter to Eulogius he duly reports 'that the miracles of the Apostles seem to be imitated in the signs which they exhibit'–

that is, Augustine and his companions. Yet in a later letter to Augustine, Gregory warns him about the danger of such miracles for his spiritual health: 'You will rejoice because the souls of the English are drawn by outward miracles to inward grace.' But Augustine is plainly warned against pride and delusions of grandeur. He is instead to realise that 'great is the grace shown to that people for whose conversion you have received the gift of working miracles.'[14] This prudence is faithfully displayed by Bede in his whole approach to miracles.

Instead the relative progress and success of the mission is seen in an eschatological perspective. Taking up a conviction from St Paul, the Whitby monk cites what he claims to be Gregory's own opinion:

When all the Apostles bring their own peoples with them and each individual teacher brings his own race to present them to the Lord in the day of Judgement, he will bring us, the English people, instructed by him through God's grace.[15]

His was the initiative, 'though absent in the body yet present in the spirit.' This vision of spiritual efficacy is eloquently stated by Gregory in his letter to his friend Eulogius in Alexandria:

I have related all this (about the mission) that you may know what you perform both among the people of Alexandria by preaching, and in the ends of the world by praying. For your prayers are where you are not; your holy works are evident where you are.[16]

For Gregory who had a lively expectation of the imminent end of the world, of which the many tribulations with which he had to deal were signs, the spread of the gospel to the very ends of the known world and with such impact heightened his sense of the quickening tide of events to their end in Christ. This hope did not induce millennarian fervour or desire for further charismatic manifestations: it was rather a sober hope, determined in its faithful following of the humble Christ, by whom in the mind of this writer Gregory and other saints should be measured. For 'St Gregory taught us to recognise that this virtue is greater than signs or miracles'.[17] In this the saint proved exemplar as much by the tenor of his writings as by his refusal at first to accept the papal office. Even the final acceptance of high office could be seen as a Christ-like surrender to the Father's will.[18]

He who first shunned the kingdom of the whole world, a fleeting, earthly kingdom, gained an empire when He was crucified; humble and meek, He offered himself for all, even praying for his enemies.

In this hallmark of a true disciple, 'St Gregory taught us by his own practice as well as by his words that "he asks nothing for his enemy who does not pray for him out of love." ' This surely is the wellspring of that unusual spirit of restraint and moderation which permeates the remembrance of the English mission, in this writer, and no less in Bede: the absence of crude compulsion to convert; the gradualist approach towards the eradication of paganism by the conversion of shrines to Christian usage; the temperate ethos of the responses of Gregory to Augustine's enquiries.

There was a deep moral basis to the manner in which the mission was conceived and sustained, a sense of accountability within a clear divine purpose which Gregory imparted to his disciples. Such was Gregory's spiritual stature that the means of evangelism could be significantly determined by the spirit and purpose of the message itself: 'the healing of souls, because it is in them that we are the image of God'.[19]

In the latter part of his work, the monk of Whitby records a catena of miracles which had by his time become associated with the memory of Gregory. What is interesting about them is the theological and spiritual points which they address, indicating by their emphasis certain common themes in early English Christianity evident also in Bede and elsewhere. One concerns the Real Presence of Christ in the eucharist; another the real presence of saints in their relics. Another conjoins Gregory's moral authority with regard to marriage and divorce to his spiritual power against hostile pagan magicians. Yet another tells how a Lombard king finally accepted the pope as his mentor. His writings, especially the *Homilies*, were such that 'Christ spoke through him'.[20] As inheritor of the keys of St Peter he was able to teach about heavenly realities vouchsafed to him in visions. But this was rooted in his Job-like sufferings about whom Gregory wrote at such length, 'that through my scourging I should better understand the feelings of a man who had been scourged himself.'[21] Hence it was believed that he could even extricate sinners from hell, endowed as he was with the common life and love of the saints in the Body of Christ.

Yet the monument to Gregory's greatness and vision lay in the way he secured the passage of the mission in 596-7 and sustained it thereafter. This Bede clearly perceived and made it his business so far as he was able to record in some detail. Through Nothelm, later archbishop of Canterbury, he secured documents from the papal archives in Rome whose import is more than corroborated by other letters remaining from Gregory's official register.[22] These testify to the extent of papal diplomacy in paving the way for Augustine's journey: they indicate also the decisive role played by those in Gaul who made the mission a practical possibility. They reveal also the fact that Gregory hoped that a successful mission to England would stimulate reform also in the Gallic church, and he clearly relied upon active support from the Frankish rulers and their bishops. There remain therefore a web of letters to bishops in southern Gaul – at Tours, Marseilles, Arles, Vienne, Autun and Aix-en-Provence, and at Lyons. To the abbot of Lérins Gregory also wrote thanking him for welcoming Augustine on his first abortive journey. Letters remain to a nobleman Arigius, and to the kings Theodoric and Theodebert, and to the queen-mother, Brunhilda. To his friend Eulogius of Alexandria he wrote in 598 describing how Augustine had been made bishop by the Frankish prelates.[23] In this detail Bede was wrongly informed when he describes how Augustine returned to Arles from Kent for consecration. But he was justified in envisaging a close tie initially with the primate of that see.[24] The political support of the secular rulers was no less important to the security of the missionaries. The Merovingian royal house had a dynastic interest in Kent by marriage, and economic ties through trade. The pope assumed contacts indicating English interest in Christianity antedating his mission, and to some extent his action was to spur the Gallic church into missionary initiative. The second wave of the mission in 601, led by Mellitus, was similarly supported by a chain of letters, directed to the principal court centres of Frankish rule as well as to the bishops.[25]

It is possible to detect from these letters certain key figures. First of these was Candidus, the papal factor and agent in southern Gaul who managed the papal estates there and collected the revenue, often with difficulty. To him the pope wrote his letter ordering the purchase of English slave boys well before the sending of Augustine. Candidus is also mentioned in several of the letters to bishops in 596, where their delay in paying up is condemned. Of some importance also was Syagrius, bishop of Autun, to whom Gregory wrote in 599 thanking him for his active part in supporting the mission and sending him the pallium as a reward. To him the pope intimated his long desire to initiate the English mission; and Syagrius' influence may lie behind the later mission of Felix to Kent and East Anglia.[26] Syagrius was also a close collaborator with queen Brunhilda, who to judge from the pope's various letters to her took the mission very much to heart. His praise for her role is fulsome, and is comparable to how he later addresses Bertha, the Frankish queen of Kent in 601. She is likened to Helena, the mother of Constantine, to whom her husband, Ethelbert, is compared by the pope in an accompanying letter.[27] There is reason to suppose that she with her Frankish bishop, Liudhard, had not been inactive in preparing the ground for Augustine's mission.[28] Like others in her family, Bertha was an educated lady to whose initiative the pope felt he could appeal.

The dynastic tie with Kent was clearly an important instrument in securing the launch of the mission in 597. Kent was the part of England closest to the Continent and probably the least de-Romanised in some respects. Trade links hinted at in Bede, when he mentions the 'interpreters' who acted as intermediaries for Augustine, have been borne out by archaeological finds: Merovingian coins in the St Martin's hoard at Canterbury include a medallion inscribed with the name of 'Liudhard bishop' – a happy coincidence indeed. The rich diversity of goods in east Kentish graves from this period include the fabulous Kingston brooch, glass vessels from Alexandria and jewellery from the Loire valley. The wealth of Kent was in part too a result of Ethelbert's 'Bretwaldaship' or overlordship over the neighbouring Anglo-Saxon kings, which almost certainly involved tribute, and may have given him command of the lucrative slave trade. Certainly his sphere of influence embraced both sides of the Thames estuary and included dominance over London as a port.[29] The island of Thanet, where the king first met Augustine, was at that time an important sheltering point of entry for traffic to the estuary, and tolls were charged which secured the wealth of Canterbury for many centuries.

It is against this general background that Bede's account is to be read. He relied heavily upon Canterbury traditions collated by his colleague abbot Albinus of the monastery of St Peter and St Paul there (later known as St Augustine's): 'he carefully ascertained from written records or from old traditions, all that the disciples of St Gregory had done in the kingdom of Kent or in the neighbouring kingdoms.' His authority lay also behind Nothelm's mission to Rome to research the papal archives.[30] The success of this historical enterprise may be judged when Bede's account is placed against the sketchy outline of the Kentish mission given in the Whitby *Life of St Gregory*, which rested entirely upon the summary of the two missions included in the *Liber Pontificalis*.

For Bede the mission sent by Gregory fulfilled the divine purpose and destiny of the English: unevangelised by the unhappy British, 'God in his goodness did not reject the people whom he foreknew; but He had appointed much worthier heralds of the truth to bring this people to the faith.'[31] As in the Acts upon which Bede closely models his account, underlying the miraculous progress of the Christian mission lies a darker note of rejection and failure: one people is chosen, another is reprobate. After relating the circumstances of the papal initiative and Augustine's false start when his companions lost heart and had to be stiffened in their resolve by Gregory, Bede tells how the missionaries finally arrived in Kent, seeking the patronage of Ethelbert its king, whose sway as 'Bretwalda' extended to the Humber. They landed in Thanet where they were accommodated by the king, encouraged it is implied by his Christian wife Bertha and her bishop Liudhard. Finally he met them with his witan outdoors for fear of magic: they were confronted by a chanting company of monks bearing a silver cross and an icon of Christ. Cautious for the sake of his retinue, Ethelbert gave them permission to come to Canterbury under his protections as guests: 'nor do we forbid you to win all you can to your faith and religion by your preaching.'[32] It was by their example, which Bede describes very much in the language of Acts 2, and their simple apostolic life-style that people became attracted to their message. This power of example was in Bede's mind the key to successful evangelism. They made use of the reconstituted Roman church dedicated to St Martin which the queen had been using as her chapel. Later they proceeded to build and to restore ruined churches elsewhere, including in due course the one which became Christ Church, the cathedral.[33]

After an undisclosed period, Ethelbert himself became Christian, and conversion became something of a fashion among the nobility:

> It is related that the king, although he rejoiced at their conversion and their faith, compelled no one to accept Christianity; though none the less he showed greater affection for believers since they were his fellow-citizens in the kingdom of heaven.

This absence of crude compulsion is striking and was sincere: 'he had learned from his teachers and guides in the way of salvation that the service of Christ was voluntary and ought not to be compulsory'. Yet it was to a heavenly kingdom that these converts were being drafted in, and where the king led those who sought his favour would follow with their households, not always for the deepest of reasons. Moreover such royal patronage inevitably integrated the bishop and his monks into the aristocratic establishment of the Kentish court: 'it was not long before he granted his teachers a place to settle in, suitable to their rank, in Canterbury his chief city, and gave them possessions of various kinds for their needs.'[34] Royal help led to the creation of the cathedral, and to the eventual founding of the monastery of St Peter and St Paul outside the city walls where archbishops and kings might be buried.[35] The very topography and church dedications recalled the origins of the missionaries from Rome itself. As the pope intended in his letter to Ethelbert, Augustine as bishop was to be the king's mentor, to be accepted as the voice of God and to be venerated as an effectual intercessor for the king with heaven.[36] Little wonder that Bede includes an encomium of Ethelbert as the principal benefactor of the Kentish mission, marking also his burial in the chapel of St Martin in the royal monastery.

A permanent memorial to this new-found position of the church in Kent is, as Bede knew, enshrined in the first code of written law in English drawn up by Ethelbert:

Among other benefits which he conferred upon the race under his care, he established with the advice of his counsellors a code of law after the Roman manner. These are written in English and are still kept and observed by the people. Among these he set down first of all what restitution must be made by anyone who steals anything belonging to the church or the bishop or any other clergy; these laws were designed to give protection to those whose coming and whose teaching he had welcomed.[37]

Examination of this law-code reveals the extraordinary privileges given to the bishop and the church, a degree of restitution in theory superior even to that of the king himself. Otherwise the code is far removed from Roman law in its content, being a summary of customary law of a Germanic tribal character. But the fact of its being written at all, and in such solemn form with clear ecclesiastical influence and address is a sign of change. The role of the king as lawgiver was being enhanced by Christian literacy and authority. In return, the position of the church was ensured against attack, in theory at least, even if the massive scale of restitution was far in excess of what Gregory envisaged in his reply to Augustine on this very issue: simple restoration not profit was his intention.[38] The writing of law, like the status of charters later, gave a sacred talismanic aura to the document containing it, placing it alongside the Bible as a symbol of the new order of religion in the land. Yet scrutiny of the content of these laws reveals no real Christian influence, and Gregory's fourth and fifth replies to Augustine on questions to do with marriage indicate the difficulty of intruding Christian principles into Anglo-Saxon customary law.

The unique monastic character of this mission from Rome has already been commented upon, and Gregory's letters bear ample testimony to the way the spirit of monastic obedience to him personally underpinned and gave strength to the progress of his missionaries. Bede, himself a monk, emphasises the monastic flavour to the English mission and the church it created throughout his *History*, possibly to an inordinate extent. The common life of Augustine and his companions in Canterbury is modelled on that of the earliest disciples in the Acts: and passages in Acts 2 and 4 had for a long time been a 'locus classicus' for justifying the monastic life as capturing and preserving the essence of primitive Christianity. In the first of Gregory's Responses, Augustine as bishop is commanded to live with his 'familia' of clergy as an abbot with his monks: 'because you are conversant, brother, with monastic rules, and ought not to live apart from your clergy in the English church . . . you ought to institute that manner of life which our fathers followed in the earliest beginnings of the church: none of them said that anything he possessed was his own, but they had all things in common'.[39] This common and if possible celibate life was to determine how the economic resources of the see were to be apportioned. The monastic ethos of the mission took embodiment in the creation of the royal monastery without the walls of St Peter & St Paul under the leadership of Peter its first abbot. At some unknown date a school was founded there, for which no doubt the 'very many manuscripts' sent by the pope with Mellitus in 601 were intended; of these the sole survivor is probably the Canterbury Gospels upon which new archbishops of Canterbury still take their inaugural oaths.[40] The cult of St Peter was not only a ploy to bind rulers like Ethelbert in loyalty to the Apostolic see; it also acted as a powerful model of suffering obedience to sustain a monastic bishop in dire moments, as the story of archbishop Laurence's chastisement when contemplating flight from Kent reveals.[41]

Gregory enunciated a clear strategy for the development of the English mission. Crucial to its continuing success was obviously the active partnership with the Gallic church. So in the second of his Responses to Augustine, he clearly states that the new English church is to benefit from customs of both the Roman and Gallic churches in an eclectic manner. In his sixth Response he indicates that Augustine should consecrate sufficient bishops to support each other and secure canonical consecrations of new bishops: 'for how often do bishops come from Gaul who can assist as witnesses at the consecration of a bishop?' In the seventh Response, Augustine is warned against asserting any primatial rights in relation to those of the metropolitan of Arles: 'you have no right to judge the bishops of Gaul, who are outside your jurisdiction'. On the other hand Augustine may by example and admonition challenge abuses, and should actively collaborate with his colleague at Arles for the reform of the church in Gaul.

This intention was supported by Gregory in a letter to the bishop of Arles.[42]

With Mellitus and his companions of the second mission in 601, Gregory sent a further letter to Augustine outlining his vision for the structural development of the English church. He envisaged the primatial see at London rather than permanently at Canterbury, with another in due course re-established at York. Each primate would be supported by twelve suffragan bishops, and seniority of consecration would determine the distinction of honour between the two primates. To this end the pope sent Augustine the pallium. This was an ambitious scheme, modelled it seems on that which pertained when Britain was a province of the Roman Empire. Gregory also intended that the archbishop of Canterbury should have primacy over 'all the bishops of Britain', and this was claimed both by Augustine when he met them in synod, and by his successor Laurence in his letters to the Irish and British churches appealing for unity in the keeping of Easter and other matters.[43] The guidance Gregory gave to Augustine about the way he was to conduct the episcopal office summarises his well-established teaching in his *Pastoral Rule*.

In reality the progress of the mission was assisted and also constrained by Ethelbert's sway as 'Bretwalda' or overlord of the other English kingdoms. To this Gregory directly appealed in his letter to the king, hailing him as a 'ruler over nations' raised up by God to advance the cause of Christianity by 'exhorting, terrifying, enticing and correcting them', destroying if need be the worship of idols after the example of Constantine the great. 'Now let your majesty hasten to instil the knowledge of the one God, Father, Son and Holy Spirit, into the kings and nations subject to you, that you may surpass the ancient kings of your race in praise and merit.' In this way the king's anxiety about his own sins before the day of Judgement might be mitigated. The key to all this lay in a working alliance with Augustine as his mentor and intercessor.[44] So in due course Augustine was able with Ethelbert's support to create episcopal sees in Rochester and also in London, because Ethelbert's nephew Saeberht ruled in Essex. The first bishops of these sees were Justus and Mellitus, and their cathedral churches were built by the king himself, who 'later bestowed many gifts on the bishops of these churches and that of Canterbury; and he also added both lands and possessions for the maintenance of the bishops' retinues.'[45] The significance of these endowments was of course reflected in the recompense prescribed in his law codes.

The pastoral theology of the mission faced challenges from at least two directions: from paganism, and from the recalcitrance of the British church. Archaeological and place-name evidence indicates the relative strength of paganism around Canterbury in eastern Kent, and this may well account for the king's reticence in receiving Augustine in 597 and too readily endorsing his message. It may account too for the apparent 'volte face' of pope Gregory in 601, for in his letter to king Ethelbert he enjoins the destruction of places of pagan worship with their idols, whereas in his letter to Mellitus written shortly afterwards he carefully advises his missionaries that:

> The idol temples of that race should by no means be destroyed, but
> only the idols in them. Take holy water and sprinkle it in these shrines,
> build altars and place relics in them. For if the shrines are well built – it
> is essential that they should be changed from the worship of devils to
> the service of the true God.

The familiarity of the people will thus be diverted into Christian worship in
already hallowed places; likewise their feasts should be converted into
Christian solemnities. This policy Gregory commended both on the pastoral
grounds of the gradual nature of conversion, and on the basis of Old
Testament practice.[46] It is likely, therefore, that the pope's appeal to the
king was more rhetorical, and this in practice was what happened, probably making a virtue out of a necessity. Nonetheless liberation from the
fear, superstition and perceived emptiness of pagan worship of idols is
something acclaimed by Bede and also by Aldhelm:

> where once the crude pillars of the foul snake and the stag were
> worshipped with coarse stupidity in profane shrines, in their place dwell-
> ings for students, not to mention holy houses of prayer, are constructed
> skilfully by the talents of architects.[47]

Gregory clearly hoped that all the British bishops would gravitate towards
his emissary and unite with him in a common life and mission to the pagan
English: 'we commit to you all the bishops of Britain that the unlearned
may be instructed, the weak strengthened by your counsel, and the perverse
corrected by your authority'.[48] As in Gaul, so in Britain, mission was to be
a stimulus to reform of the church under the guidance of Rome. What
Gregory seems to have failed to reckon with were two things, not unrelated:
the tenacity with which the Irish and British Christians clung to their customs
out of reverence for their own holy men; and the deep hatred of the British
towards their Anglo-Saxon conquerors. So when 'Augustine, making use
of king Ethelbert, summoned the bishops and teachers of the neighbouring
British kingdom to a conference' he was already a compromised figure in
their eyes.[49] His appeal for unity in missionary activity and in the keeping of
the catholic reckoning of Easter fell on deaf ears. A trial healing miracle –
the only one actually recorded by Augustine – did not clinch the matter
either: 'his adversaries agreed unwillingly and a man of *English* race was
brought forward who was blind. He was presented to the British bishops,
but no healing or benefit was obtained from their ministry,' which was
perhaps hardly surprising given the racial barrier. Augustine's prayers
succeeded, and the British were obliged to agree to a second conference.

To this 'seven British bishops and many learned men came, chiefly from
their most famous monastery called Bangor Iscoed' ruled by an abbot
Dinoot. Significantly 'they went first to a certain holy and prudent man
who lived as a hermit among them to consult him as to whether they ought
to forsake their own traditions at the bidding of Augustine'. The holy man
indicated that Augustine's demeanour should determine his trustworthiness:

if he rose to greet them, all would be well. But for a Roman bishop to receive sitting was quite normal, and so antipathy set in because of a cultural clash. The British dismissed Augustine as arrogant, fearing to fall under his sway, and perhaps also that of the Anglo-Saxon overlord. The pivot of the issue was threefold:

> to keep Easter at the proper time; to perform the sacrament of baptism ... according to the rites of the holy Roman and apostolic church; and to preach the word of the Lord to the English people in fellowship with us.

But this was overtly presented as an act of submission to Augustine as the pope's envoy. At their refusal, he is remembered as having predicted their eventual defeat at the hands of the English as an act of divine judgement. This occurred later in 615 at the battle of Chester when many of the monks of Bangor were massacred by Ethelfrith of Northumbria. Bede's chapter on this unedifying exchange reveals both his own bias against the unfortunate British Christians, and also the likely British provenance of the traditions he is handling, which portray Augustine in a less than flattering light. Even if Augustine were haughty or just ill-briefed, he may have been doomed to failure from the start given the defensive stance of the British for wholly understandable reasons. This tragic conflict grumbled on throughout the seventh century. Augustine's successor as archbishop of Canterbury, Laurence, complained in his letter to the Irish bishops and abbots of the refusal of both British and Irish Christians to share table-fellowship with the Roman missionaries and their converts.[50] Later Aldhelm wrote to Geraint the British king of Devon and Cornwall in similar vein. He criticised the lack of unity in the church in Britain, the rancour over interpretation of doctrine and customs such as styles of monastic tonsure and the date of Easter. He lambasts the Welsh bishops

> glorying in the private purity of their own way of life, who detest our communion to such a great extent that they disdain equally to celebrate the divine offices with us in church or to take courses of food at table with us for the sake of charity. . . . No greeting of peace is offered, no kiss of affectionate brotherhood is bestowed according to the word of the apostle.

He concludes: 'Surely catholic Faith and the harmony of brotherly love walk inseparably with even steps'.[51] Yet these appeals apparently did little to overcome the depth of bitterness and resentment which ruled the hearts of the British church leaders. But it may well be that neither Aldhelm nor Bede, being utter devotees to the Roman tradition, and of the first well-established generation of English Christians, could do sympathetic justice to the British position and plight.

There is another angle on the nature of this rancour and division. The last two of Gregory's Responses to Augustine deal with matters of ritual purity: 'all these things the ignorant English people need to know'. The implication is that there is confusion of moral teaching among some of the English converts for which Augustine needs an authoritative verdict from Rome.

There is reason to suppose that these address the teaching of the British church, under Irish influence, on issues such as sexual purity and divine worship. Certainly that which is addressed by Augustine bears closer resemblance to what is found in the early British and Irish codes of penitential discipline than to what is known of pagan Anglo-Saxon proclivities or to the moral theology of Rome under Gregory. To all this the pope responds with moderation and human good sense, basing himself upon a characteristically spiritual interpretation of scripture. It is just possible that these replies furnished Augustine with powerful ammunition for his second and fateful conference with the British church leaders, the issues having surfaced at the first meeting perhaps. What is most significant, however, is that indirect light is shed upon likely British evangelism of the English, probably along the western border of the conquest where the populations were evenly balanced, the boundaries of the Hwicce and the West Saxons where Augustine's conferences occurred.[52]

The degree to which the Roman missionaries were dependent upon Ethelbert's favour and support as Bretwalda was revealed immediately after his death. His pre-eminence was already slipping to the king of the East Angles, Redwald, even during his lifetime, and on his death a reaction against Christianity set in. His son, Eadbald, refused baptism and married his father's most recent wife. Bede describes him as 'apostate', and portrays him like Saul of old as mentally unstable. Meanwhile in Essex, the death of Ethelbert's nephew, Saeberht, ensured the succession of his three sons. These resumed their worship of idols, and mocked bishop Mellitus for refusing them the eucharist, banishing him from London. He and Justus, bishop of Rochester, departed for Gaul. While the archbishop, Laurence, was weighing up a similar move, he received in a vision a reprimand from St Peter which so impressed Eadbald the king that it led to a reverse of policy in favour of the church: 'he banned all idolatrous worship, gave up his unlawful wife, accepted the Christian faith and was baptized; and thereafter he promoted and furthered the interests of the church to the best of his abilities'.[53] Whereupon Mellitus and Justus returned from their self-imposed exile; but Mellitus was unable to return to London 'for king Eadbald had less royal power than his father had and was unable to restore the bishop to his church against the will and consent of the heathen'. The king built instead a church dedicated to the holy Mother of God to the east of the monastery church of St Peter and St Paul in Canterbury.

The mission continued, firstly under the leadership of Laurence, then of Mellitus, with active support from pope Boniface V. Like his earlier namesake, Boniface IV, his interest was genuine, and his letter to Justus who succeeded Mellitus at Canterbury is included by Bede in his *History*.[54] The support from Rome was clearly important to the establishment of the Kentish church: Bede records how in 610, Boniface IV held a synod to deal with harmony in the monastic life, at which Mellitus attended. The 'needs of the English church' were deliberated also, and the bishop returned with letters to the archbishop and the king.[55] The link with Rome by Mellitus was sustained in personal terms, and he may have known Boniface V before he became pope; certainly the new pope wrote to him soon after his accession. His letter to Justus is full of encouragement, noting a letter from the king upon his conversion, and sending the pallium. The work of mission is described as 'cleansing the hearts of unbelievers from their inherent disease of superstition'. Of Mellitus is recorded a miracle by which he checked a fire in Canterbury through prayer at the church of the four crowned martyrs. This dedication was another echo of Rome, for a church of this name stood also upon the Coelian hill close by their home monastery of Gregory's own foundation.

The first phase of the mission to Kent concluded with the labours of Paulinus in the north, at the court of Edwin king of Northumbria, who married Ethelbert's daughter, Ethelburh, during the reign of Eadbald. Like Bertha before her, this was allowed upon condition that she were permitted to practise her faith unmolested. To this Edwin agreed, indicating a sympathetic attitude himself towards Christianity. So Paulinus came with her as bishop and private chaplain. The story dominates the second part of Book II of Bede's *History*, and this represents the strength of tradition he was able to tap from various sources. The significance of Edwin's final conversion is also demonstrated in the Whitby *Life of St Gregory*, whose middle section describes the cult of the king after his death as well, and also in fragmentary British sources. In these, the *Historia Brittonum* (sometimes referred to as Nennius), it is alleged that the baptism of Edwin was in fact carried out by Rhun son of Urien in the midst of a more general conversion. This may be polemical; or it may reflect some more ancient tradition of British Christian influence upon the Northumbrians.[56] Bede's account must stand as a skilful collation of traditions, corroborated independently by the Whitby *Life*.

Disentangling the strands woven together by Bede, the story of Edwin's conversion begins when he was a young man in exile from his predecessor, king Ethelfrith. The authority for the story seems to have been the king himself and it is recorded at length by Bede and more briefly in the Whitby *Life*. Behind it lies also Welsh tradition about Edwin's sojourn at the court of the Christian king of Gwynedd.[57] For a time he remained under the protection of the Bretwalda, Redwald of East Anglia, who at one stage was almost bribed by Ethelfrith to betray Edwin. Apprised of his danger by a friend at court, Edwin contemplated flight again. While in this agony of uncertainty 'he saw a man silently approach him whose face and attire were strange to him'. As a sign and promise the stranger laid his right hand on the young man's head and disappeared. Edwin thought he had seen a spirit; the writer of the Whitby *Life* more cannily concludes that the one who appeared to him 'crowned with the cross of Christ' was no other than Paulinus himself, who would much later fulfil the sign and call him to obedience and faith. If so, this might indicate a mission by Paulinus to East

Anglia in Redwald's day. According to Bede, Redwald had received Christianity while in Kent, but had lapsed under the influence of his wife: 'he seemed to be serving both Christ and the gods whom he had previously served, for in the same temple he had one altar for the Christian sacrifice and another small altar on which to offer victims to devils'.[58] This flagrant example of royal syncretism indicates how difficult it was for kings to depart from the traditions of their ancestors whose guardians they were. Indeed the whole clutch of stories surrounding Edwin's conversion afford an unique insight into the psychology of royal conversion.

Paulinus proved an energetic but not initially successful missionary. A sequence of private crises within the royal household began gradually to dispose the king's heart: a narrow escape from assassination and the safe delivery of a daughter, Eanflaed, who was baptised at Pentecost as a pledge of the king's own conversion should God give him victory against his enemies in Wessex. This occurred, and the king relinquished the worship of idols and sought lengthy preparation from his bishop, Paulinus. His procrastination was partly prudent with regard to his followers, partly also personal: 'in his innermost thoughts he was debating with himself as to what he ought to do and which religion he should adhere to'.[59] Meanwhile Paulinus had secured a papal letter from Boniface V to the king urging conversion, using the example of Eadbald in Kent as a spur. It is an eloquent appeal for the rejection of idolatry in favour of worship of the true God and baptism. The pope concludes by sending a handsome gift – 'the blessing of your protector, St Peter, chief of the Apostles'.[60] A companion letter was sent to the queen, to whose Christian influence and example the pope could appeal. She is called to fulfil St Paul's prediction: 'the unbelieving husband shall be saved by the believing wife'. To speed a reply, the pope sends some tactful gifts to her too: 'a silver mirror and an ivory comb adorned with gold'.[61] The most likely source for these two particular letters seems to have been Paulinus himself.

Finally, reminded by Paulinus of the heavenly sign and its promises fulfilled by political success, the king resolved to become a Christian provided he could carry his council with him. It is in this context that the famous speech by the pagan high-priest, Coifi, is told in which he testified to the emptiness of his faith. A nobleman likened the brevity and uncertainty of human life to the flight of a sparrow through a hall, loitering 'for the briefest moment of calm'. In short, hope of reasonable prosperity and some inkling into the afterlife swayed the hearts of men, and here Christianity seemed to break fresh ground and give a sense of security. Coifi himself broke all taboos and desecrated the ancestral shrine at Goodmanham. There is in the Whitby *Life* a comparable tale about the debate with paganism: cruder and more ordinary it carries a ring of truth. During the period of the king's instruction, he and his court were arrested on the way to church by the croaking of a crow 'from an unpropitious quarter of the sky'. To break their superstition, the bishop ordered a youth to shoot it down. The arrow became a sign of the vanity of pagan belief in the omens attributed to such natural events: if the bird could not avoid death, it could hardly foretell the future! Yet in the next breath this monk records how the death of Paulinus himself was marked by the departure of his soul in the form of a beautiful swan.[62] Taken together these stories afford a lively window into the way the merits of the new faith were debated, and absorbed both at the time and in Bede's day also.

So king Edwin, with all the nobles of his race and a vast number of the common people, received the faith and regeneration by holy baptism in the eleventh year of his reign, that is in the year of our Lord 627 and about 180 years after the coming of the English to Britain. He was baptized at York on Easter Day, 12 April, in the church of St Peter the Apostle, which he had hastily built of wood while he was a catechumen and under instruction before he received baptism. He established an episcopal see for Paulinus, his instructor and bishop in the same city. Very soon after his baptism, he set about building a greater and more magnificent church of stone, under the instructions of Paulinus.[63]

Thus Gregory's strategy was being fulfilled, and pope Honorius sent the pallium to Paulinus, and wrote encouragingly to Edwin. He reminded him that he was a king only on condition that he offered due worship to the true God, and urged him to read frequently the works of Gregory, 'your evangelist and my lord'. The king is to support his bishop, and the significance of the pallium for both archbishops is explained to him to ensure a stable succession of bishops in England. This in due course occurred, and when Justus died, his successor, Honorius, came north to Lincoln to be consecrated by Paulinus. In the pope's letter to the new archbishop he assumes the active co-operation of the kings of Kent and Northumbria in this, in order to obviate the need for recourse to Rome in person for primatial consecration.[64] Bede indicates the degree of active papal interest and involvement in the affairs of the church in the British Isles by citing letters to the Irish by Honorius and his successors concerning the vexed issue of the date of Easter, and alleging a revival of Pelagianism. Honorius was a worthy successor to Gregory the great, consciously following the policies of his distinguished predecessor. His authority and interest lay behind the sending in 634 of Birinus as missionary bishop to Wessex, and probably also the arrival of Felix from Burgundy whom the archbishop of Canterbury, Honorius, sent as missionary bishop to the East Angles.[65]

The initial impact of Edwin's conversion was considerable, and opened many doors of missionary opportunity. A visit north by Paulinus to the royal palace at Yeavering is described to baptize and catechise for a whole month; likewise at Catterick near the royal residence. It was Edwin's influence as Bretwalda that persuaded Eorpwold, son of Redwald of East Anglia to convert. Despite his premature death, his brother, Sigebert, came to the throne there as 'a devout Christian and a very learned man in all respects': during exile he had received Christianity in Gaul, and it must be presumed his education also.

He at once sought to imitate some of the excellent institutions which he had seen in Gaul, and established a school where boys could be taught letters with the help of bishop Felix who had come to him from Kent and who provided him with masters and teachers as in the Kentish school.[66]

Sigebert and Felix proved a formidable partnership, and a see was created at Dunwich, where Felix served for 17 years. The king at that time welcomed the Irish 'peregrinus', Fursey, whose preaching and sanctity won him a following. A man of visions, one of which Bede relates in some detail, he founded a monastery within the walls of the old Roman fortress of Burgh Castle with some Irish companions. From this he finally retired to become a hermit, departing for Gaul where he died at his monastery of Lagny, to be buried and venerated at Peronne.[67] So strong was the monastic impulse of these missionaries that in the end the king, Sigebert, himself retired to a monastery, from which he was pressed to emerge to engage in battle, dying unarmed.[68]

Edwin's reign was remembered as a time of peace and stability throughout the north of England. Paulinus meanwhile made headway in the sub-kingdom of Lindsey, converting the reeve of Lincoln and building a 'stone church of remarkable workmanship' where he consecrated Honorius. Although in ruins in Bede's day, it became something of a shrine where miracles of healing occurred still. Bede received at first-hand a description of Paulinus from an old man, a priest and abbot, who had been baptised by him as part of this mission: 'he was tall, with a slight stoop, black hair, a thin face, a slender aquiline nose, and at the same time he was both venerable and awe-inspiring in appearance.'[69] He was assisted by a deacon, James, 'who survived right up to our days'. He remained at York after the death of Edwin and the flight of Paulinus in 633: he was 'a true churchman and a saintly man', who continued the work of catechism and baptism, and later instructed the rising generation of Northumbrian Christians in the Roman and Kentish manner of singing in church.[70]

Edwin fell in battle to an alliance between Cadwalla, the Christian king of Gwynedd and the pagan ruler of Mercia, Penda. It spelt ruin to his family and a time of cruelty for his people. Once again Bede does not hide the antagonism between British and English. Cadwalla's intention was to 'wipe out the whole English nation from the land of Britain'. It was in fact the last concerted resistance by the British to their northern conquerors and it came within an ace of success.

Nor did he pay any respect to the Christian religion which had sprung up amongst them. Indeed to this very day it is the habit of the Britons to despise the faith and religion of the English and not to co-operate with them in anything any more than with the heathen.[71]

Paulinus fled to Kent, taking with him the queen Ethelburh and the royal children, including Eanflaed who would become abbess of Whitby. Some of these children were sent on to Gaul to shelter with king Dagobert. Meanwhile Paulinus became bishop of Rochester because Romanus its bishop had died on an embassy to Rome to pope Honorius.

The memory of Edwin, the first Christian king of Northumbria, was kept alive at Whitby in particular. It became the royal monastery, presided over by Eanflaed and her daughter Aelfflaed. The writer of the *Life of St Gregory* recounts how, long after its burial, the body of Edwin was rescued from the battlefield by a miracle. According to Bede, the king's head had been salvaged at the time of the battle, and brought to York to the cathedral to be placed in the chapel of St Gregory. He notes also the later burial of the king's body at Whitby; but the full story is treasured in the Whitby *Life* in the monastery created by Edwin's grand-niece, Hilda, who had been one of the first to be baptised by Paulinus in 627, and who had received her vocation to the monastic life while in exile in East Anglia, hoping initially to go over to Chelles in Gaul.[72] The Whitby *Life*, asserts that the relics of Edwin worked miracles, being venerated in the church of St Peter at Whitby 'on the south side of the altar which is dedicated in the name of the blessed apostle Peter and east of the altar dedicated to St Gregory'.[73] Edwin was regarded as a virtual royal martyr, as well as, like Ethelbert, the patriarch of Christianity among his people. The strength of the tradition associated with him at York and Whitby in the next generation is testimony to the fact that although his death was a setback for Christianity in the north, the ground had been well-prepared by Paulinus for the prosperity of the faith in those parts. Indeed Paulinus emerges as the missionary whose labours are best recorded. He with Honorius, whom he consecrated to Canterbury and who served there for the next 25 years, must be acclaimed as those who did most in the first generation of the Roman mission to secure its long-term success.

VI. AIDAN AND CUTHBERT

The death in battle of Edwin proved a severe if in the end temporary set-back for Christianity in Northumbria. The kingdom was divided into its two constituent entities – Deira in the south and Bernicia in the north, and thus weakened was again attacked by the British king, Cadwalla, who killed both kings and maintained a rule of terror for a year. It was later viewed as 'annus horribilis' by the Northumbrians on account of their humiliation, and because both kings, Osric and Eanfrith turned apostate from the Christian faith, which Eanfrith had received while in exile among the Irish, and Osric from Paulinus himself. Eanfrith was the son of Edwin's predecessor Ethelfrith, as was Oswald his brother who finally regained the kingdom by killing Cadwalla at the battle of Heavenfield in 634. This victory broke forever British resistance to English rule in the north and was regarded as a turning-point in the Christian destiny of Northumbria. Bede's account is corroborated by a prominent memory in the *Life of St Columba* by Adomnan.[1] According to this tradition Columba appeared to the young prince Oswald on the eve of the battle, covering his camp with heavenly protection. In biblical language, he was promised victory. When told of this portent, his followers promised to accept baptism if it came to pass. The monks at Iona clearly saw this as the key which opened the door to Christian mission in Northumbria, and the sign that Oswald 'was afterwards ordained by God as emperor of all Britain'. Sometime during his reign, Oswald returned to Iona and told the story to abbot Segene who had probably baptised him while in exile there. This is an important window also into the mind of the Ionan monks, accounting for their profound veneration of and loyalty towards their founder, Columba.

In Bede's account of the battle, Oswald's actions echo those of the great Constantine himself. He set up the 'sign of the holy cross', and prayed for divine help, 'for He knows that we are fighting in a just cause for the preservation of our whole race'. So 'as dawn was breaking they gained the victory that their faith merited'. Bede further recounts how in later years it became a place of pilgrimage for the clergy at Hexham, fragments of the cross wrought miracles, and in due course a church was built.

Oswald's own response was to send to Iona for missionaries to come and evangelise the Northumbrians, and the story of this mission is in many ways central to Bede's own understanding of the theology behind the history he is recounting. Abbot Segene's first choice was not a success: he found the English 'intractable, obstinate and uncivilised'. He returned from Northumbria to Iona in disgust. Aidan's appeal for a gentler and more gradual approach to the work of evangelism led to his being appointed instead:

They agreed that he was worthy to be made a bishop and that he was the man to send to instruct those ignorant unbelievers, since he had proved himself to be pre-eminently endowed with the grace of discretion which is the mother of all virtues.[2]

The king gave Aidan the tidal island of Lindisfarne for his monastic headquarters, and co-operated with him actively in 'seeking to build up and extend the church of Christ in his kingdom', even at times serving as interpreter for the bishop to the nobility. Lindisfarne offered physical security and the ascetic remoteness of Iona; it was also in sight of the royal fortress at Bamburgh. Aidan was followed by others, mainly monks, loyal to Iona and its dependent houses. Aidan's example was long remembered, and was treasured by Bede as a notable example of effective evangelism. 'The best recommendation of his teaching to all was that he taught them no other way of life than that which he himself practised among his fellows.' He refused possessions and travelled on foot; he was fearless towards the rich using gifts to him as alms for the poor or to redeem slaves, some of whom he trained for the priesthood.

In Bede's mind Aidan was an exemplary bishop, and his portrait of him is primarily a theological disquisition resting undoubtedly on solid historical memories. In his 'preface' he indicates how close were his connections with the Lindisfarne community, from whom he had already drawn material and traditions for his *Life of St Cuthbert*. Although by Bede's day the cult of St Cuthbert at Lindisfarne was perhaps beginning to eclipse the memory of St Aidan, in his *History* Bede with great determination sets up Aidan as the spiritual founder of the whole Lindisfarne tradition with which he shows such sympathy. This is most evident in the formal encomium with which Bede concludes his account of Aidan's death.[3] 'All these things I greatly admire and love in this bishop and I have no doubt that all this was pleasing to God. But I neither praise nor approve of him in so far as he did not observe Easter at the proper time.' Bede appears concerned to rescue the memory of Aidan from those who would still use him in defence of the non-Roman calculation of Easter, and to reclaim him as a pillar of catholic orthodoxy and a true saint of the universal church.

Despite his almost passionate obsession with the importance of the Roman computation of Easter, Bede is prepared to give Aidan the benefit of the doubt, confident that

> In his celebration of Easter he had no other thought in his heart, he reverenced and preached no other doctrine than we do, namely the redemption of the human race by the passion, resurrection and ascension into heaven of the one mediator between God and men, even the man Christ Jesus.

So for Bede, Aidan is set up in his *History* as the yardstick by which all other bishops are measured:

> such were his love of peace and charity, temperance and humility; his soul which triumphed over anger and greed and at the same time

despised pride and vainglory; his industry in carrying out and teaching the divine commandments, his diligence in study and keeping vigil, his authority, such as became a priest, in reproving the proud and the mighty, and his tenderness in comforting the weak, in relieving and protecting the poor.

His was in Bede's mind a truly apostolic ministry. So the stories he relates concerning Aidan exemplify the virtues included in this very important definition, 'a man of outstanding gentleness, devotion and moderation'.[4] Bede's account is clearly in part polemical, against the 'modern slothfulness' and acquisitiveness of clergy in his day! 'Aidan taught the clergy many lessons about the conduct of their lives but above all he left them a most salutary example of abstinence and self-control. . . . All who accompanied him had to engage in some form of study. . . . This was the daily task of Aidan himself and of all who were with him.'[5] Bede selects two significant stories of how Aidan related to kings. In the first he portrays Aidan commending the generosity of Oswald towards the poor at his gate at an Easter feast, blessing the king's right hand with the words, 'May this hand never decay!' In Bede's day the severed right hand of the king was venerated as an incorrupt relic in the royal chapel at Bamburgh.[6] The second story is no less famous, of how Oswald's successor, Oswine, insisted that the ageing bishop should relent and use a horse, gave him one of his best. This Aidan promptly gave away to a beggar. Chided by the king for his over-generosity, Aidan stood his ground with the words: 'Surely this son of a mare is not dearer to you than that son of God?' At which the king's abject repentance moved the saint to tears.[7]

Likewise the three miracles recorded by Bede have a profound political as well as symbolic significance. The first concerns the embassy sent to collect Eanflaed, Edwin's daughter, from Kent to be the wife of king Oswy. To the priest accompanying them, Utta, Aidan gave a phial of oil to pour on troubled water during a storm. As in its gospel exemplar, power over a storm in nature pointed to a deeper power over the unruly wills and affections of sinful men. This is evident also in the second miracle, when after the death of Oswald, the Mercian ruler Penda raided far into Northumbria and besieged the royal fortress at Bamburgh and tried to burn it down. Aidan in retreat on the Farne Island witnessed the spectacle and by his prayers prompted a divine alteration of the wind which 'carried the flames in the direction of those who had kindled them' so that they fled in terror. The final miracle also concerns fire. Aidan died on a preaching mission, lying in a tent propped up against the end of his church and cell on a royal estate by Bamburgh. The wooden buttress later survived a serious fire during another of Penda's raids and in due time was preserved and venerated as a miracle-working relic.[8] Thus was this simple and ascetic bishop a stay and prop to the political order which made his mission a practical possibility. Even as a critic he was its true servant, standing for the values of an eternal kingdom as a monk who had 'died' to the world. So Aidan embodied the authority of

Christ, 'who came not to be served but to serve'. His ministry and vocation called forth that also of the king as his interpreter and support. Theirs was an alliance built upon a genuine friendship and mutual respect. Underpinning it was a sacrificial monastic way of life which was no sham, enabling Aidan and those who truly followed him to relate to and so to evangelise all manner of folk, high and low. In many ways the figure of Aidan is an important key to unlock the theological purpose of Bede's writing of the *History*.

The example of the bishop illumines and throws into sharp relief also that of the king: there is a double act here upon which Bede dwells with consummate care and emphasis. Oswald, and to a lesser extent Oswine also, is as Bede portrays him the model Christian king – another yardstick by which others may be measured. But Oswald is remembered by both Bede and Adomnan in his *Life of St Columba* as a formidable military leader, a northern 'Bretwalda' with 'greater earthly realms than any of his ancestors', a ruler of British, Pictish, Irish and English, an 'emperor of all Britain'.[9] He did not achieve this 'supreme power over the whole land' by meekness and prayer alone! Yet Bede nowhere speaks directly of his political activities or even how he found himself trapped and killed by Penda and the Welsh near Oswestry after an aggressive campaign far from home.[10] His interest lies elsewhere; and the picture he paints of this young and vigorous king is highly selective.

To some extent Bede's criteria are influenced by Old Testament portraits of kings like David and Solomon; they are coloured too by the example of Jesus. His purpose is not only ethically to edify, as he states in his 'preface' to the Northumbrian king Ceolwulf who commissioned his work; it is also to raise a potent antitype to pagan ideas of the heroic king. Whereas in *Beowulf* there is a transformation of values underway in a Christian direction more implicit than explicit: in Bede the Christian goal is set forth with radical clarity and theological sophistication in a manner that would direct the biblical thought of the monks towards moulding the values of the Christian aristocracy from which their leaders in Northumbria sprang. In Bede's mind, and upon patristic authority, there was a direct line of duty in Christian kingship which was interpreted by a vision of episcopacy moulded by monastic life. This is a powerful and fundamental nexus running throughout his work, and never more evident than in this conjunction of Aidan and Oswald.[11] So for Bede, 'lordship' is defined by Christlike humility, prayer and service; 'true nobility' is expressed in the practice of Christian virtues guided by bishops; 'power' resides supremely in the occurrence of miracles signifying divine favour, of which earthly prowess and success in battle might be a sign; 'fame' is relocated in relation to heaven and eternal life, by which earthly memory is now perceived and remembered. The picture Bede paints, the points he chooses to highlight, are all determined by these overt principles. Yet his selection must rest upon accurate memory to which by implication his interpretation is appealing. This is both a theological statement and a potent political point: its root lies deep in the Old Testament, in I Samuel 8 and elsewhere, where prophetic authority indicates the accountability of monarchy towards God and its moral purpose, and warns against tyranny.

Oswald was therefore venerated in Northumbria and upon Iona as a king who had shown biblical faith before battle, who had been subject to a lengthy and obscure 'preparatio' by divine providence while in exile, whose victory was enjoined by heavenly intercession and whose triumphant sign was the Cross. He proved himself a guardian of his people's very life against a mortal enemy, and demonstrated this further by his initiative in asking for a mission, and then acting as active interpreter and protector of it. So he offered a spiritual 'cure' to his own nobility, sustaining the progress of Christianity by investing in education: 'lands and property were given by royal bounty to establish monasteries, and English children, as well as their elders, were instructed by Irish teachers in advanced studies and in the observance of the discipline of a Rule'.[12] The king's generosity towards the poor was an expression of true magnanimity springing from a following of the divine example of Christ. As ruler of Northumbria he was a reconciler of its constituent parts and like Edwin before him a bringer of peace to his people. 'He held under his sway all the peoples and kingdoms of Britain' and used his position and influence to advance Christianity, as Ethelbert of Kent had done before him. Bede recounts how Oswald played an active role in support of the Italian bishop, Birinus, in the evangelisation of Wessex. Birinus had been sent by pope Honorius 'having promised in the pope's presence that he would scatter the seeds of the holy faith in the remotest regions of England, where no teacher had been before'.[13] His landfall was in Wessex and there he laboured for fifteen years. Oswald was married to the king's daughter probably as a result of the alliance forged when as Northumbrian 'Bretwalda' he stood sponsor at the baptism of Cynegisl of Wessex. Both kings endowed Birinus with lands for a see at Dorchester-on-Thames, near Oxford, from which later in the century his remains were translated to the new see at Winchester. Oswald's influence extended also for a time over Sussex where later his memory was venerated.[14]

He died in battle, defeated by Penda of Mercia and the Welsh near Oswestry; but like Edwin before him he was regarded as a royal martyr and his remains were rescued and venerated as relics. Bede records the tradition that he died with prayer on his lips; indeed he was remembered generally as a man of prayer.[15] Beasts and men were healed at the spot of his death, and soil taken from the place was claimed to have miraculous properties.[16] By Bede's time Oswald's cult was well-established, his body being translated to Bardney, his head to Lindisfarne and his hands and arms to Bamburgh: he had been mutilated by his enemies. Bede tells how the reputation of the sainted king spread to Germany and to Ireland upon the authority of the great missionary, Willibrord;[17] and it was at Wilfrid's monastery at Selsey that a young sick convert had a vision of St Peter who confirmed that the heavenly intercession of Oswald had secured a cessation of plague for the monks.[18] His efficacy and compassion transcended the racial divide between south Saxons and Northumbrians, as is also made clear in the story surrounding the translation of relics to Bardney: there the monks resisted receiving the king's remains because he was an ancestral enemy and erstwhile conqueror. A column of heavenly light changed their minds.[19] His feast on the day of his death, 5 August, was commemorated in the calendar of St Willibrord who took some relics with him on his mission, and his cult spread wherever Irish and Anglo-Saxon influence was felt on the Continent.[20] Thus portrayed, Oswald combined perfectly the role of Anglo-Saxon royal hero and Christian patriarch and martyr-king.

Bede's portrayal of his kinsman and successor, Oswine who initially ruled over Deira after Oswald's death, while Oswald's brother, Oswy, ruled in Bernicia, is equally significant. Oswine ruled in 'the greatest prosperity, beloved of all', being 'a man of great piety and religion'.[21] Tension arose between the two kings which led to the murder of Oswine, who having forgone an unequal battle was betrayed by a friend of Oswy. Later the royal family raised a monastery there in atonement for the crime. Bede's story of Aidan giving away the gift of a horse from Oswine reflects creditably upon both bishop and king. It is the 'graces of virtue, modesty and humility' which marked out this ruler in Bede's mind. His reaction to Aidan's remonstrance so moved the bishop by its sincerity and lack of self-regard that he exclaimed: 'I know that this king will not live long; for I never saw a more humble king. Therefore I think that he will very soon be snatched from this life, for this nation does not deserve to have such a ruler.' As Aidan only lived for twelve days after Oswine's murder, it may be assumed that the tragedy which befell his friend was the last straw.

Aidan's remembered words touch upon a profound paradox at the heart of Bede's portrayal of the Christian model of kingship. For Oswine was not the only example of a humble king: Sigebert of East Anglia, the patron of St Felix, resigned his throne to become a monk and died unarmed in battle.[22] Likewise later Sebbi of Essex who after a reign of thirty years finally went into a monastery, despite his wife's long-standing protests, receiving his habit from the bishop of London and divesting himself of his personal wealth. 'He was given to religious exercises, constant prayers and the holy joys of alms-giving. . . . For this reason many people thought and often said that a man of his disposition ought to have been a bishop rather than a king.'[23] So finally he became a monk, exemplifying the nexus and affinity between the three offices as Bede understood them. Other kings, notably Ine and Cadwalla of Wessex, in due time resigned their thrones to make pilgrimage to Rome.[24] Rome symbolised the eternal kingdom of God and proximity to the apostles, and Cadwalla assumed the baptismal name of Peter from pope Sergius and died while still in his baptismal robes. He was duly buried in St Peter's as a 'pilgrim king' who had 'come from the very ends of the earth, inspired by loving devotion'. This flight from rule over a temporal kingdom out of loyalty to an eternal one was implicit in Bede's theology of kingship; but it remained perforce exceptional. Instead in the case of key rulers like Edwin, Oswald and Ethelbert it was the heavenward dispositions in their rule that Bede highlighted as being of lasting significance and value.

Aidan died in 651 and was succeeded by Finan 'who had been sent from the Irish island monastery of Iona'.[25] He built the church on Lindisfarne 'after the Irish method, not of stone but of hewn oak, thatching it with reeds'. It is thanks to Bede that so full a picture may be obtained of the activities of the missionaries from Lindisfarne. Outside this tradition there are only fragmentary hints of Irish missionary activity elsewhere in England during the middle of the seventh century. They are mentioned in passing by Bede. When Wilfrid came to Sussex he found there

a certain Irish monk named Dicuill who had a very small monastery in a place called Bosham surrounded by woods and sea, in which five or six brothers served the Lord in humility and poverty; but none of the natives cared to follow their way of life or listen to their preaching.[26]

It is possible that the founder of the monastery at Malmesbury was an Irish monk called Maildub, and by inference from a letter addressed to Aldhelm he may have been an influence upon Aldhelm himself.[27] Later traditions claimed Irish influence at Glastonbury also though whether as early as the seventh century is unclear: its connections at that time with the British and Welsh churches were, however, strong enough for the kings of Wessex, notably Ine, to recognise and endow it as a significant religious community.[28] The activity of Fursey in East Anglia and the company of Irish monks who joined him at Burgh Castle has already been noted, and is discussed by Bede between the missionary episcopates of Aidan and Finan.[29] What these places all have in common apart from Irish connections is a certain remoteness and isolation congenial to Irish asceticism.

The episcopate of Finan saw a steady extension and consolidation of the Irish mission through Lindisfarne. The kingdom of the Middle Angles came under the political sway of Oswy of Northumbria, and Penda's son, Peada, secured a marriage alliance in return for his converting to Christianity. He was baptised by Finan and returned with a mission of English and one Irish priest. Even Penda was moved to permit evangelisation elsewhere in Mercia and in due time bishops were appointed to serve in this area.[30] One of these missionaries, Cedd, went on to play a key role in the re-conversion of Essex. Again Oswy's personal influence upon its king, Sigeberth, proved crucial, and Bede records a summary of the arguments the Northumbrian ruler used against idolatry. Finan baptised him too, and a mission was requested which was led by Cedd who became in due time bishop for those people. 'He established churches in various places and ordained priests and deacons to assist him in preaching the word of faith and in the administration of baptism.' He created monastic headquarters within the old Roman fort at Bradwell-on-sea, where his church still stands, and also at Tilbury.[31]

He did not become bishop of London, however, remaining an itinerant monastic pastor to the people as a whole.

After a while, their king was murdered by some of his kin. They killed him because they resented him 'because he was too ready to pardon his enemies, calmly forgiving them for the wrongs they had done him, as soon as they asked his pardon'. Although Bede deftly presents this fate as a divine judgement for the king transgressing a commandment of his bishop, it in fact sharply illuminates the collision between Christian values fully adhered to and the realities of politics in a still largely pagan and warlike society. The bishop is portrayed acting in a prophetic manner like Samuel of old, and in a spirit frequently demonstrated by his Irish mentors. But once again it raises the question of how humble a Christian king might safely be!

The career of Cedd is full on interest and significance as representative of an English disciple of the first Irish missionaries active in partnership with their successors in advancing the monastic mission. Bede recounts in some detail how he also founded the monastery of Lastingham in Yorkshire at the behest of the king of Deira who intended it as a royal mausoleum. Cedd's brother was the king's chaplain. Lastingham lies in the north Yorkshire moors, in Bede's day a site 'amid some steep and remote hills', though actually not far from the Roman road from York to Malton. He spent the whole of Lent in vigil there to cleanse it of evil influences and 'to consecrate it to the Lord by prayer and fasting'; in this he was assisted by another of his brothers. The new monastery followed the customs of the mother-house at Lindisfarne and remained under Cedd's rule even while he was away in Essex. In 664 he died from plague and was buried at Lastingham, leaving his own brother Chad as abbot. Thither came some of the monks from the Essex monastery to live and die near their spiritual father.[32]

Chad was not left in peace at Lastingham but became caught up in the confused church politics surrounding Wilfrid who had gone to Gaul for his consecration as bishop of Northumbria. During his absence, Oswy made Chad bishop, perhaps as an auxiliary or more likely as a rival. Because there was at that time no archbishop at Canterbury, Chad was finally consecrated by the bishop of Wessex, assisted by two British bishops. Later this would compromise him in the eyes of the new archbishop, Theodore. But meanwhile he returned to the north as a bishop in the mould of St Aidan, 'preaching the gospel, travelling not on horseback but on foot after the apostolic example'.[33] Although retired by Theodore to Lastingham, having been re-consecrated in the catholic manner, Chad went on to become bishop at Lichfield in succession to Jaruman, who had himself been a missionary in Essex after Cedd's death when plague induced the kingdom to revert to paganism.[34] Theodore had to command Chad to ride a horse because of his age, and 'following the example of the early fathers, he administered the diocese in great holiness of life'.[35] Bede clearly valued the memory of Chad as an exemplar of the monastic episcopal life. But there is no less an eloquent testimony to his holiness in Eddius' *Life of Wilfrid* which is generally forcefully partisan towards those who opposed his hero or who in any way obstructed his path. Of Chad he writes: 'they consecrated to the see of York a deeply pious servant of God and admirable teacher named Chad, who came from Ireland, but they did it ignorantly and in defiance of canon law'. In his response to Theodore's remonstrance he showed himself 'a true and meek servant of God' and his eventual appointment to Lichfield was a friendly arrangement made with that true servant of God.[36] Bede writes at some length about the manner of his dying in 672 during another outbreak of plague 'sent from heaven which came upon them and through the death of the body translated the living stones of the church from their earthly sites to the heavenly building'.[37] Chad had a more secluded cell near his cathedral where he could retire for prayer with his brethren. On one occasion his companion, Owine, witnessed the moment when Chad received a heavenly summons by the hand of his own deceased brother, Cedd. A week later he died, fully prepared, being ruled by a healthy fear of the Lord which he used to demonstrate whenever there was a storm, which he regarded as a reminder of divine judgement and an occasion for earnest intercession. His passing was also witnessed by an English monk in Ireland, Egbert. At the place of his burial miracles later occurred: 'Chad's place of burial is a wooden coffin in the shape of a little house, having an aperture in its side, through which those who visit it out of devotion can insert their hands and take out a little of the dust'.

At one level the Irish mission based at Lindisfarne suffered a major set-back as a result of the Synod of Whitby. The story is told at great length by Bede, and the essence of the issue is more briefly recounted by Eddius in his *Life of Wilfrid*. It revolved around the correct and uniform calculation of the date of Easter in which Bede had a keen professional interest. But it also arose as a result of politics within the Northumbrian court between Oswy and his son, and rivalries between clergy of the Irish persuasion and those nurtured by contact with the Gallic church. Bede clearly regarded the row as regrettable if inevitable and he did not let it prevent him from continuing to portray the impulse derived from the Irish missionaries in a favourable light. Because the queen came from Kent, the situation could arise that Easter was being kept by different members of the royal family at different times. An Irishman, Ronan, educated in Gaul antagonised Finan by his polemic and 'fierce temper' and upon his death the issue blew open, although since Aidan's day the divergence had been widely tolerated in Northumbria because of the esteem in which he and his disciples were held. The king and his son, Aldfrith, took opposing sides, and Wilfrid made his mark as an advocate of the Roman and Gallic position. The new Irish bishop, Colman, was summoned to a synod at the royal monastery at Whitby where Hilda presided as abbess, to resolve the issue. Cedd acted as interpreter. The king declared his interest in achieving uniformity. Colman appealed to the sanctity of the Columban tradition of Iona, Wilfrid to the practice of the universal church, and worsted Colman in argument. In the end the authority of Columba was unfairly ranged against that of St Peter to which Oswy the king had to defer. In the words of Eddius: 'Tell me which is greater in the Kingdom of Heaven, Columba or the Apostle Peter?'[38] By this verdict the whole Irish position in these matters was undermined, and Colman returned to Iona, taking with him some of the relics of Aidan. But he still retained the respect and affection of the king whose hand had been somewhat forced by Wilfrid's polemic. An Irishman educated among the southern Irish who had accepted the Roman Easter succeeded him as bishop, and a disciple of Aidan called Eata became abbot of Lindisfarne. In due course Eata became bishop there also.

Bede is at his most direct in summing up exactly why the Irish missionaries made the impact that they did:

How frugal and austere he and his predecessors had been, the place itself over which they ruled bears witness. When they left, there were very few buildings there except for the church, in fact only those without which the life of a community was impossible. They had no money but only cattle; if they received money from the rich they promptly gave it to the poor; for they had no need to collect money or to provide dwellings for the reception of worldly and powerful men, since these only came to the church to pray and to hear the word of God. The king himself used to come, whenever opportunity allowed, with only five or six thegns, and when he had finished his prayers in the church he went away. If they happened to take a meal there, they were content with the simple daily fare of the brothers and asked for nothing more. The sole concern of these teachers was to serve God and not the world, to satisfy the soul and not the belly. For this reason the religious habit was held in great respect at that time, so that whenever a cleric or a monk went anywhere he was gladly received by all as God's servant. If they chanced to meet him by the roadside, they ran towards him and, bowing their heads, were eager either to be signed with the cross by his hand or to receive a blessing from his lips. Great attention was also paid to his exhortations, and on Sundays the people flocked eagerly to the church or the monastery, not to get food for the body but to hear the word of God. If by chance a priest came to a village, the villagers crowded together, eager to hear from him the word of life; for the priests and the clerics visited the villages for no other reason than to preach, to baptize, and to visit the sick, in brief to care for their souls. They were so free from all taint of avarice that none of them would accept lands or possessions to build monasteries, unless compelled to by the secular authorities. This practice was observed universally among the Northumbrian churches for some time afterwards. But enough has been said on this subject.[39]

The fruitful marriage and collaboration between Irish and Northumbrian Christianity continued to determine many aspects of church life in the north for the next hundred years. When Colman left his bishopric at Lindisfarne after the Synod of Whitby, he was accompanied by a group of 'about thirty men of English race' in addition to his Irish followers: these were all monks. They migrated via Iona to create a monastery first upon Inishboffin, and then another for the English at Mayo who had found the vagaries of Irish habits impossible to live with.[40] By Bede's day it had become an important centre of English monastic life in Ireland. Two of the correspondents of Aldhelm may have been sojourners there: Wihtfrith is warned by Aldhelm of the pagan distractions of Ireland, and Heahfrith is greeted upon his return from a six year course of study 'in the north-west part of the island ... sucking the teat of Wisdom'.[41] In this letter Aldhelm challenges the attraction of Ireland to English scholars now that excellent learning has been established by archbishop Theodore at Canterbury, who is portrayed as 'hemmed in by a mass of Irish students'. Bede had no mixed feelings towards the Irish and their learning, fully recognising the debt the English church owed to them for both the beginning and the consolidation of the Christian mission. He describes how 'there were many in England, both nobles and commons, who in the days of bishops Finan and Colman had left their own country and retired to Ireland either for the sake of religious studies or to live a more ascetic life. In course of time some of these devoted themselves faithfully to the monastic life, while others preferred to travel round to the cells of various teachers and apply themselves to study. The Irish welcomed them all gladly, gave them their daily food, and also provided them with books to read and with instruction, without asking for any payment.'[42]

Significant in Bede's mind was the career of Egbert, whose name crops up at several key points in the *Ecclesiastical History*.[43] Of noble birth, he went with others to Ireland where he narrowly escaped death by plague. One of his friends and companions was Chad, whose death he witnessed from afar. While ill, he had promised God a life of perpetual exile from Britain in return for life and health. This he would devote to a full repentance, marked by a daily recitation of the entire psalter and a 24 hour fast once a week. His ascetic example won many to the faith, both Irish and Picts: 'he lived a life of great humility, gentleness, temperance, simplicity and righteousness.'[44] Exile from Britain did not mean, however, no contact with his homeland; indeed it enhanced his reputation. He tried in vain to restrain king Ecgfrith of Northumbria from warlike attacks on the Irish, 'a harmless race that had always been most friendly to the English'. Instead the king's army 'spared neither churches nor monasteries'. This was in 684; the next year the king launched an attack against the Picts, against the advice this time of St Cuthbert, and on this occasion he was trapped and killed.[45] Some glimpse of his venerable reputation as a holy man and bishop may be found in Aethelwulf's *De Abbatibus*, which is a monastic poem springing from some unknown daughter house of Lindisfarne early in the eighth century. Egbert's advice was sought about the site for the founding

of the monastery, and his blessing requested for the altar: 'a table, consecrated in the name of great Peter to God, sped and strengthened the monastery against the dark enemy'.[46] The exiled bishop also intimated a spiritual vision of the 'small hill' on which the monastery was to be built, and
sent a letter later commending the progress of the foundation which had
taken place within some former fortified haunt of violent men.

The latter part of Egbert's life was clearly of great spiritual fruitfulness.
For Bede this bore a two-fold significance. Firstly because Egbert initiated
the mission of Willibrord to Frisia. He had himself wished to go as a
missionary and perhaps also as a pilgrim to Rome. In this he was prevented
by a vision of Cuthbert's mentor, Boisil, to one of his fellow-monks. When
Egbert tried to depart he only just survived a storm. Instead he sent a monk
called Wihtbert who was unable to make headway against the pagan king
of Frisia. Finally he was able to commission Willibrord to the task with
lasting success.[47] For Egbert there remained the no less taxing task of
winning the monks of Iona to the keeping of the catholic Easter. His
reputation for being 'learned in the scriptures', revered for his 'long and
holy life' in exile in Ireland,[48] paved the way: 'being a gracious teacher and
a most devout doer of all that he taught, he was gladly listened to by them
all.'[49] For Bede there was a fitting and providential reciprocity about this
particular embassy by an English Christian to the place from which the
northern mission had sprung. Egbert remained upon Iona for 13 years,
dying there in 729 on Easter day. 'So the most revered father, being as-
sured of their conversion, rejoiced to see the day of the Lord: he saw it, and
was glad.' The schism at Whitby was thus reversed, and Iona was once
again enfolded within 'the gracious light of ecclesiastical fellowship and
peace'.[50]

A notable feature recorded in Bede and testified to also in the writings of
Aldhelm is the steady growth of royal female monasticism during the seventh
century in England. The initial impetus for this came from Gaul where it
was already well established. Bede tells how Eorcengota, daughter of Eadbald
king of Kent, went to the royal monastery at Faremoutier-en-Brie. It was a
double monastery of men and women, whose founder had been blessed
for it by St Columbanus. 'At that time, because there were not yet many
monasteries founded in England, numbers of people from Britain used to
enter the monasteries of the Franks or Gauls to practise the monastic life.'[51]
Thither also went their daughters as nuns, and Bede mentions Chelles and
Andelys-sur-Seine along with Brie: these were similar royal double houses.
Among such devotees were two daughters of Anna, King of the East Angles,
and notably Eorcengota of whom several miracles and heavenly visitations
were related signifying her holiness. Her aunt, the daughter of the king of
East Anglia, called Aethelburh became abbess and was found to be incorrupt
after death. The impetus to found royal nunneries continued in Kent throughout the seventh century, with houses founded at Lyminge, Sheppey and in
Thanet.[52]

Another circle of female monastic life was associated with the saintly bishop, Eorcenwald, who in 675 became bishop of London. He founded two monasteries, at Chertsey and at Barking, the latter for his sister Aethelburh.[53] Bede refers to a lost *Life* of this saint, giving vivid insight into the dire impact of plague upon such a community, and the attitude to illness current in monastic thinking at that time. A manifestation of brilliant heavenly light indicated a suitable burial-ground; finally to a sister was vouchsafed a vision of the heavenly ascent of Aethelburh herself, who died not long after. This nun had been afflicted for nine years 'so that any traces of sin ... might be burnt away by the fires of prolonged suffering'.[54] Another crippled nun implored the heavenly intercession of the departed mother and was thus enabled to die in peace, as did the nun who had witnessed Aethelburh's impending death. This catena of stories is a moving and psychologically valuable window into the impact of suffering upon a Christian community at that time. In later years the very remains of these holy nuns were deemed to be able to work miracles.[55]

It was to Hildelith, the long-serving abbess of Barking and successor to Aethelburh, that Aldhelm dedicated his famous tract, *In praise of Virginity*.[56] This was a work of signal importance and abiding influence in Anglo-Saxon monasticism at this period and also in the tenth century revival of the religious life. Barking was another double house, and Aldhelm clearly addressed a noble audience of men and women who had renounced the world, either to adopt a celibate life or to abandon marriage. He cites male and female martyrs from earlier Christian history who had made similar choices, and distinguishes between virginity, chastity by which he means virtuous renunciation of marriage, and marriage itself as integral Christian vocations. His work was not without patristic precedent; but its adaptation was singular in addressing the precise social situation now fashionable among the Christian Anglo-Saxons. It is hardly felicitous in its style but it is sound and vigorous in its theology: 'carnal integrity is in no way approved of unless spiritual purity is associated with it as its companion'.[57] In support of this view he cites St Augustine from the *City of God*, reminding his hearers also of the caution of St Gregory the great: 'I, a loathsome painter, have painted a beautiful man; and I who am still tossed on the waves of sin direct others to the shore of perfection'.[58] The work is at once a 'florilegium' culled from numerous patristic sources, and a kind of martyrology to inspire those who felt called to this path of noble self-denial and asceticism, to whom he bids farewell as 'flowers of the church, monastic sisters, pearls of Christ, jewels of Paradise, and participants in the celestial homeland'.[59]

Bede in his turn sets before his readers two outstanding examples of such royal monastic vocation, whose commitment led them along very diverse paths, but who were each representative of many others at this time. The first was Etheldreda, founder of Ely. She also was a daughter of king Anna of the East Angles and was succeeded as abbess by her sister,

Seaxburh, queen of Kent and mother of Eorcengota. For twelve years she had refused to consummate her marriage to king Ecgfrith of Northumbria, supported in this singular vocation by bishop Wilfrid whom she in turn patronised and endowed with lands at Hexham,[60] where he created the church whose crypt remains today. Finally she was permitted to retire to Coldingham, a royal nunnery on the north-east coast above Lindisfarne, 'receiving the veil and habit of a nun from bishop Wilfrid', and living a life of extreme austerity under the king's aunt, Aebbe. After a year there she moved to Ely to found the monastery where she remained for seven years, dying of plague in 679. In 695 her sister the abbess had her body translated and it was found to be incorrupt by bishop Wilfrid and more significantly in Bede's mind by the doctor who had tended her: an incision he had made for a tumour had apparently healed up. Even the coffin and clothes in which she had been first buried were miracle-working and her burial-place became a major shrine. Bede marks the extreme spiritual importance in his mind of this event by an elaborate poem in elegiac verse and alphabetical form, in honour of 'this bride and queen of Christ': he takes the example of the Bible 'in which many songs are inserted into the history'.[61] He places her within an almost identical list of Christian virgins as those recounted by Aldhelm in his tract, and regards her choice of virginity as a 'mimesis' of the virginity of Mary. The important thing in his mind is that this holiness has occurred in his own age, thus bringing the Christian past to life in the present. Her incorruption is a demonstration of divine power, an intimation of the reality of the resurrection, and a sign that she is numbered among the virgin followers of the Lamb in heaven.

Bede then proceeds to outline the career of another very different royal nun, Hilda, abbess of Whitby. She was a contemporary of Etheldreda's and died in 680. She was related to king Edwin and received baptism from Paulinus as a young girl. For the first half of her life until she was 33 she lived a noble married life. This she relinquished and departed for East Anglia in the hope of going abroad to Chelles. This was prevented by bishop Aidan who gave her land on the Wear for a small monastery, from which she removed to become abbess of Hartlepool. The rule of life she built up there owed much to the teaching of Aidan and his disciples. From here she moved to Whitby where in due time she created the foremost royal monastery in Deira, and a significant educational centre: 'so great was her prudence that not only the ordinary people but also kings and princes sometimes sought and received counsel when in difficulties'. She presided over the contentious synod of Whitby and was succeeded in office by two royal princesses under whose aegis the first *Life of St Gregory* was written. Bede lists the number of northern bishops who emerged from her tuition[62] and indicates the extent of her influence and stability of example. Both her birth, final suffering and death were highlighted by heavenly intimations to those close to her. It is in the context of her inspired leadership at Whitby that Bede tells the charming story of Caedmon who became by divine grace a poet of Christian theology in the English tongue. This was a true charism of the Spirit and led to a holy and gifted life and edifying death. Hilda imbued to the full the threefold stream of Christian mission to the north: Paulinus, Aidan and the attraction and example of Gallic royal monasticism. To her church she proved a true mother.

Bede perforce gives only a highly selective view of the development of royal female monasticism in the seventh century; other sources give some fragmentary glimpses of the scope and influence of this phenomenon which proved one of the most permanent features of the Anglo-Saxon church. But immediately after his encomium of Hilda, he does discuss in a homiletic fashion the fate of the royal double monastery at Coldingham.[63] This house finally burned down, Bede believed, as an act of divine judgement for its lax life. An Irish ascetic living among them had warned the inmates of the need to reform, but the extremity of his life-style failed to impress in a decisive manner the monks and nuns of noble extraction who were ruled by Aebbe, a royal princess. Bede's source, Eadgisl, a priest who lived there for a while attested that they were unconcerned with their souls' welfare, being 'sunk in slothful slumbers or else awake for the purposes of sin'. The whole presentation is minatory, advocating a penitential and ascetic approach to the religious life. The implication is clear: that many such houses were hardly divorced from noble and lay society in their social mores, and so lay vulnerable to charges of corruption, either from their stricter brethren or from more worldly critics.

The preceding story about Caedmon the Christian poet is no less illuminating. It heralds the genesis of a whole tradition of Christian poetry in the vernacular as Bede asserts.[64] It indicates that singing lays to the harp was a regular feature of monastic life at Whitby; it reflects also the impact subconsciously of preaching and teaching in the vernacular. Bede portrays him in an exemplary light and the manner of his dying foreshadows that of Bede himself. Bede was of course keenly interested in poetry, composing a book on the 'art of metre'. What was striking about Caedmon was that he appeared to receive this gift of converting Christian theology into Anglo-Saxon verse by divine charism during his sleep, rather like St Dunstan in a later century. By creative and prayerful memorization and 'rumination' of 'the whole course of sacred history' he was able to communicate with great power the vast spectrum of Christian belief: he became a poetic catechiser. As with the missionaries themselves, he began with the Creation, which seems to have been the most successful point of contact with pagan and semi-Christian audiences. It is interesting to note that in *Beowulf*, this theme is also harped, and this great poem affords a fascinating insight to how Christian beliefs permeated the traditional values and hopes of noble saga.

The most striking monument to Christian creativity during this period in England is found in the cult of St Cuthbert.[65] He was born around the year 634 and died in 687, and within a few years of his death was venerated as the foremost saint of Northumbria. In 651 he became a monk at the Irish monastery at Melrose, and for a time served under Eata at the new foundation at Ripon until political conditions led to their withdrawal. By 676 he was prior at Lindisfarne where in due time he withdrew to lead the life of a recluse upon the inner Farne island. Against his inclination he was made bishop of Hexham which he exchanged with Eata for Lindisfarne, where he remained for two years until his death upon Farne. When in 698 his body was translated into the church at Lindisfarne, it was found to be incorrupt, and so it remained throughout the Anglo-Saxon centuries, becoming the focus for a major cult. His life-style was closely modelled on that of Aidan and Chad, and he was therefore very much a beneficiary of the Irish spirituality which had formed Lindisfarne and fuelled its mission. He was himself an active missionary, both as a monk and as a bishop. But Cuthbert was of the generation which accepted the decrees of the synod of Whitby and so became, and certainly was perceived and portrayed as being, a unifying figure in the northern church, during his lifetime and after his death. Due to the activities of Willibrord and others his cult spread rapidly to the Continent wherever Anglo-Saxon missionaries operated.

The crystallisation of his memory and example, and the emergence of his cult may be closely observed, both in the hagiography which remains and also in the remarkable artefacts found in his coffin at Durham. His pectoral cross and portable altar remain, both works of the greatest skill and artistry, and extensive fragments of the carved wooden coffin in which his body was laid at its first translation. There is reason to suppose also that the famous Lindisfarne gospels were commissioned to commemorate this momentous event within the life of the community there, their initiator being the holy abbot Eadberht under whose direction the translation and veneration of Cuthbert occurred.

The earliest life of St Cuthbert is by an anonymous member of the monastery at Lindisfarne, offered to the community as a collaborative witness to their memories. Although clearly influenced by classical Christian hagiographies, it is an unsophisticated collation of the key events in Cuthbert's life which were already probably well-recognised, and it is in style similar to Adomnan's *Life of St Columba* with which it is contemporary. It was composed shortly after the translation of the body in 698 and finished before the death of king Aldfrith in 705. It is unusual in that it falls into four distinct chapters dealing with different phases of the saint's life, in the Irish pattern of one predestined to sanctity and engaged in an alternating pattern of pastoral mission and ascetic seclusion, rather like Fursey. If it has a conscious model it is probably the figure of St Martin of Tours as a holy monk-bishop, and in its mingling of healing and prophecy it is similar to the life of St Columbanus by Jonas. Cuthbert like Martin, Columbanus and also Columba had an influence which reached beyond his cell into the politics and fortunes of the ruling house and the nobility. But it was the role of the prophet and holy man that he was called to play, not the political adventurer like his contemporary Wilfrid whom the monks of Lindisfarne regarded with some reason as a rival and even a threat.

The first life of St Cuthbert is effective in its relative simplicity and directness; as the writer avers – 'it is a ready path of virtue to know what he was'. The first section deals with his childhood in which his vocation to become a saint was intimated. It was a vision of the heavenly ascent of the soul of St Aidan while tending sheep that led him to seek a monastic life. As in the life of St Columba, angels play a discreet but significant part, and Cuthbert's spiritual life was rooted in a lively sense of and contact with the heavenly. From this there flowed an ease with animals and nature, and in due time the capacity to heal others of various ailments. The third part of the life deals with his search for seclusion as a monk at Melrose and then at Lindisfarne: this becomes the key to his sanctity, and his cell upon Farne, with its well of water provided by a miracle, and his physical labour there to secure a harvest are all recounted in detail. Yet his contacts with his own community and with the wider world of the nobility were not severed, and in the end he was compelled to serve as bishop, sacrificing his life as a recluse for an active ministry of preaching, confirmation, healing and evangelism in the remote parts of his diocese. The life concludes with the story of how Cuthbert retired for the last time to Farne to prepare for death, and of how his body was found to be incorrupt after burial and became the source of miracles. It therefore provides a lucid and balanced framework within which the still active common memory of stories and teachings of the saint might be secured, interpreted and passed on.

At an early stage in his own monastic life as a scholar, Bede became interested and involved in promoting the cult of this saint. Shortly after the death of king Aldfrith in 705, Bede composed a metrical poem, based upon the anonymous life, of which an early draft has recently been found at Besançon.[66] Influenced in its style by the works of Arator, it was intended to be an intricate meditation on the spiritual meaning of the life of St Cuthbert. It was perhaps motivated also by emulation of the work of Venantius Fortunatus in popularising the life and miracles of St Martin in verse. In substance it is quite close to the anonymous life, but it adds miracles subsequent to that work and is thus an attempt to update and fortify the memory upon which the cult was being fostered.

Later in his career, Bede essayed a full-blown life of the saint, which assumes and builds upon that of the anonymous monk. It is a very sophisticated piece of theology, but it adduces new material also about Cuthbert which Bede is careful to vouch for, and concludes with a moving, lengthy and probably verbatim account of the saint's death by the monk who knew him most closely, Herefrith. To this work Bede makes reference in his *History*; he summarises it and adds to it two further miracles.[67] By contrast with the anonymous life it makes demanding reading and lacks some of the immediacy and charm of that work. But this is because Bede's *Life* is a reflection upon an already well-established cult, and a direct contribution to its furtherance within the wider life of the English church with which he was so deeply concerned.

Bede had at least four or five theological aims in the way he composed his life of St Cuthbert, and his mode of writing was an application of the classic approach to biblical exegesis of which he was a master to the deeper significance of hagiography. In his exposition of the Bible, Bede identified the four levels of interrelated understanding: the actual history; its moral meaning; its bearing upon the life of the church in its sacraments and spiritual life; and its eternal meaning as a window into the kingdom of heaven. So in this *Life of St Cuthbert*, Bede places the well-established frame of the saint's life within these subtle perspectives. He adds to the history directly with his usual care, and in his preface proffers the work to the Lindisfarne community with which he had close personal ties as an adornment and amplification of the cult. But he has so presented the life of the saint as to be an exemplary sermon, a detailed commentary upon how the saint's life illuminates the Bible, and how the Bible in turn determines the true meaning of what happened to the saint. To reinforce this and give it veracity, he presents nuggets of Cuthbert's own teaching. Cuthbert was haunted by the prediction of his father-in-God, Boisil that he would finally end up as a bishop. When probed by his brethren about this, he would lament: 'Even if I could possibly hide myself in a tiny dwelling on a rock, where the waves of the swelling ocean surrounded me on all sides, and shut me in equally from the sight and knowledge of men, not even thus should I consider myself to be free from the snares of a deceptive world: but even there I should fear lest the love of wealth should tempt me and somehow or other should snatch me away'.[68]

This example touches upon the deeper interest of Bede in Cuthbert's life: how he reconciled the active and contemplative life. Here the influence of Gregory's *Dialogues* is seldom far away, and Bede portrays Cuthbert as someone who indeed managed to fulfil this double vocation. He summed it up in these words attributed to the saint:

He held that to give the weak brethren help and advice was a fit substitute for prayer, for he knew that He who said, 'Thou shalt love the Lord thy God', also said, 'Thou shalt love thy neighbour as thyself'.

He accepted the yoke of episcopacy as another obedience on the spiritual path. As a recluse he had deepened the spring within to ensure its free and pure flow; now as bishop, as indeed formerly as prior to the monastery, the water within flowed out in charity, evangelism and pastoral care. This metaphor of the living water within flowing out was in Bede's mind the key to the creative resolution of this double spiritual movement within Christianity. It came to a focus in the charism of the eucharist:

When Cuthbert offered up the saving Victim as a sacrifice to God, he offered his prayer to the Lord not by raising his voice but by shedding tears which sprang from the depth of his heart.[69]

The life of Cuthbert, so close in time to Bede's own, gave him ample opportunity to examine the heart of what constituted a saint. Held thus within this strong biblical and subtle moral and spiritual frame of reference, the inner working of God rendering Cuthbert a truly Christ-like figure might be discerned.[70] At the start of his work, Bede cites the words of the prophet in Lamentations 3 which indicate that the ascetic and eremitic path is a true following of Christ and bearing of the Cross. In the light of this stern and lifelong vocation, every event recorded in the life of Cuthbert becomes a glimpse into the great sacrifice of divine love reaching out through the compassion and obedience of the saint. Healing, exorcism, prophecy, familiarity with nature, teaching about the spiritual life, carrying the gospel to places where others feared to tread were all acts of grace, made possible by obedient and faithful love on the part of Cuthbert. In the end the return to Farne proved to be a share in Calvary, as the moving testimony of Herefrith makes clear. To turn aside from pastoral care as an active bishop was to seek again 'the strife of a hermit's life', his final sufferings a preparation 'by the fires of temporal pains for the joys of perpetual bliss'.[71] The account by his friend of his passing is presented as a true passion narrative, as Cuthbert succumbed to the rigours of tuberculosis which appears to have dogged his life. The saint remained on the island isolated by a great storm for five days to the anxiety of his brethren on Lindisfarne. With hindsight this was the period of sternest refinement: 'God wished to test him by bodily pain and by a still fiercer contest with the ancient foe, cutting him off from mankind for that space of time'. To his friend Herefrith Cuthbert intimated the gravity of the spiritual affliction which had pursued him, and the hostility which had now brought him to the threshold of death. He would only say: 'I have fought my fight for the Lord', urging them to let him remain buried on Farne, reduced in the end to silence by his sufferings.

Hidden throughout this life is perhaps another theme dear to Bede's heart: the importance of spiritual friendship within the monastic vocation. He was himself the ardent practitioner and steady beneficiary of this throughout his life, and his many writings depended heavily upon its fruitfulness. In the *Life of Cuthbert* four friends of the saint play a crucial role: Boisil, who was his father-in-God and sponsor at Melrose, whose prayers healed him and whose wisdom was his mentor even as Cuthbert sat by his bedside while Boisil was dying; Eata, with whom he went first to Ripon and then to Lindisfarne, and with whom he later served as fellow bishop; Herefrith who was a lifelong companion in the monastic life and who was Bede's authority for the manner of Cuthbert's dying and other stories; and finally Eadberht his successor as bishop of Lindisfarne who supervised the translation of the body and the proper establishment of the cult of the saint upon the Holy Island. Such spiritual friendship, built as much upon affinity of vision as upon natural human affection, provided the context within which the distinctive and elusive inner life of the saint might be recognised, communicated and preserved as a living memory. As in the life of St Columba, these bonds of spiritual affinity lay close to the heart of the tradition, and Bede takes up and subtly amplifies the story in the anonymous life of how Cuthbert used to meet while at Carlisle his friend the hermit Herbert who lived on an island in Derwentwater, and promised him that they would both die and pass to heaven at the same time.[72]

The extreme care given by both writers, implicit in the case of the anonymous monk, elaborately explicit in the case of Bede, and the wealth of artefacts surrounding the earliest stage of the posthumous cult of St Cuthbert on Lindisfarne indicate the supreme significance they attached to the phenomenon of so commanding a saint within the life of their church. Within a century of the evangelisation of England, Cuthbert's memory could be ranged alongside that of St Martin of Tours and be commemorated with all the wealth of Christian culture and literacy. Yet as Bede indicates in his *History* this was not an isolated instance, even if it proved the pre-eminent one. Sanctity was the first fruit of evangelism, and in its turn gave to evangelism new impetus and power. It occurred within a community as a result of prayer, and drew to itself the patronage and devotion of rich and poor alike. It affirmed the presence of the kingdom of heaven within the life of the church, holding out the hope of miracles in this life, and the reality of eternal life in which the saint already shared, and to whose intercession and compassion his fellow-countrymen might appeal. For in Bede's own words placed now above his tomb in Durham cathedral:

Christ is the morning star who when the night of this world is past, brings to his saints the promised light of life and opens to them eternal day.

VII. THEODORE AND WILFRID

From the beginning of the missions, southern and northern, the creation of an indigenous clergy had been a major priority. Gregory had instructed the purchase of English slaves with a view to their education; Aidan had acted similarly, and in Chad and Cuthbert had found worthy successors. So upon the death of Paulinus, who having withdrawn from York after Edwin's death in battle had become bishop of Rochester, archbishop Honorius 'consecrated Ithamar, a man of Kentish extraction but the equal of his predecessors in learning and holiness of life'.[1] This was in 664, and the next decade saw a small but significant flow of appointments to episcopal office of English Christians. The death of Felix of East Anglia in 647 led to the succession of an East Anglian deacon called Thomas, and when he died by Berhtgisl, also called Boniface, who came from Kent. In due course Ithamar of Rochester was succeeded by a south Saxon called Damian, and upon the death of Honorius in 653, the first English archbishop of Canterbury was appointed, Deusdedit, after a vacancy of 18 months.[2] He presided there for nine years. This was clearly a significant stage in the development of the English church, and these appointments reflect well on the work of the Kentish and East Anglian schools, of which otherwise so little tangible remains. It was only the ravages of plague in the 660s. which decimated the leadership of the English church and left it in the weakened state in which Theodore found it upon his arrival from Rome in 668. He of course became primate almost by default, at the pope's insistence, because the nominee of the kings of Kent and Northumbria, the Englishman Wigheard, 'a good man and well fitted for the office of bishop', had died of plague while in Rome.[3] In his *History of the Abbots*, Bede gives a fuller insight into the rationale behind this nomination: 'Wigheard had been trained in Kent in every branch of church tradition by the Roman disciples of pope Gregory. Egbert was eager to have him consecrated in Rome, reckoning that if he had a bishop of his own race and language, he and his people would be able to enter all the more deeply into the teachings and mysteries of their faith, since they would receive them at the hands of someone of their own kith and kin, and not hear them through an interpreter but in their own native tongue.'[4] His predecessor Deusdedit had been a West Saxon, not a man of Kent.

The West Saxon origin of Deusdedit may be more significant than Bede's passing remark would indicate: there must have been a centre of education suitable for his formation, so that he appeared the best candidate for the primatial see despite his not being Kentish. This possibility is strengthened by consideration of where Aldhelm obtained his own extensive education in theology and classical learning before he went to study under abbot Hadrian in Kent as a mature priest sometime after 670. His time in Canterbury though in his own mind significant and formative, comprised two brief spells interrupted by other ecclesiastical duties before he became abbot of Malmesbury around the year 673. There he remained until at the end of his life he was made the first bishop of Sherborne in 706 where he served until his death in 709-10.[5] He was a man of very wide learning indeed, both in theology and also in the classics. He became a fluent master of Latin, versed both in grammar, rhetoric and metre: he claimed to be the first Englishman 'to have toiled so mightily in a pursuit of this sort' and his style had an immediate and extensive influence upon that of his peers and successors. Although both style and content of his learning reveal familiarity with Irish scholarship, and traditionally he was nurtured by an Irish hermit called Maildubh the eponymous founder of the monastery at Malmesbury, it has been established that the roots of his knowledge of Latin were derived from continental sources, probably from Spain, and his attitude emulates the work of Isidore of Seville.[6] The decisive evidence is that his early education in Latin was thorough and effective, and the possibility that this was obtained at a centre of British learning in the south-west cannot be ruled out. There is indeed an anonymous letter to him in later life attributing influence to a 'certain holy man of our race': this may be an allusion to Maildubh, or it could be to a British father. It mentions also a visit by Aldhelm to Rome and his reputation for his 'Roman eloquence'.[7] Although later in his life Aldhelm rather depreciated the limitations of the learning he had received before he went to Canterbury, nonetheless it was the foundation for a long and formidable scholarly career. Unlike Bede he was quite as much at ease using classical authors as with the Bible and patristic thought. He was by no means as severe in subordinating the former to the latter.

In a letter to his bishop, Leuthere, written while he was studying under abbot Hadrian at Canterbury, Aldhelm confirms at first hand the advanced learning which was now available there: metrical composition of which he became a master, computation of dates, astronomy with astrology, and the study of Roman law; a transcription of one such law-book remains in a later copy. [8] His enthusiasm and degree of absorption comes across in his letter: for him it was a stimulating vista of fresh scope upon not unfamiliar material. He forged a close friendship with Hadrian as a later letter indicates, and pays glowing tribute to the work of archbishop Theodore and Hadrian in establishing such a centre of excellence in England: 'Britain, although situated in the outer limit of the western world, possesses the lucent likeness of the flaming sun and moon, Theodore . . . and Hadrian'.[9] Aldhelm's own understanding of the curriculum of learning is solidly classical: 'arithmetic, geometry, music, astronomy, astrology, mechanics, and medicine', a sevenfold division of universal significance to his mind.[10] He was a firm believer in higher learning, encouraging a former pupil, Heahfrith, who had spent six years in Ireland now to settle down in England and to contribute to its intellectual life under his direction.[11] Aldhelm's own written contributions demonstrate the range of his learning: poetry, the treatise on virginity, epigrams and riddles, a treatise on metre dedicated to king Aldfrith of Northumbria, who was a spiritual protégé and scholarly friend, and the small collection of remaining letters which afford clues to the many-sided aspects of his ecclesiastical activities. The multiplicity of copies of his main works, in England and on the Continent in the eighth century and beyond reflect his abiding influence. As Bede says, 'he was a man of wide learning . . . remarkable for his erudition in both ecclesiastical and in general studies'.[12]

Aldhelm had an ambivalent attitude towards the prevalent Irish learning which at that time still dominated much of the English church. He did not wholly approve of the steady migration of Englishmen to Ireland in pursuit of learning when high standards were now available at Canterbury and perhaps elsewhere too. With some irony he portrays archbishop Theodore 'hemmed in by a mass of Irish students' whom he parries with his higher learning. Although it is an admitted lampoon it clearly reflects the confident assertion by an Englishman of the new Latin culture forming in the Anglo-Saxon church which was already displacing the tutelage of the Irish. Yet Aldhelm was of course in regular contact with Irish scholars and their books, as in a fascinating fragment of correspondence with the monk Cellanus, an Irishman living at the monastery at Peronne founded by Fursey. Within his lifetime the fame of Aldhelm's writings had spread there: Cellanus had read his books, probably on virginity, and now asks for copies of some sermons; Aldhelm's reply is not without a certain irony in its tone.[13]

Bede's lapidary obituary of Aldhelm indicates that if learning lay at the heart of his life, he was an active churchman enmeshed in royal and ecclesiastical politics in a way that Bede himself was not. Even in old age he proved an energetic bishop, and is remembered in the west as an active church builder and patron. For some of these churches he composed dedicatory verses comparable to those of Bede. The creation of the see of Sherborne marked a significant advance in organising the church in Wessex. Aldhelm also seems to have played something of the role of mediator between the English and British churches in the south-west, with some success as Bede observes: 'he led many of those Britons who were subject to the West Saxons to adopt the catholic celebration of Easter.' Evidence of Aldhelm's role in this is found in his letter to Geraint, the British king of the western peninsula, written shortly after and at the behest of the council of Hertford in 672 convened by Theodore. In it he adopts like Bede the Roman line, appealing in the end to the authority of St Peter to secure the unity of the church. But it is relatively eirenic in tone, and free of racial denigration. He challenges the persistence in the non-Roman tonsure and explains carefully the theology of the orthodox practice and its symbolic significance. He is firm about the date of Easter, and criticises the pharisaic ostracism shown by the church in south Wales towards English Christians. This by implication he is concerned to prevent in the south-west: 'surely the catholic faith and the harmony of brotherly love walk inseparably with even steps.'[14] His courtesy towards the king and his bishops is striking and his apparent success may perhaps be accounted for if for some time he had been educated among them. The West Saxon power inter-penetrated rather than conquered absolutely in Somerset, Dorset, and beyond. Constructive coexistence, particularly in the life of the church, seems to have been likely for much of the seventh century, and in this Aldhelm may have played an important part. It is interesting to note that when Chad came south for consecration and found that Deusdedit had died, he went to bishop Wine of Wessex and was duly consecrated by him 'with the assistance of two bishops of the British race',[15] an act that caused him later complications, but which probably indicates amicable co-operation between the British and English churches in the south-west.

The case of Glastonbury, though shrouded in obscurity, legend and tampered sources may shed further light on the process whereby the interests of the two churches were peacefully intermingled under Aldhelm's leadership. There had been a British monastery and shrine on what was then an island in the Somerset fens for some long time before the West Saxons became dominant in those parts. During Aldhelm's lifetime its patronage was assumed by the kings of Wessex, notably Ine, who is portrayed in the later Glastonbury traditions as a principal benefactor and builder of the church of St Peter there. In these negotiations Aldhelm features regularly as abbot of Malmesbury, so much so that William of Malmesbury at first thought that he was founder of Glastonbury until he examined the charter evidence more closely.[16] It is perhaps significant in this connection that it was at Doulting, hard by Glastonbury, that Aldhelm died: his friendship with the place may well have been long and deep. Both as an aristocrat and as a lawyer Aldhelm's influence upon Ine was probably considerable; he became king in 688 when Aldhelm was well-established as a senior cleric in his kingdom. Aldhelm may well have been a moving spirit behind the formulation of Ine's laws which contain direct if discriminatory provisions for the British population and landowners.[17] Ine's personal devotion to the vision of Roman Christianity evident in Aldhelm's theology expressed itself finally in his abdication and pilgrimage to Rome where he was venerated as a saint.[18] It was under Ine that the see of Winchester was divided and that of Sherborne created and given to Aldhelm. He was clearly not averse to political intervention as his letter in defence of Wilfrid indicates, and he was able to write to king Aldfrith of Northumbria on virtually equal terms. In the popular memory too he was remembered and even venerated as a great pastor and local saint, a man who would play his harp on the bridge of Malmesbury to attract ordinary folk into church.

The appointment by pope Vitalian in 668 of Theodore to become archbishop of Canterbury must rank as the most remarkable turn of events in the history of the English church during this period. Despite his age – he was over 66 – he effectively reconstituted and revitalised the entire church in England in a way which was never reversed, giving it unity under the leadership of the primate in Kent. No less significant was his impulse to education and learning in England, primarily at Canterbury, but indirectly also in the north as well: of this impulse Bede knew himself to be a direct beneficiary. For Theodore's guide to England, at the pope's command, had been Benedict Biscop, the founder of the monastery in which Bede grew up.[19] To Benedict was entrusted the community of St Augustine's at Canterbury until such time as Theodore's companion Hadrian was free to join him in Kent and become its abbot.

Theodore was a Greek monk from Tarsus in Cilicia. Before he came to Rome in the company of many other Greek monks he had spent time in Antioch, Athens and Byzantium, and sprang to prominence in Rome as a partisan of pope Martin I and his successors in their resistance to the pressure being exerted by the Emperor to acquiesce in the monothelite controversy. The imperial line was to impose a settlement in the interests of unity, asserting that in Christ there was only one divine will operating. In this he was opposed by Sophronius of Jerusalem and Maximus the Confessor, and in due course both Martin and Maximus suffered horribly for their stand. Theodore's links with the next pope, Vitalian, were close; and it appears also that Hadrian had acted as envoy twice to Gaul already on political business on behalf of the Emperor. Hadrian was a north African and abbot of a monastery near Naples whom the pope approached first to become archbishop of Canterbury. He declined but named Theodore instead, and was sent as his companion to England. The monothelite controversy continued to affect Theodore even far away in England: in 678 the Emperor pressed the pope for a resolution of the debate ecumenically, and pope Agatho, before summoning a general council of bishops in Rome, to which he hoped in vain that Theodore would be able to come, sought declarations of orthodoxy from the western churches. So in 679 a council of the English church was held at Hatfield to affirm the faith of Nicea and Chalcedon against monothelite interpretation.

Bede recounts the matter quite fully with great emphasis on the orthodoxy of the English church. He also provides insight into the wider context of the Roman church's involvement at this time. On a visit to Rome Benedict Biscop brought back with him the monk John, precentor at St Peter's, to help supervise and train the community at Wearmouth and to conduct a teaching mission throughout the church.[20] He came also as pope Agatho's commissary to ascertain the doctrinal position of the English bishops, and to communicate the decrees of the council of pope Martin in 649 concerning the monothelite issue. He represented the Roman see at the council of Hatfield and duly took a copy of its proceedings back with him to Rome. He died in Gaul and was buried at the shrine of St Martin at Tours. But the pope received the statement of the English bishops, and it was also subscribed by Wilfrid who was then pursuing his cause in Rome.[21] The council of Hatfield under Theodore's leadership endorsed the Roman line, and advocated orthodox Christology, adding also affirmation of the double procession of the Holy Spirit from the Father and the Son. Despite the later division between the eastern and western churches over this clause in the creed, it would appear that at this time Theodore was echoing the teaching of Maximus the Confessor to whose influence he may well have been indebted.[22].

Theodore brought to the English church a truly ecumenical perspective, and he was able to guide it with reference to customs in both western and eastern churches, as his *Penitential* makes clear.[23] Many indications remain of Greek and Syrian liturgical and hagiographical traditions in England at this time: saints of Naples commemorated in early calendars; Greek prayers inserted into liturgy books; Bede's own translation of the *Passion of St Anastasius* correcting an earlier bad rendering from the Greek.[24] Little tangible remains from the school which Theodore and Hadrian created at Canterbury. Bede and Aldhelm are unanimous in their praise of it:

Both of them were extremely learned in sacred and secular literature. . . . They gave their hearers instruction not only in the books of holy Scripture but also in the art of metre, astronomy, and ecclesiastical computation. . . . Some of their students still survive who know Latin and Greek as well as their native tongue.[25]

They gave impulse also to the knowledge and use of music in church, and according to Aldhelm to the study of Roman law as well.

Fortunately it is possible to catch a glimpse of the quality and scope of the learning they made available from some manuscripts derived from their time. These indicate a strong historical interest in the text of the Bible, reflecting the approach of the school of Antioch in this matter, a preference for eastern fathers, some knowledge of Syriac theology, and little dependence on the classic Latin theologians like Jerome and Augustine. One of the teaching books remains – the *Laterculus Malalianus*.[26] This is a simple commentary on the life of Christ in the gospels with supporting references and explanations which reveal a traditional Semitic and typological approach to the text. Biblical glosses have also been detected on the vulgate text of the Pentateuch and the gospels in the Leiden glossaries.[27] These reveal a strongly philological approach, well-informed in the fields of medicine, philosophy, rhetoric, metrology and chronology, and indicating first-hand knowledge of topographical and geographical phenomena in the near east. Fragments of this kind of teaching may be detected in the writings of Aldhelm and Bede also.[28] Certainly the quality of Bede's learning, the absolute priority he gave to the exegesis of scripture, and his evident familiarity with Greek are a tribute to the standard and vision which Theodore and Hadrian imparted to the study of the theology in England in the latter part of the seventh century. Pope Agatho's verdict upon Theodore is also significant: in a letter to the Emperor in 680 he describes him as 'a colleague,

fellow-bishop and philosopher'. As an experienced witness of the whole
monothelite controversy, Theodore would have added great weight to the
Roman synod of 680; but his advanced age clearly precluded his coming.

Shortly after his death, his disciples in Kent collated a body of his penitential teaching and directions for the governance of the church.[29] In these
Theodore reveals a thoroughly eclectic pragmatism, endorsing the established
Irish pattern of private penance and spiritual cure. In the eighth century he
was regarded as a prime authority on matters of moral theology by Egbert,
archbishop of York, who compiled his own penitential modelled in some
respects upon Theodore's.[30] Theodore addresses drunkenness among the
clergy, sexual immorality of all kinds, homicide, heretical sacraments,
perjury, eating tainted food, clerical breaches of discipline, rebaptism, ignoring
Sundays and fast-days, public penance and reconciliation, pagan
observances and magic. The ethos of his advice is summed up in the last
provision:

A person who would receive the eucharist should make confession
first, and the priest ought to consider the age and education of the
person and what is appropriate. Priestly authority is to be moderated in
proportion to infirmity, and this principle applies to all penance and
confession – what will most enable God to help people and what may
be obeyed in all diligence.

The second part of this material deals with various aspects of running the
church – the proper use of church buildings and their ordering; the duties
and limitations of bishops and other clergy; rules for baptism and confirmation drawing on traditions eastern and western; masses for the dead,
and a long section regulating monastic life. He deals too with the position of
women in church, and communion with British and Irish Christians: here
the unity of the church is the key. He treats also of coping with demonic
possession, which animals ought to be eaten or not eaten, and engages in a
lengthy debate over how Christian marriages are to be constructed and
upheld in a semi-pagan society, concluding with decrees concerning slavery. This corpus of 'iudicia' clearly enshrines the powerful memory of a
great teacher, and reflects the manifold duties and achievements of his time
as archbishop of Canterbury. They mirror too the 'mores' of a society in
transition from pagan to Christian social habits. As such they proved of the
utmost value to the English missionaries on the Continent and to the Irish
church as well, and became part of the common foundation to penitential
discipline throughout northern Europe in the early middle ages.

Theodore's interest in canon law and its implementation is evident also in
the decrees of his first synod, held at Hertford in 672: his declared aim was
the 'unity and peace of the church',[31] although only four of his bishops
were present in person. Its 'capitula', though not original, set the agenda
for Theodore's primacy: a common Easter; no episcopal intrusions into
others' sees, nor into monasteries; stability of monastic life and control of
the movement of clergy; simplicity of life-style for bishops and clergy, and

mutual obedience. He prescribed also an annual synod, regulated episcopal precedence by order of consecration, and indicated a desire to increase the number of bishoprics as the church grew. Finally he asserted Christian marriage. In all their deliberations the bishops in council had the support and guidance, and perhaps active persuasion also of 'many teachers of the church who knew and loved the canonical institutions of the fathers'. Only the 'capitula' on the future multiplication of sees was deferred, and each bishop signed the agreed text of the canons to keep the record straight for the future. This occasion was the first national synod of the English church, and appears to have been free of royal control. It established the over-riding authority of the archbishop of Canterbury as metropolitan and leader of the English church.

This leadership Theodore proceeded to exercise with some vigour, not at all inhibited by his age or race. His first task was to strengthen the bench of bishops.[32] Plague had decimated its ranks so that there was only Wine as bishop of London, and Chad at York, with Wilfrid at Ripon in the wings. Theodore travelled the land, reconsecrating Chad and appointing Putta to be bishop of Rochester.[33] He was a musician devoted to the Roman chant, 'very learned in ecclesiastical matters but with little interest in secular affairs being content with a simple life'. Wilfrid resumed the reins at York, while Chad was moved to become bishop of Lichfield. When Chad died, he put in Winfrith, 'a good and discreet man' and one of his own deacons.[34] In East Anglia, Theodore placed Bisi, 'a man of great sanctity and devotion', with the assistance of two suffragans at Dunwich and Elmham.[35] One of his most significant appointments was that of Eorcenwald to London, a man of holiness and political weight; this was in 675. Early in his primacy, Theodore had made the Frankish cleric, Leuthere, bishop in Wessex, and on his death he appointed Haeddi, who became a close friend and ally; a poem remains which the archbishop composed for him, and he was a friend too of Aldhelm's.[36] In 676 the Mercian king raided and destroyed Rochester. Putta fled his see, retired 'and went around wherever he was invited teaching church music.'[37] Theodore had difficulties filling the see; his first nominee departed 'for lack of means'. By 680 he had created new bishoprics at Worcester and Hereford, and possibly at Leicester as well. One of his most gifted and energetic disciples, Oftfor, served in the Worces-ter diocese under its bishop Bosel as a suffragan missioner. Of similar calibre was Tobias who after Theodore's death became bishop of Rochester, 'a man of great learning, familiar with Latin, Greek and English'.[38]

Yet Theodore did not entirely get his own way nor was he able always to secure a consensus among his bishops. Bede records how he had to depose Winfrith, his own nominee, from the Mercian see after only a few years in office; likewise Tunberht, bishop of Hexham was unseated to make way for Cuthbert.[39] It was some time before Theodore was able to replace the simoniac Wine at London with a more congenial and able colleague, Eorcenwald, in 675. According to Eddius, Winfrith attempted to travel to

Rome most probably to protest his cause before retiring to his own monastery at Barrow.[40] All this may hint at the context for the celebrated defiance Theodore endured from Wilfrid, for a time bishop of Northumbria. Eddius alleges that initially Wilfrid had the support of some of his fellow-bishops, and certainly Wilfrid implied this to the pope.[41]

The story of Wilfrid's stormy episcopate is told both by Bede and by the bishop's disciple and apologist, Eddius. Bede's account is the more judicious and reserved, filtered in fact of many of its contentious aspects: perhaps Wilfrid was too political a bishop for Bede's taste, or else Bede was privy to details of the quarrels which he regarded as unedifying and therefore unsuitable for the kind of history he was writing. Nonetheless he devotes a substantial chapter to an appraisal of Wilfrid's career, and includes a number of significant details omitted by Eddius.[42] The story as told by Eddius is clearly a partisan account, impassioned in places, and trying to portray Wilfrid within the long tradition of persecuted prophets in the Bible. In its ethos it is close to the *Life of St Columbanus*, and Wilfrid emerges as a bishop in the mould in some respects of St Martin. It is quite evident that Eddius was prompted to write in response to the first *Life of St Cuthbert*, from which he lifts whole passages to communicate the sanctity of his hero. Behind both writers stands the shadowy figure of Acca, bishop of Hexham, who had been Wilfrid's personal chaplain in the closing years of his life. Eddius was commissioned by Acca directly to compose his *Life of Wilfrid*; Bede on many occasions in his writings intimates his devotion and debt to Acca as a spiritual father and personal friend. The picture he paints of him immediately after his obituary of Wilfrid is a fitting tribute to both master and disciple.[43]

Of no other figure is it possible to build up so composite and many-sided an impression than that of Wilfrid because of the qualities of his two biographers. He is unique in the way in which then and subsequently he has aroused conflicting emotions and judgements. Bede's reserve has been interpreted as disdain, and it is only recently that a fairer and more sympathetic evaluation has been attempted of Wilfrid's position.[44] In many ways his life, and the controversies it provoked, constitute a crucible in which it is possible to discern the many strands being woven together at this time in the formation of the English church.

Wilfrid is the only member of the first generation of indigenous clergy of whom details are known. He was born of a noble family and like several of the Celtic saints his birth was accompanied by heavenly portents. His own mother died and his step-mother was 'harsh and cruel' so with his father's blessing he left home with a suitable retinue and made his ways to the court of queen Eanflaed who became his patron, 'for he was comely in appearance and exceedingly sharp of wit'.[45] She directed him to Lindisfarne to serve a noble monk who was retiring there. At Lindisfarne he was well-received and educated 'because with a loving heart he sought to live the full monastic life in all humility and obedience', devoting himself to the learning of scripture especially the psalter. With the queen's approval he migrated to Kent as the protégé of king Erconberht to wait for a suitable opportunity to make a pilgrimage to Rome – 'a road untrodden by any of our race'.[46] Though not yet fully a monk, Wilfrid was clearly the beneficiary of the best education that was available in the English church at that time.

In order to appreciate the many-sided significance of his career it is perhaps better to look at it thematically rather than simply chronologically. But the outline of his episcopate may be baldly recounted: in 664 he was nominated bishop and went abroad for consecration in Gaul; when he returned Chad was already bishop of York and the situation was only resolved by Theodore in 669 when Wilfrid became bishop of the whole of Northumbria. In 678 he fled his see while it was divided without his consent and appealed to Rome where he obtained the pope's support. But on his return to Northumbria in 681 he was arrested and eventually banished to Sussex. In 686 with a change of king he returned to the north but in 691 he fell out with him and retreated to Mercia where he remained until 703 when a new archbishop, Berhtwald, presided over a synod at Austerfield which effectively ousted him from his see and possessions in the north. Again Wilfrid appealed successfully to Rome and in 705 returned to be reinstated to part of his original see at Hexham, and to his monasteries. In 709 he died aged around seventy-six. The dynamics which caused this so turbulent a career shed much light on the formation of the English church in the second half of the seventh century.

First and foremost was Wilfrid's devotion to the see of Rome. He claimed to have been the first to make pilgrimage there from England; he was certainly the first bishop actually to appeal to the pope, and on more than one occasion. In this devotion he was undoubtedly encouraged initially by Bede's own spiritual father, Benedict Biscop, founder of the monastery of Monkwearmouth-Jarrow. Their careers and inclinations are closely parallel. Benedict too was of noble birth and an established thegn when he relinquished it all to go on pilgrimage to Rome for the first time, accompanied part of the way by Wilfrid. Both were friends and protégés of Alchfrid, son of king Oswy of Northumbria, who would have joined them.[47] Both derived their orders and profession from Gallic churchmen from whom they drew considerable resources and support in church affairs. Benedict made the journey to Rome no less than six times, Wilfrid three times, and he would have stayed there if he could. Devotion to Rome centred around the cult of St Peter as the prince of the Apostles, and to only a slightly lesser extent that of St Andrew as well. It was to St Andrew that Wilfrid made a personal profession of devotion which was to underpin his own vocation and mission. Of more practical value on his first visit he secured the friendship of the archdeacon Boniface who late became pope.[48] By his patronage and instruction he returned to England with a papal blessing. When in due course he constructed the monastic church at Ripon it was to St Peter that it was dedicated, and his church at Hexham was dedicated to St Andrew, and both by the style of their stone building clearly reflected his memory of what he had seen in Rome and Gaul. The way in which Eddius described Wilfrid's stand at the synod of Whitby and during his various disputes with the Northumbrian kings is open propaganda for an almost 'ultramontane' vision of the authority of the Petrine see. Even upon his death-bed, Wilfrid's thought and hopes turned again to Rome.

Wilfrid as a young man was clearly a person of ability and promise, so much so that on his way to Rome he was detained and patronised by the bishop of Lyons and by the count there, and stayed there for three years before returning finally to England.[49] There he was professed a monk, just as Biscop was at Lérins, and from there he hardly escaped with his life when his patrons fell foul of queen Baldhild. But it was due to the promotion of prince Alchfrid in Northumbria that Wilfrid first obtained prominence in the northern church as founder and abbot of Ripon, being ordained by the Gallic bishop of Wessex, Agilbert, with whom he played a decisive role at the synod of Whitby. It was in the wake of this triumph that Wilfrid was first nominated to become a bishop, probably at Alchfrid's behest. Because of the dissensions within the northern church over Easter, and perhaps for other reasons too, Wilfrid sought consecration in Gaul. He was sent forth as the blue-eyed boy of the Northumbrian court and church!

> The plan met with the cordial approval of the kings. They prepared him a ship and a force of men as well as a large sum of money, so as to enable him to enter Gaul in great state. Here at once there took place a large meeting consisting of no less than twelve catholic bishops, one of whom was bishop Agilbert. When they heard the testimony to his faith they all joyfully consecrated him publicly before all the people with great state, raising him aloft in accordance with their custom as he sat in the golden chair.[50]

This vivid picture in Eddius is passed over by Bede who simply recounts how the ceremony was carried out 'with great dignity'. Yet it is the key to understanding why from the start Wilfrid was never so secure in his episcopate in the north. The routing of the Irish at Whitby, though presented by Bede as a victory for Roman observances, was in reality the high-point of Gallic influence in the new English church. Wilfrid was perceived as the protégé of foreign bishops, and even before he returned the tide had turned back somewhat, and king Oswy had ordered the consecration of Chad to York having quarrelled with his son Alchfrid. Chad, as Eddius admits, represented the Irish interest, and for three years Wilfrid operated from Ripon as abbot, while on occasion sallying south to Mercia and Kent to function as bishop at the behest of the kings there who were his friends.[51]

One of Theodore's first acts was to restore Wilfrid to the see of York, displacing Chad who with Wilfrid's support became bishop at Lichfield. Under Wilfrid the cathedral in York was restored and the church at Ripon built, both in great state, and there is a vivid account in Eddius of the solemn consecration of Ripon 'in the presence of the kings' and the lay and ecclesiastical nobility. This was the period of Wilfrid's greatest favour in the north, but his position unravelled due to a conflict of interest with both king and archbishop.

Theodore had declared his firm intention of dividing the vast tribal dioceses of the English church as soon as he could at the synod of Hertford in 672, although he did not secure a consensus there for this move. In 678, with the active collusion of the king, Theodore consecrated for Northumbria three bishops, all of whom were English disciples of the Irish bishops.[52] This provoked Wilfrid's first appeal to Rome. But the background seems to be an alliance of hostile interests led by Theodore, determined if he could to divide the great Northumbrian see and perhaps also to prevent a rival to his metropolitan status, for Eddius more than once refers to York as a metropolitan see (as indeed Gregory had intended).[53] Resentment by the Irish party in the northern church remained long after the synod of Whitby, and Theodore's three consecrations probably reflect the active influence of those moulded by the founding tradition in the north to which Bede himself pays such eloquent tribute. The style of Wilfrid's episcopate stirred envy among churchmen as well as at court and with the king, though Eddius alleges that Wilfrid was supported in his desire to appeal to Rome by his fellow-bishops, who themselves may have feared the alliance of monarch and archbishop.[54] By this bold move Wilfrid was to test the reality of papal authority in the church which was so evidently the product of Rome's own mission. In so doing he was of course challenging the position of Theodore as archbishop of Canterbury and the pope's own nominee. It seems more than likely that at the root of it lay jealousy by Wilfrid towards Theodore, and there is an echo of this when Eddius asserts that towards the end of his life the primate sought reconciliation with Wilfrid, mediated significantly by Eorcenwald, bishop of London, seeking to commend Wilfrid as his successor at Canterbury.[55]

Wilfrid's position was undermined by the active hostility of king Ecgfrith, who clearly regarded him as a threat. Initially Eddius implies a fruitful alliance between them:

> Thus that most pious king found his kingdom extending both north and south by his triumphs, while at the same time the *ecclesiastical kingdom* (regnum ecclesiarum) of St Wilfrid of blessed memory increased also.[56]

Eddius asserts that it was the malice of the king's second wife that provoked him to envy and fear of Wilfrid:

> She eloquently described to him all the temporal glories of St Wilfrid, his riches, the number of his monasteries, the greatness of his buildings, his countless armies of followers arrayed in royal vestments and arms.[57]

If this is true, then Wilfrid was in danger of becoming the Wolsey of the seventh century. There was a momentum in his progress as the foremost ecclesiastical aristocrat. But there may have been also more personal rea-

sons for the king's resentment and the new queen's fear. For according to
Bede Wilfrid had persuaded Ecgfrith's first queen, Etheldreda, to resist
intercourse with her husband and finally to become a nun. As abbess of Ely
she remained his friend and protector. In this he had double-crossed the
king who 'had promised him estates and money if he could persuade the
queen to consummate their marriage, because he knew that there was none
whom she loved more than Wilfrid himself'.[58] This scenario went on for
twelve years: Bede portrays it as a miracle; but for the king it was probably
a nightmare and humiliation. He finally relented and she fell into the hands
of Wilfrid, founding Ely outside her husband's domains. It is another example in Wilfrid's life of open collision between the beliefs and values which
were forming Christian aristocratic society in England. But in political terms,
Wilfrid was a leader capable of inspiring unshakeable devotion among his
many followers and admirers, as his dispositions upon his death-bed reveal. It is surely significant that he managed to alienate three very different
kings in due course. Those with whom he lived in Northumbria found him
impossible, while he retained influence and respect among rulers elsewhere
who worked with him only occasionally and from a distance. The long-
term opposition of someone like Hilda of Whitby to him is also notable.

Undoubtedly Wilfrid's view of episcopacy and the status and trappings
pertaining to it were coloured by his experiences in Gaul.[59] There, as heirs
in part of Roman civic order, bishops were local potentates who lived in
great style, whose political pretensions often landed them in conflict with
local rulers as the writings of Gregory of Tours reveal. Wilfrid's own friendship with the archbishop of Lyons nearly placed him in fatal danger. On the
other hand there is a sense too in which Wilfrid's stature in Northumbria
mirrored for a time the military brilliance and prowess of its secular ruler at
the height of his power. As bishop of the kingdom he had become a great
lord, wielding influence and patronage alike well outside the confines of the
territorial kingdom. The kind of loyalty he could command as a spiritual
ruler was compelling, as Aldhelm reminded Wilfrid's clergy in his letter of
support.[60] As 'sons of the same tribe' they must expect to face exile with
him: 'what will be said of you if you cast into solitary exile the bishop who
nourished and raised you?' He contrasts this prospect tellingly with the
loyalty owed by a retainer to his lord in the secular life.

The collision with Theodore was to say the least unfortunate if possibly
inevitable, for both bishops were committed to advancing Roman order in
the land. When confronted by archbishop Berhtwald at Austerfield in 703
and the machinations of his enemies in Northumbria, Wilfrid made this
apologia:

> Was I not the first, after the death of the first elders who were sent by
> St Gregory, to root out the poisonous weeds planted by the 'Scots'?
> Did I not change and convert the whole of Northumbria to the true
> Easter and to the tonsure in the form of a crown. . . . Did I not instruct
> them in accordance with the rite of the primitive church to make use of

the double choir singing in harmony, with reciprocal responses and antiphons? And did I not arrange the life of the monks in accordance with the rule of the holy father Benedict which none had previously introduced here?[61]

These achievements, in conjunction with the style of his building work and overseas contacts in Gaul and Rome were formidable. But to his critics it seemed that he would bow to the authority of a distant pope in the way he would not co-operate with the pope's surrogate, the archbishop of Canterbury. Meanwhile his great wealth laid him open to the envy and greed of those who would despoil him.

The paradox of Wilfrid's person was that conjoined with this love of the splendour of his office was a strongly ascetic streak, imbued no doubt while a young man at Lindisfarne, and which Eddius did not hesitate to compare with that of Cuthbert himself, at least by implication. For his followers he was a holy man and a true spiritual father. Even for his critics this does not appear to have been in doubt. In many respects he was closer in style and power to St Columbanus or St Martin of Tours, and there are many aspects of Eddius' story which compare closely with their hagiographies: the sense of being an exile among his own people, in conflict with other bishops and rulers, but welcomed by strangers far away, a prophetic figure measured by the great figures of the Bible who was prepared to seek martyrdom. Many of Wilfrid's miracles fit this genre, and there is no doubt that he was a formidable church leader in his generation, perhaps the most outstanding English bishop yet to emerge.

Wilfrid was also a person of great courage and enterprise, as his initiatives in mission among pagan peoples reveal. He seized opportunities, most notably in Sussex and in Frisia where he launched active evangelisation incidental to his own immediate interests. On his way back from consecration as bishop in Gaul he was beached by a storm in Sussex. His company was assailed by wreckers and cursed by a magician. But in true biblical manner his armed retinue fought back while the bishop prayed and the tide lifted them off just in time to escape to Kent.[62] Later during a period of exile Wilfrid returned to Sussex to undertake its evangelisation. Eddius' account is corroborated and amplified by Bede.[63] With the support of king Wulfhere of Mercia, the king of Sussex became Christian having married a Christian queen from the Hwicce. Bede tells the story of how Wilfrid taught the people how to fish and so rescued them from destitution, commending the gospel by his pastoral and practical care. In due time the king gave the bishop land at Selsey for a monastery and for five years he served there as missionary bishop, and Bede recounts a miraculous vision of St Oswald by a child there.[64] But Wilfrid was ever an opportunist and sponsored the exiled prince Cadwalla in his efforts to conquer Wessex. This he duly achieved, and Cadwalla then overthrew Wilfrid's erstwhile protector the king of Sussex, and conquered the Isle of Wight. Idolatry there was suppressed and the ruling house destroyed; Wilfrid received a share of the spoils being given a quarter of the lands.[65] After a brief reign, Cadwalla abdicated and went as a pilgrim to Rome to receive baptism there and to die.[66]

Wilfrid's initiative in Frisia was no less portentous: he was driven there by a gale while going into exile in 678, trying to avoid his enemies in both England and Gaul. Eddius wishes to contrast the welcome he received among pagans with the treachery of so-called Christian rulers. He was protected, preached the gospel, and many were converted and baptised. It was a small but not unforgotten beginning. According to Bede, a friend of Egbert's called Wihtbert who with him had lived in exile among the Irish for some time, went also as a missionary to the new king of the Frisians, but in vain.[67] It fell to Wilfrid's disciple from Ripon, Willibrord to make progress many years later with a mission that was not overturned.[68] He secured the support of the papacy, sent a colleague to Wilfrid for consecration as another missionary bishop, and was himself consecrated by the pope as archbishop of the Frisians in 695 with a see at Utrecht. Thither Wilfrid went on his final journey to Rome with his chaplain Acca, where they heard tell of the miraculous fame of St Oswald on the continent.[69] Thus Wilfrid by his own initial vision laid the foundation and nurtured the first English mission abroad, and in many ways the career of Boniface is best understood as modelled on Wilfrid's example. For mission lay close to Wilfrid's heart as his activities as a roving bishop in Mercia and Wessex indicate, for example in consecrating Oftfor as bishop of Worcester.[70]

Without a doubt, Wilfrid posed a formidable but by no means negative challenge to the bishops and rulers of his generation. In his own manner he asserted the energy, vision and independence proper to a bishop of the church in his own right: he was a creature neither of king nor archbishop. In his career the conflicts of Offa's reign with the church were foreshadowed, as well as some of the struggles of Boniface in Germany. The dynamics within episcopacy evident in his experience, and the reactions to them, were to haunt the medieval church until the Reformation.

Yet Wilfrid, like Theodore, believed deeply in holiness, as his promotion of the cult of Etheldreda indicated. The framework of the church's institutional structure, over which there might be disagreement, existed solely to make possible the inner transformation of human nature evident in a saint, and to mediate through the saint divine grace for the healing and welfare of human society. Even while Wilfrid was pursuing his battles one such a saint was emerging at Lindisfarne – Cuthbert. Another more hidden but no less potent a hermit and thaumaturge of the next generation was Guthlac.

Like Wilfrid and Benedict Biscop, Guthlac was a noble thegn who experienced a 'conversio' to the monastic life at the age of twenty-four, after an energetic career as a warrior and leader of men in Mercia. But even then he had had reservations about his life of plunder: 'he would return to the owners a third part of the treasure he had collected'.[71] His *Life* was written by Felix, an east Anglian monk, at the behest of the king of that land, although many of the stories speak of Guthlac's relationships with friends and rulers in Mercia. Felix was influenced by Bede's *Life of Cuthbert*, and by classical hagiographies like those of St Antony and St Paul. In his style he was a follower of Aldhelm; and it seems that the *Life of Guthlac* was composed around the year 730.[72] Guthlac himself was born around 674; in 698 he became a monk at Repton, and in 699 retired to become a hermit on the fenland island of Crowland where the drama of his *Life* was centred. He died in 715 having enjoyed the friendship of king Aethelred of Mercia and that also of Aethelbald who became king shortly after Guthlac's death, and to whose patronage his cult and shrine owed their existence and promotion. Like St Antony, Guthlac proved himself a true warrior of Christ, living up to the meaning of his name – 'reward of battle'. In its way this life is a Christian counterpart to *Beowulf*: a story of a hero in his struggle with evil in the fenland fastnesses on the edge of society, winning for himself a true glory and for his people celestial blessing.

It is a compact and well-informed work, resting upon the testimonies of a circle of intimates of the saint's as well as his sister, Pega, herself a recluse. It is a story of ascetic struggle, overt and persistent, with demons anxious to overthrow Guthlac's determination and frighten him with visions of hell. On one occasion they appear in the guise of Britons, stirring no doubt bitter memories of earlier conflicts in which he was engaged while a thegn in Mercia. He lived on the island in an ancient barrow converted into a cell, with the support of his community at Repton, and claiming the active protection of St Bartholomew, who appeared to the saint more than once.

His relationships with fellow-clergy and monks were chequered. To his brethren at Repton his asceticism seemed harsh and they mocked him. He was nearly murdered by a jealous companion, Beccel, and did not hesitate to advise abbots about the state of their own monasteries or to challenge the love of ease and duplicity of visiting clergy. He was endowed with prophetic insight as a holy man and spiritual father to many. Like St Cuthbert he became familiar with animals and birds, and Felix includes a 'dictum' of the saint's about this: Guthlac said,

> Have you not read how if a man is joined to God in purity of spirit, all things are united to him in God? and he who refuses to be acknowledged by men seeks the recognition of wild beasts and the visitations of angels; for he who is often visited by men cannot often be visited by angels.[73]

At the very close of his life Guthlac confessed to an intimate that twice a day he had enjoyed an angelic visitation; in this respect his life is similar to that of St Columba.

After a period of enclosure and spiritual conflict, Guthlac emerged as a healer and exorcist. One such beneficiary was an East Anglian noble youth called Hwaetred whose cure his parents had sought at numerous shrines. They heard of Guthlac and journeyed to him; after three days of prayer and baptismal lustrations the boy was delivered.[74] His fame did not go uncriticised, and the story is told of the scepticism and caution of a visiting priest who had had experience in Ireland of false hermits. These doubts the saint later exposed. There is at this point a vivid account of Guthlac as a preacher and teacher:

> Now there was such a glory of divine grace in Guthlac, the man of God, that whatever he preached seemed as if uttered by the mouth of an angel. There was such an abundance of wisdom in him that, whatever he said, he confirmed by illustrations from the divine Scriptures.[75]

Guthlac died in an odour of sanctity, and after a year his body was found to be uncorrupt: the parallel with Cuthbert is manifest in the whole way Felix recounts this climax. He died in Easter week after a short but sharp illness, giving instruction to his intimate circle, his sister Pega and the anchorite Ecgbert, concerning his burial and the inner meaning of his spiritual life.[76] On the night of impending death his cell was seen filled with heavenly light, and after receiving holy communion he died. His companion saw 'the house filled again with the splendour of heavenly light and a tower of fire stretching from earth to heaven. . . . The whole air was heard to thunder with angelic voices, while one would have thought the island to be filled with the sweet scents of many kinds of spices'. The experience was too overwhelming and the monk fled the island by boat to tell the saint's sister. A posthumous appearance to Aethelbald the future king, and the healing of a blind man, together with the incorruption of his body, initiated the cult which grew up at the shrine in which he lay at Crowland.

PART THREE

VIII. BEDE

The most vivid and complete picture of monastic life in England in the seventh century is to be found in the two contemporaneous accounts of the monastery where Bede grew up, Monkwearmouth-Jarrow in Northumbria. The anonymous life of Ceolfrith, and Bede's own *Lives of the Abbots*, together with scattered references to life in his own community in his other writings, build up a picture of a large and lively monastery, closely moulded on continental models, and sustained by a web of friendships over several generations. Bede's own labours of learning during more than thirty years were a direct product of the favourable conditions thus created, and his own life was nurtured and assisted by numerous friends and mentors.

The founder of this monastery was Benedict Biscop, the friend of Wilfrid. After two years formation in the monastic life at Lérins where he was professed, he returned to England via Rome in the company of archbishop Theodore, and for another two years presided over the monastery of St Peter and St Paul (later St Augustine's) at Canterbury. After which he went for a third pilgrimage to Rome, collecting a library of books on the way and returned to Wessex hoping to found a monastery there under the patronage of his friend Cenwalh, the king of that land. But Cenwalh died in 674 as Benedict returned and so he went north and gained the confidence of king Ecgfrith of Northumbria. The king's endowment was lavish; seventy hides at the strategic mouth of the Wear, where a church was dedicated to St Peter and a community created to house all the books and relics Benedict had brought back from abroad. From his friend, abbot Torthhelm, an Englishman in Gaul, he obtained builders capable of erecting 'a stone church in the Roman style he always loved so much'.[1] Thence he also drew glaziers and other craftsmen, together with suitable artefacts for divine worship. Fragments of this glass have been found at the site at Jarrow, where a second part of the monastery was created some years later and dedicated to St Paul.

Meanwhile Benedict went again to Rome in 679-680, and Bede lists clearly what was significant about this visit, and discusses it also in his *History*. Books and relics head this list, and a complete sequence of icons of the apostles and the Mother of God and scenes from the Apocalypse;

> Thus all who entered the church, even those who could not read, were able, whichever way they looked to contemplate the dear face of Christ and His saints, even if only in a picture, to put themselves more firmly in mind of the Lord's incarnation and, as they saw the decisive moment

of the Last Judgement before their eyes be brought to examine their conscience with all due severity.[2]

In addition to all this Benedict secured a papal privilege similar to that obtained by abbot Hadrian for the monastery at Canterbury, which guaranteed the monastery's independence and integrity. This was sought 'with king Ecgfrith's permission and indeed at his wish and exhortation': there was no conflict over this between Benedict and the king, despite the ongoing quarrel with Wilfrid at the time. Finally, Benedict brought back to England John the precentor of St Peter's in Rome, and abbot of the monastery of St Martin there. They came via Tours to venerate the shrine of the saint, and John came to Monkwearmouth to teach the monks how to sing and celebrate the Roman rite. During his visit he exercised a wide teaching ministry, as well as attending on the pope's behalf the council held by Theodore to declare against the monothelite heresy. John died on his way home to Rome and was buried at Tours.[3]

Eight years after the foundation at Monkwearmouth, the king initiated the new sister-house at Jarrow, where Bede grew up. The creation of this monastery was entrusted to Ceolfrith who had also travelled with Benedict to Rome. He had been his close companion since the creation of the first house, serving there as prior and for a time being driven out by the antagonism of some of the noble monks there to the strictness of the regime. He too was of noble birth, but by eighteen had become a monk at the royal foundation of Gilling. He was related to Tunberht, later bishop of Hexham, and with him for a time a member of Wilfrid's monastery at Ripon. There he was ordained priest before going south for a visit to the church in Kent 'to learn fully the practises of the monastic life' there. Later he went for the same purpose to the house of St Botulf in East Anglia.[4] Meanwhile his own brother Cynefrith under whom he had entered the monastic life at Gilling had withdrawn to Ireland 'in his zeal for the study of the scriptures, combined with his desire to serve the Lord more freely in tears and prayers'. Ceolfrith thus was beneficiary of every aspect of monastic life that had so far formed the English church, and was in his own lifetime regarded as an expert; for that reason he became Benedict's collaborator and in due time his successor. The friendship between these two, and the affectionate loyalties they long inspired was the foundation upon which the whole enterprise rested.

Nine years into its life, Monkwearmouth received a new abbot, Eosterwine, a kinsman of Benedict, appointed by him effectively to run the monastery because the king frequently summoned Benedict to court for advice, and because of Benedict's extensive travels abroad. Bede gives an exemplary account of Eosterwine's sanctity and humility in language redolent of the *Rule of St Benedict*. But he died of plague while Benedict was abroad, and Ceolfrith appointed in his place Sigefrith, 'a deacon of wondrous sanctity, amply learned in the scriptures and singularly devoted to their study'.[5] But he was a sick man, and both he and Benedict lingered on for several painful years, and Bede tells the story of their friendship to the end, preparing for death side by side. For a time Ceolfrith's community at Jarrow hung by a thread, decimated by plague so that only the abbot and a young schoolboy, perhaps Bede himself, remained to sustain the singing of the divine office. On his last visit abroad Benedict had again obtained numerous books and further icons for the chapel of the Mother of God he had built, and for the church of St Paul at Jarrow, comprising a sequence of Old Testament and New Testament stories which typologically interpreted each other.[6]

In chapter 11 of his *Lives*, Bede records at some length and with great care Benedict's last instructions to his community. He claimed that the rule he had set up, resting as it did, in part at least, upon that of St Benedict, nonetheless distilled the best of what he had witnessed in seventeen monasteries at home and abroad.

> He gave orders that the fine and extensive library of books which he had brought back from Rome and which were so necessary for improving the standard of education in this church should be carefully preserved in a single collection and not allowed to decay through neglect or be split up piecemeal.

Here is the firm voice of the most spectacular beneficiary of this great library: examination of Bede's own writings reveal how extensive and comprehensive was the range of works available to him as the result of Benedict's labours. Reminding his brethren of the dictates of the *Rule of St Benedict* and of the intentions of the papal privilege granted them, Benedict insisted that any successor be chosen from within their own ranks and not on grounds of kinship. This is a persistent theme throughout Bede's account: 'Let them reckon as the eldest son (i.e. as heir) among their spiritual children him who is endowed with the more abundant spiritual grace'. Upon which principle Ceolfrith assumed the abbacy of the double monastery at Benedict's command and ruled for twenty-eight years.

Ceolfrith consolidated admirably and consistently the work of Benedict Biscop, and to judge from the tone of the anonymous *Life* and from Bede's own response to his final departure on pilgrimage to Rome he was an abbot of great charisma. He was undoubtedly Bede's immediate spiritual father and true heir to Benedict's singular vision. 'He doubled the number of books in the libraries of both monasteries with an ardour equal to that which Benedict had shown in founding them.'[7] He commissioned three whole copies of the Bible, one of which – the *Codex Amiatinus* – he later took to Rome and during the time of pope Sergius I he obtained a privilege for Jarrow comparable to the earlier one for Monkwearmouth which king Aldfrith and his witan ratified. He also sent a lengthy letter to Nechtan, king of the Picts, setting out the catholic position on Easter and related matters, and sent architects to build him a church in the Roman manner. Bede cites the letter at length, in which it is revealed that at an earlier date Ceolfrith had helped entertain Adomnan of Iona and persuade him to accept the orthodox position.[8] What is interesting about this exchange is the emphasis

Ceolfrith placed upon devotion to St Peter and fidelity to the practices of the Roman see going hand in hand. Under the leadership of Benedict and Ceolfrith, the double house of Monkwearmouth-Jarrow became a mirror of Rome, in its liturgy, learning and art.

So at the end of his life, Ceolfrith surprised his community by deciding to relinquish office and make a final pilgrimage to the holy city. The drama and poignancy of this move is recounted in some detail by the anonymous biographer and by Bede also, whom it clearly upset very profoundly. In his commentary on Samuel, he tells how he was unable to write for some time as a result of the loss of his spiritual father. After his solemn departure from the monastery, the monks elected his successor, Hwaetberht, and sought Ceolfrith's approval for it. They sent a letter of commendation to the pope to accompany him on his voyage to Gaul, but he died at Langres and was buried there for a while until his relics could return home to lie with those of Benedict, Eosterwine and Sigefrith, which Hwaetberht had translated into the sanctuary of St Peter's church.[9] Some of his company pressed on to Rome bearing gifts, including the precious Bible, and returned with a papal letter to Hwaetberht.[10] Meanwhile at Langres his burial-place became something of a local shrine. He died aged seventy-four, having been abbot for forty-three years and priest for forty-seven. Bede records also his devotion to the psalter and to the daily eucharist.[11] The anonymous biographer reflects on his generosity towards the poor, a trait he inherited from his father who on one occasion turned a feast he had laid on for the king into a banquet for 'the poor, the strangers and the sick' instead, with his wife serving them herself; thus 'he entertained the highest king in the person of his lowly followers'.[12] Bede, for whom monastic obedience channelled natural self-effacement, is never more quietly emphatic than in his account of these founding fathers whom he knew and loved, both in his *History of the Abbots* and in his homily for the commemoration day of Benedict Biscop. Indeed the whole tenor as well as the quality of his copious learning and writing was their lasting memorial. He wrote from and for a community bound together in its vision and values by the example and energies of these remarkable men. For a brief while the marriage of idealism and friendship within the Christian life appeared complete and left a lasting mark. To find a comparable moment would lead back to St Basil, or perhaps forward to the Cistercians of the twelfth century. Bede was therefore the unique product of a singular milieu.

All Bede's extensive learning was devoted to building up the life and mission of the church. At the end of his *History* he outlines his achievement, giving prominence to the many works of exposition of Scripture. To this his whole life within the monastery was devoted:

I have spent all my life in this monastery, applying myself entirely to the study of Scripture; and, amid the observance of the discipline of the Rule and the daily task of singing in the church, it has always been my delight to learn or to teach or to write. . . . For my own benefit and that of my brothers I have made it my business to make brief extracts from the works of the venerable Fathers on the holy Scriptures, or to add notes of my own to clarify their sense and interpretation.[13]

In addition to this exegetical 'corpus' he composed hagiographies and a martyrology, works on poetry and metre, and works on chronology and science. Everything was concerted to undergird the intellectual and spiritual life of the church whose *History* has been regarded by posterity as his crowning labour. It too reflected his understanding as a biblical theologian, and his keen interest in the calculation of sacred time and the evidence of that reality to be seen in the lives of recent saints among his own people.

Bede's *History* is both a monument to the remarkable missionary enterprise of the seventh century among the English peoples and a penetrating and subtle examination of the mission of the church. There is, therefore, theological comment and interpretation of this phenomenon throughout the work. The *History* is closely modelled upon the Bible and is permeated by the steady conviction that the eternal life experienced by saints, in this life and after death, interweaves and influences the unfolding development of the church's life. This is indeed its true story and significance, and Bede and those for whom he wrote clearly saw a divine pattern running through the history of the formation of their church, comparable to that in the historical sections of the Bible, the books of the Kings and the Acts of the Apostles. It was significant too that the hagiography which they absorbed from the earlier story of the church should become real and embodied in the lives of their own saints, like Cuthbert or Guthlac. This was proof of the reality of the gospel and its power to recreate human nature; the emergence of sanctity brought the Christian past into the present, and consequent miracles pointed to the imminence of the supreme miracle of human salvation. In Bede's mind emerged a clear vision of the work of Him who 'makes all things new', within and through the manifold influences moulding the English church and nation. The sense that the English were indeed one people under God was the corollary to this perception, and the culminating message of the *History*.

Elements of this missionary ecclesiology emerge early in Bede's writing, for example in his commentary on the Acts.[14] It is not an elaborate or lengthy work, but already certain typical traits emerge. Of St Peter curing the sick by his shadow, Bede writes:

Now he does not cease to strengthen the infirm among the faithful by the invisible screen of his intercession. . . . So the church, concentrating her mind and love on heavenly things, passes like a shadow on the land, and here on earth, with sacramental signs and temporal figures of heavenly things she renews those whom there in heaven she rewards with everlasting gifts.[15]

Of saints he comments: 'As they dwell on high by the merits of their works, through mental contemplation they direct their attention with wisdom towards things above, while always watching out for themselves with prudent discretion'.[16] Here speaks a true disciple of St Gregory the great.

The Acts of the Apostles is, of course, the first missionary history of the church, and Bede was bound to address the issue common to the time of the apostles and of his own – idolatry. When discussing St Paul's speech at Athens, Bede carefully outlines the classic approach adopted by the missionaries of his own day also.

The order of the apostle's argument deserves careful examination. Among gentiles the treatment of his subject takes the form of a series of steps. First, he teaches that the one God is the originator of the world and of all things. . . . Thus he demonstrates that God is to be loved not only because of his gifts of light and life, but also because of a certain affinity of kind. Next, he disposes of the opinion which is the explicit reason for idols by saying that the founder and Lord of the entire world cannot be enclosed in temples of stone, that the grantor of all blessings has no need of the blood of victims, that the creator and ruler of all men cannot be created by the hand of man, and that God, in whose image man was made, should not be appraised in terms of the value of metals. He teaches that the remedy for such errors is the practice of repentance. Now if he had begun by destroying the idolatrous rites, the ears of the gentiles would have rejected him.[17]

Belief comes instead step by step, and so virtue is made out of the necessity confronting Paul and Bede's contemporaries that neither was normally in a position to secure by direct action the destruction of idols. Bede, consonant with the instructions, of Gregory indicates by implication that persuasion rather than force addresses the inner errors of the heart and mind.

The exigencies of active mission become at Bede's hand exemplars of the spiritual life. Paul's narrow escape from death by shipwreck is treated in a most beautiful allegorical sense:

No one escapes the tempests of this world except those who are nourished by the bread of life, and one who in the night of present tribulations depends for all his strength on wisdom, fortitude, temperance, and justice will soon, with the shining forth of divine help, reach the port of salvation which he had sought, provided that, unencumbered by things of the world, he seeks only the flame of divine love with which he may warm his heart.

In Bede's *Life of St Cuthbert* just such a spiritual scenario was acted out in the manner of the saint's dying. Thus the *History* is both a record and also a spiritual guide for those who in their several vocations would lead the church further through its temporal voyage. The quiet authority behind the way Bede writes is drawn both from scripture and tradition, and from active listening to the living testimonies within his own generation and community.

This commentary on Acts was dedicated, like much of his other biblical work, to his friend and mentor, bishop Acca of Hexham, and it was to him that he sent the work which he composed while writing the *History* – the

De Templo.[19] This is a theological 'tour de force' and at the same time an indirect commentary upon the theology implicit throughout the *History*. It rests upon and clearly presupposes an earlier work, an exposition of the spiritual meaning of the Tabernacle for the life of the Christian church. But it is in the *De Templo* that Bede's own thought takes wings, and it is perhaps the finest compendium of his own theology and spiritual vision. As he wrote, Acca had been unseated from his see and was in difficulties for reasons unclear.[20] Very much in the spirit of Gregory commenting on the book of Job, Bede reminds Acca that 'we must have patience', supported by the consolations of scripture and the examples of the fathers, 'that we may call to mind how much dark affliction those eminent fathers of the church and the bright luminaries of the church have often borne even during this life' before passing to glory.[21] Acca is bidden to emulate St John upon Patmos and to use this exposition of the mystical meaning of the Temple as a ladder of divine ascent:

> Through the Spirit to the contemplation of the unfathomable mysteries of the heavenly mansions, so that in the very place where the deluded enemy imagined him to be deprived of the help and companionship of human friends, he was privileged to enjoy the sight and conversation of angelic friends.[22]

This too had been the privilege of hermits like Columba, Cuthbert and Guthlac.

Once again saints' lives are crucial witnesses to this heavenly 'transitus' at the heart of the church's life. As preachers of the gospel by word and example they are the beams supporting the structure of the Temple. But these are only the outward signs of an inner grace and vision which cannot be fathomed:

> Although we are as yet unable to see clearly the inner glory of the saints, nevertheless from what we have been able to see from the outside we faithfully adhere to the members of the church who are in heaven. We can also apply this to the saints who are still in this life.[23]

This attraction and adhesion leads to a participation in the divine patience which to Bede's mind is the supreme hallmark of sanctity. In this judgement Bede is reinforced by his strong sense of history: indeed the life of the church, visible and hidden, is the true meaning and purpose of human history. So he draws this meaning from the biblical description of the walls of the Temple:

> The temple walls are the *nations* of believers of whom the holy universal church consists and whose widespread distribution throughout the whole world is denoted by the width of the walls; whereas the height denotes the hope and whole upward thrust of the church towards heavenly things; or at any rate the height of the wall which consists of courses of stones laid one on top of the other denotes the state of the present church where the elect are all built upon the foundation of Christ and follow each other in succession through the course of the

ages and, by supporting each other, fulfil the law of Christ, which is charity.[24]

Here is a dynamic but at the same time a very concrete understanding of apostolic tradition. It is also a vital model for understanding the unity of the church in its very diversity.[25] One of the most striking things about this commentary, like that concerning the Tabernacle also, is the strong sense of architecture and visual imagery and colour with which Bede invests his writing. It is an indirect testimony probably to the very physical environment in which he had grown up at Jarrow as well as to his own interests and aptitudes.

Although it is in many ways a profoundly contemplative work, the *De Templo* does address many elements of church life vital for the progress of the Christian mission in England and abroad at that time. As usual Bede attaches great importance to the suitability and formation of teachers and preachers. He reminds his readers that the word 'priest' in the scriptures embraces not only the ordained ministers but also all called to a holy life:

all who are outstanding by reason of the loftiness of their good life and salutary teaching, and are of benefit not only to themselves but to a great many others as well. For while they offer their bodies as a living sacrifice, holy and pleasing to God, they truly exercise the priestly ministry spiritually.[26]

For to this all Christians are called; equally ordained ministers are thus reminded of the particular and decisive demands of their office also. The generation of sanctity is the true apostolic succession:

In the universal assembly of the elect various righteous persons succeed each other and the lesser ones are glad to follow faithfully in the footsteps of the greater and of their predecessors, and to rely on their sayings or writings, lest perchance they should lapse into error.[27]

Thus the life of divine love within human nature forms an unbreakable and actual chain within which the present generations are called to be partakers.

Baptism and evangelism are symbolically at the heart of the Temple – in its central pillars and in the great bronze laver of universal regeneration. But baptism is a call to present purity in order to obtain heavenly glory, and Bede directly chastises the dilatory clergy of the younger generation,

When some want to have the appearance and the name of being teachers, priests and pillars of the house of God though they have absolutely none of the firm faith needed to despise worldly ostentation and make invisible goods their ambition, none of the strength needed to administer correction, none of the diligence even to understand the errors of those to whom they have been preferred.[28]

This for Bede is a very stern judgement, borne out also in his famous letter to his pupil, Egbert the new archbishop of York.[29] But its quiet force prompts immediate comparison with the criteria deployed in the *History* to set forth exemplary leaders of the English church as a yardstick by which contemporary ministers and leaders might be measured and guided.

As in the *History of the Abbots* there is in this work an eloquent defence of icons,

> For if it were permissible to raise up the brazen serpent on a tree that the Israelites might live by looking at it, why is it not permissible that the exaltation of the Lord our saviour on the cross whereby he conquered death be recalled to the minds of the faithful pictorially, or even his other miracles and cures whereby he wonderfully triumphed over the same author of death, since the sight of these things often tends to elicit great compunction in the beholders and also to make available to those who are illiterate a living narrative of the story of the Lord.

For Bede such representations are, like the details of the Temple as he is expounding it, a 'living writing'. There is a wider context to these observations – the iconoclastic controversy, and the remarkable visual presentations of the gospel story and particularly of the Cross in Anglo-Saxon art and literature at the time, resting as they did upon a steady enrichment of liturgy derived from Rome.[30] Bede's verdict is that the Law prohibited idolatry, not the making of suitable images as such for the House of God.[31] Thus, in a striking exposition, the very structure beneath the great bronze laver becomes symbolic of the work of evangelism, with a direct reference to the mission to the English which Bede has set forth in his *History*:

> The wheels placed underneath to support the laver of the Temple raised the base from the ground when the blessed pope Gregory recently in our own day ruled the Roman church on the strength of the words of the Gospel; the same wheels fitted beneath God's chariot transported people long distances when the most venerable fathers, Augustine, Paulinus and the rest of their companion backed by the oracular sayings of the gospel came to Britain at his command and a short while ago entrusted the word of God to unbelievers.[32]

This is a classic example of the connection made by Bede between the different levels of meaning implicit within the precise text of the scripture and actual historical and moral developments. It is a matter of discerning the hidden but consistent pattern to divine action in history, and so experiencing how 'these very same words of sacred history, which are to us an entirely new lightning-flash of divine wisdom, open the door to a new understanding of the old'.[33]

Bede firmly believed that the divine was a matter for experience and not just for study, and that this possibility of participation in the divine life was mediated by the living past of scripture and tradition to form a living present encountered in the liturgy and in the lives of saints. Expounding how vessels for sacred use in the Temple were first cast in moulds of clay, Bede indicates the making of saints 'in the fire of tribulation' and the humiliation of physical and mental suffering. After death, 'when they had reached the point of contemplation, the casings of the moulds were broken and they were brought out into the light and each of them arranged in its proper place in the temple of the Lord'. Then the true resplendence of their glory is revealed, accomplished on the inner altar of the heart, the true Holy of Holies.[34] Herein lies the hidden unity of the church's life and teaching throughout history. Angels constitute the doors to the Holy of Holies in heaven just as 'holy teachers and priests' are the initial doors of the Temple of the church itself. The hinges are made of gold which represent 'the minds and hearts of these angels or saints by which they cleave fixedly to the contemplation and love of their creator' and in that spirit fulfil their proper ministry.[35] This is why in his *History* Bede highlights the lives of those saints whose lives most clearly embodied a Christ-like love. Like the silent golden hinges of the Temple, their movement might appear imperceptible, but upon them the doors of evangelistic witness and opportunity in fact turned, opening the way into the Kingdom of God.

In Bede's vision 'precious in the Lord's eyes is the dying of his saints', and his own proved no exception. It is described by Cuthbert, one of Bede's own pupils, who later presided over Monkwearmouth-Jarrow as abbot. After an illness stretching from Easter to Ascension in 735, during which he continued teaching and the daily recitation of the psalter, Bede began to prepare to die, singing in both Latin and English, and drawing comfort from words of St Ambrose: 'I have not so lived, that life among you now would make me ashamed; but I am not afraid to die either, for the God we serve is good'. He was still working on translating St John's gospel into English, and preparing a selection of Isidore's *De natura rerum*. He dictated almost to the last moments of his life, when he dispensed some small gifts to his brethren and friends. A boy called Wilbert, acting as ammanuensis pressed him for the last sentence, and having done so, Bede died on the floor of his cell where he used to pray, reciting the Gloria. 'All who heard or saw the death of our saintly father Bede declared that they had never seen a man end his days in such great holiness and peace', full of thanksgiving to God for everything.[36] He had left to his own church the learned instruments for the reform and development of Christian life in England and also on the continent, thus proving himself a worthy disciple of St Gregory.

If Bede was an idealist in many ways, and a theologian of eloquent vision and formidable learning, he could also be a stern critic and mentor, as his letter to his former pupil, Egbert the new archbishop of York, reveals.[37] This was in effect his last will and testament, for in it he apologises that illness has prevented him from meeting Egbert in person to communicate his concerns. The letter was sent in November 734: the next year Bede died, and Egbert received the pallium from the pope to serve as archbishop of York for over thirty years. His brother in due course became king of Northumbria, and together they built up the church, developing a strong centre of learning and a library in York itself. To Egbert was attributed a *Dialogue* and the substance of a *Penitential* also. It fell to his generation of bishops to attempt the reform and further development of a church already prey to corruption. Bede's letter is therefore important because it reveals his very practical understanding and concern about church life. His zeal for active reform sheds further light on the significance of his *History* and other writings as providing a yardstick by which his church might measure and enhance its life.

Bede's letter provides both a commentary on the fundamental concerns evident throughout his writing and a blueprint for the many attempts at reform and development evident in the Anglo-Saxon church from the council of Cloveshoe in 747 onwards into the ninth and tenth centuries. In England at least, the era of straight missionary activity was coming to an end, and Bede's writings mark the period of transition. From now on the case for reform would be presented as restoration of pristine conditions, distilled from the collective memory in the hagiographies of Bede and others. The last capitula of Egbert's *Dialogue* reveals this perspective graphically:[38] he writes that in preparation for Christmas the English used to fast for the full twelve days beforehand, both clergy and also laity and their families, making confession and so receiving the eucharist on the festival. 'This custom developed in the English church during the times of pope Vitalian and archbishop Theodore of Canterbury, and was kept as if by law.' It is clearly a standard and practice to which Egbert wishes his flock to return.

Throughout his letter, Bede stresses the importance of sound teaching and a tradition of learning within the life of the church. His theology of the episcopate is openly culled from the writings of St Gregory the great which he commends to the newly consecrated bishop. The bishop is to take an active and determining lead by both word and example. Bede had a horror of bishops demeaning their office by gossip and intrigue, and he urged that a bishop live in a community which might uphold him in his office, and protect him from a lax life-style. Bede urges Egbert to tackle the provision of priests and teachers for far-flung villages, reminding him of the bishop's duty to visit and to confirm, and not simply to draw in taxes from places in his diocese which were effectively uncared for. Central to Bede's mind was the widespread learning of the Creed and the Lord's prayer, either in Latin or English, and Bede refers to translations of these he has written for unlearned priests to use. He regards avarice as the main besetting sin of bishops, undermining the credibility of their ministry as 'protector' of their people.

Bede is surprisingly forthright in commending a programme of reform backed by royal authority 'to attend to the restoration in your days of the ecclesiastical condition of our race better than it has been hitherto'. He urges the creation of new bishoprics, a continuation of Theodore's policy, so that the archbishop of York might preside over the twelve suffragans envisaged by pope Gregory. This leads Bede to expose with considerable candour a major abuse whereby 'through the carelessness of preceding kings it has come about that it is not easy to find a vacant place where a new episcopal see should be made'. Bede's advice is a synod to elect a monastery which might receive and support a new see, its bishop being chosen if possible by the community concerned. To endow the new creation lands might be transferred by royal authority from so-called monasteries which have slipped into corruption and laxity of life. Bede describes how certain nobility, with the collusion of bishops who made money out of the transactions, had set up monasteries which were in name only, and which were effectively a way of evading taxes and military service. The result has been a lack of land suitable for the rising generation of young noblemen and veteran thegns to settle upon: unmarried and footloose they venture to fight abroad and so weaken the defence of the realm. The connivance of bishops in obtaining charters for such creations draws Bede's forthright condemnation. The life of such 'monasteries' brings discredit to the whole church, and especially to the religious life; yet Bede alleges that it has been going on for thirty years unchecked, since the death of king Aldfrith. 'Such persons suddenly receive the tonsure at their pleasure, and at their own judgement are made from laymen not into monks, but into abbots.' A sharper contrast with the ideal of monastic life portrayed in Bede's historical and biblical writings could hardly be imagined.

Bede commands Egbert to emulate the Good Shepherd, and to investigate wrongdoing in the monasteries of his diocese: it is 'your duty to provide that the devil may not usurp a kingdom for himself in places consecrated to God'. False abbots and unruly monks alike need exposure and correction, and bishops should not hide behind claims of immunity from royal authority. For those in secular life, Bede commends clear moral guidance and the provision of teachers, emphasising prayer, making the sign of the Cross, and daily reception of the eucharist, in harmony with the universal church. Confining communion simply to the major feasts is denying grace to the many blameless laity of all ages who would benefit from more regular sacramental life, which it is the duty of the bishop to provide. Bede's letter closes with a lengthy biblical exposé of the sin of avarice which he believes is paralysing leadership in church life: 'it deposed Judas from the glory of the apostolate, injured even with death the body of Ananias and Sapphira as unworthy of the society of monks, and, to come to higher things, cast out the angels from heaven'. Thus, the picture of Christian common life in the beginning of the Acts, as in his own *History* of how the English church came to be, is the goal for all Christian life, monastic, clerical or lay; it is indeed protection against 'the venom of avarice'. It would appear that Bede laboured on unceasingly with his scholarship and teaching and prayer against a prevailing tide in the church life of his day. Yet at the same time it was the inner strength of the Northumbrian church found in the genuine monasteries which enabled a person like Egbert to emerge as archbishop, and to attempt as he could to implement many of the reforms which Bede described.

The most tangible fruit of such steady reform and development was the growth of the school of York under Egbert and his successor. Egbert died in 766, and was succeeded to the primacy by Ethelbert, who lived till 780.

But Ethelbert's fame lay in the way in which under Egbert's rule and with his active encouragement he presided over the school at York, and built up its library. Of this we have a very full picture in Alcuin's poem on the saints of the church of York.[39] Alcuin himself had been educated at York under Ethelbert to whom he gives fulsome praise. The stature and significance of Egbert and the continuity of policy which he established, and his successor maintained, for fifty years is clear. He is portrayed as a generous, holy and devout bishop, working with the king his brother to secure the prosperity of Northumbria. He is also openly associated in Alcuin's mind with Bede himself. But it is of Ethelbert that Alcuin writes at great length, paying tribute to his old master. For him he is an ideal father-in-God. He proved a natural scholar, dedicated from childhood by his parents to be educated in a monastery. He was a kinsman and protégé of Egbert, who made him master of the school where he taught grammar, law, verse, music and astronomy; also the natural sciences and computation, and of course theology rooted in the Bible. He travelled abroad, as did Egbert, as far as Rome to collect books 'in love of learning making pilgrimage', like Benedict Biscop before him. By popular acclaim he was made archbishop, and 'graced his office with his scholar's gifts'. He stood up to kings and nobility, and maintained his studies: 'as learned teacher and as worthy priest, his thought enlarged his love, his love his thought'. Both bishops adorned the cathedral church, and after the fire in 741 supervised its rich reconstruction. In this project Alcuin himself was heavily involved, as was also Eanbald who succeeded Ethelbert. It is while describing Ethelbert's primacy that Alcuin gives his picture of some of the contents of the library collected there during this time. It is a list with which Bede would have been broadly familiar, though perhaps with an enhanced classical range, and certainly containing Boethius with whom Bede was unfamiliar, but whose impress is everywhere in Alcuin's writings.[40] Ethelbert resigned the see in favour of Eanbald, to assume the life of a hermit before his end. Alcuin's sense of perpetual bereavement is evident in the lines of his poem. It would appear that Ethelbert was to Alcuin what Ceolfrith had been to Bede.

The inherent intellectual strength of the Northumbrian church owed much, as Alcuin perceived and indicated, to Bede's teaching. In a way perhaps Egbert's primacy was his memorial. Certainly it was to this part of the English church that the Anglo-Saxon missionaries on the continent partic- ularly looked for encouragement and resources, both in personnel and in books, carrying with them Bede's reputation and drawing from his legacy fresh strength. The spread and importance of his writings for the growth first of mission then of reform in the continental church may be discerned throughout the eighth century.[41] For example in the first part of his ministry, Boniface did not know about Bede's works. Then by 746 or so he writes in general terms to Egbert archbishop of York requesting them. In another letter to a former pupil, the abbot Duddo, he specifies his works on St Paul, and in a later letter to Egbert he thanks him for further copies sent and requests Bede's homilies and writing on Proverbs. Cuthbert abbot at Jarrow sent Lullus a copy of the verse and prose *Lives of St Cuthbert* by Bede in 764. Later Lullus wrote seeking further precise titles including the *De Templo*; he wrote also to Ethelbert archbishop of York seeking Bede's biblical commentaries, and from the way he lists them it is evident that he is familiar with a copy of the *History* also.[42] Alcuin's familiarity is evident and extensive and this pattern is confirmed by the spread of early manuscripts in monastic centres on the continent. Bede's work by its tenor and comprehensive sweep of Christian learning, provided the bedrock both for the work of mission, and for the Carolingian reform and renaissance of theology. His vision of Christian mission and the life of the church proved central to what his compatriots and successors were able to achieve.

IX. WILLIBRORD AND BONIFACE

Bede carefully records the genesis of the Anglo-Saxon missions to the Continent, and unlike Eddius sees their true significance. Whereas Eddius is content to use Wilfrid's enforced visit to Frisia as another example of how his hero proved a prophet not without honour, being protected by a pagan king, it is Bede who pays close attention to the unfolding pattern of contact throughout the later stages of his *History*. Nonetheless the account in Eddius reveals once again Wilfrid's practical energy as a missionary and the sympathetic response he received. A prosperous harvest by land and sea was turned by the missionaries to their advantage as they proclaimed faith in the true Creator, and Eddius indicates the eventual continuation of the mission by Wilfrid's disciple, Willibrord, whose work was continuing as he and Bede were writing.[1] Trade links with Frisia were close: Bede tells a story about a Frisian merchant in London purchasing an English slave who had a miraculous escape;[2] and he also indicates Wilfrid's continuing interest in the mission of Willibrord. Wilfrid visited him on the way to Rome for his final appeal in 703, and consecrated the first bishop to work there, Swithberht, who later evangelised a German tribe near the Ruhr.[3]

But the prime mover behind the mission to Frisia was in Bede's mind Egbert whose spiritual authority permeated the monastic contacts between Northumbria and Ireland at the end of the seventh century. Although an exile by choice in Ireland, he yearned to evangelise the Germanic folk from whom the English sprang, and perhaps himself proceed as a pilgrim to Rome. In this wish he was prevented by divine intimations and a storm, and in due course he sent forth a companion, another English hermit and exile, Wihtbert. He spent two years in Frisia, encountering a far less sympathetic king, Radbod, and in the end he retired to Ireland frustrated. But Egbert was not to be thwarted, and in 690 sent Willibrord with eleven others to Frisia, who worked under the protection of Pippin in the western part of the country which the Franks had newly conquered. Willibrord had been educated at Ripon under Wilfrid before a twelve year sojourn in Ireland with Egbert.[4]

Bede also mentions the activities at this time of two brothers, both called Hewald, among the Old Saxons. They were brutally killed, and their bodies were rescued from the Rhine and enshrined at Cologne. The active involvement of Pippin was part of a much wider missionary impulse under royal patronage in which the churches along the northern frontier of the Frankish realm had been engaged on and off throughout the seventh century. Early efforts had been made by Eligius of Tournai in Flanders, and St Amand near Antwerp, and Willibrord found the ruins of his church there. Utrecht had been given to the see of Cologne as a missionary base by

Dagobert before 612, but again when Willibrord made his headquarters there the church was reduced to footings.[5] At the end of the century, missions followed military subjugations by the Frankish kings, along and across the Rhine. In this Pippin and his queen Plectrudis played a key role, supporting missions from Cologne, and refounding religious life in and around Trier. This active policy provided the context for their support of first Willibrord and then later Boniface: the English initiatives were part of a wider missionary and monastic enterprise without which they could have hardly succeeded.[6]

Willibrord's first action upon receiving royal approval for his missionary activities was to seek also that of the pope, Sergius. In this as in many other details of his mission he seems consciously to have emulated the actions of St Augustine at Canterbury. He returned from Rome armed with saints' relics to be placed in the altars of new churches. In 696 he was sent again to Rome by Pippin to be consecrated archbishop of Utrecht, during which he received the name of Clement. His bond with the pope was clearly personal and strong, and he makes mention of this moment in his life in the kalendar which was in his possession and which still remains. Boniface in a later letter to pope Stephen III recounted the foundation of the see of Utrecht and the earlier papal action to defend Willibrord's successors against the claims of the bishop of Cologne.[7] His cathedral was dedicated to Christ, and the ruined church he found from earlier days he dedicated to St Martin – a replica of the Canterbury pattern. The death of Pippin in 715 marked a setback to the mission and a revolt in Frisia; but after 719 the work was resumed with support from the new ruler, Charles Martel. For the next twenty years Willibrord laboured on, dying at the advanced age of eighty-one in 739 at the monastery he had founded at Echternach near Trier with land granted to him by queen Plectrudis, and other members of the royal family. His kalendar reflects his close associations with the church there as well as with his own native land, with Ireland and also with Rome.[8]

Although little can be deduced about Willibrord's character or the nature of his spiritual teaching, the richness and significance of his missionary activities are reflected not only in the testimonies of Bede, Eddius and later Boniface, who had for a while worked with him, but also in the manuscripts which remain from Echternach from this period.[9] These are of interest both intrinsically as a corpus of material from one place, and also for their affinities to Northumbrian manuscripts of the same period, notably the Lindisfarne gospels and the Durham gospels. The calligrapher of the Durham and Echternach gospels seems to have been the same person, perhaps the master of Eadfrith the artist of the Lindisfarne gospels. Links between Willibrord's foundation and the mother house of Northumbrian Christianity are confirmed by a story in both lives of St Cuthbert about the miraculous cure of one of Willibrord's monks at the shrine of the saint while on a visit to Lindisfarne.[10] These gospels reveal an interesting fusion of Irish and Italian influences as might be expected, being evidence for active collaboration between artists of different traditions. The Echternach gospels may indeed have been a gift for Willibrord from the community at Lindisfarne, perhaps upon the foundation of his monastery. Other manuscripts associated later with Echternach also reflect this blend of traditions.

There is a window upon the way in which the marriage of learning and art might serve to express and deepen the essential spirituality of this monastic missionary world in the poem *De Abbatibus*. It is a text rich in visual imagery capturing the manifold aspects of monastic life in the Lindisfarne connection, and as such amply reflects the rich beauty of the illuminated manuscript material remaining from that period. At one point it describes the sanctity and posthumous miracles of a monastic artist, Ultan:

> He was a blessed priest of the Irish race, and he could ornament books with fair marking, and by this art he accordingly made the shape of the letters beautiful one by one, so that no modern scribe could equal him. It is no wonder if a worshipper of the Lord could do such things, when already the creator spirit had taken control of his fingers and had fired his dedicated mind towards the stars. . . . He taught the brothers, so that they might seize the light above.[11]

Behind this glimpse of an artist at work lay a community whose spiritual roots also lay with Egbert in Ireland. In its theology it echoes directly Bede's description of Caedmon's gifts displaying the glory of the Creator; but in its spirituality of the heavenly light it perpetuates the vision of Iona, the transfiguration of saints like Columba himself.

There is an important retrospect upon the career and significance of St Willibrord in the life of him written by Alcuin and commissioned by Beornrade, abbot of Echternach almost fifty years after the saint's death. It is heavily dependent upon Bede's account in his *History* and perhaps also upon an earlier Irish life, now lost.[12] Beornrade was a kinsman as well as a successor, so the account begins with a description of the monastery founded by Willibrord's father on Spurn Head, dedicated to St Andrew, a similar foundation to that described in *De Abbatibus*. Alcuin's sources augment Bede's outline in several important respects. They tell how, when Willibrord went first to Frisia with his companions they lodged at Utrecht until, frustrated by king Radbod's scepticism, they made their way to seek the assistance of Pippin. Alcuin emphasises the momentous significance of papal support, and the metropolitan status of Willibrord, empowered by the gift of the pallium as the pope's mandate for his work. This reliance upon Roman support was to hallmark the English missions, and it sprang directly from the example of Augustine and the memory of St Gregory the great. It was also to initiate important patterns for church reform in the Frankish lands, though these could hardly have been anticipated by Willibrord and later Boniface at the time.[13] When Willibrord could make no headway without Radbod's support, for a time he went north to try and evangelise the Danes. This was not a success, but like Aidan before him he drew to himself a group of young Danes whom he baptised before taking them home by sea. In the course of this expedition Alcuin describes a notable clash with pagan belief on the island of Heligoland. When challenged by the king for breaching a taboo, Willibrord asserted that 'the object of your worship, O King, is not a god but a devil . . . for there is no God but one, who created heaven and earth'.[14] His courage won him great respect, and secured a safe passage. In a summary manner Alcuin intimates the development of a widespread mission church with its clergy and monasteries, and the miracles which accompanied the saint's activities and confrontations with heathenism. They recall also his generosity and compassion, but likewise his sternness towards unjust landowners in a pattern reminiscent of St Columba. In that tradition he proved a strong exorcist, and also a foreteller of the doom of kings. At his death in Echternach his sanctity was revealed by 'a sweet and marvellous fragrance', evidence of the ministrations of angels it was believed. Like Aidan before him, his soul's departure was witnessed by a monk as a column of heavenly light. His shrine became a place of healing and deliverance.

Frisia remained throughout the eighth century a frontier zone for Christian mission. But Willibrord's persistence and example laid a sure foundation already evident in his own lifetime. One of his disciples from England, Boniface, proved perhaps the most remarkable missionary of the whole period. It is fortunate that his extensive remaining correspondence affords an unique insight into his mind as well as his manifold activities.[15] Boniface, born Winfryth, came from Devon, perhaps near Crediton, and received his monastic formation first at Exeter then at Nursling near Winchester. In his formal education he was beneficiary both of Aldhelm and of Theodore's school at Canterbury, and during the reign of Ine of Wessex emerged as an able cleric capable of handling a delicate diplomatic mission on behalf of the church in Wessex to the archbishop of Canterbury. But like some of his Northumbrian contemporaries his heart lay not in a career in England but in missionary work overseas. In 716 he went for the first time to Frisia but found the area in a state of uprising against Frankish rule. Frustrated he returned to England and was pressed by his brethren to become abbot of Nursling. This he refused and returned with the support of bishop Daniel of Winchester to the continent and made his way to Rome.

The diplomatic overtures which secured the support of pope Gregory II are obscure; but the papal commission to Boniface remains charging him to evangelise the heathen and to use only the formularies of the Roman see in the creation of churches and converts.[16] His approach was to be one of persuasion and teaching 'in a spirit of love and moderation and with arguments suited to their understanding'. He was ordered also to assess the state of the German people on his route north with a view to missionary work at a later date, and this he did in Bavaria and Thuringia. But the death of Radbod laid Frisia open at last to extensive missionary work and thither Boniface went and worked with Willibrord for the next three years. The old bishop wished to make him his coadjutor, but Boniface refused, pleading his obedience to the pope. To Rome he returned, in 722, after a mission to Hesse, to be made bishop by the pope himself on the feast of St Andrew and given the name 'Boniface'. His oath of allegiance to the Roman see remains, as do the commendatory letters sent by the pope to Christians in Germany and in particular in Thuringia which was to be Boniface's first arena of activity. This was a very deliberate act of papal mission strategy as the documents reveal, dependent nonetheless on the active support of the Frankish ruler, Charles Martel.[17] This policy remained the solid foundation for the rest of Boniface's career in the north.

Thuringia and Hesse were the principal areas of Boniface's missionary work. His work was to revive and extend Christian influence in a sensitive and at times dangerous frontier zone, following the footsteps of a venerated Irish martyr and missionary, St Kilian, who had died around 690. Throughout his ministry, the Irish element was never far removed from the scene, sometimes causing difficulty and conflict with Boniface's organising zeal. Nor was he the only missionary from the Frankish church, his most famous contemporary being St Pirmin, the founder of Reichenau. As Boniface's ecclesiastical empire became established and extensive along the eastern side of the Rhine, he ran into opposition also from some of the existing Frankish bishops. Indeed his relations with them were uneven, as he regarded himself bound to the holy see and a pilgrim in a strange land.[18] Some of them were hardly inactive in promoting their own spheres of church and landed interest with the active support of the royal court. One of Boniface's most outspoken critics was the Irish bishop of Salzburg, Virgil, whose heterodox beliefs Boniface reported to Rome. In all his work Boniface relied heavily upon royal assistance, which he received from Charles Martel, and especially later from his successor Carloman, who was a devoted church reformer and ended up as a monk. Like Martin of Tours before him, Boniface professed to stand aloof from court intrigue, condemning worldly prelates among whom he felt an outsider. 'Boniface's authority was derived from Rome; his interpretation of it came from St Paul.'[19] His scruples about the obedience due to the see of Rome in reality enabled him to operate with considerable independence and consistency of aim. Nor was his stance apparently resented by the king, and in the end Boniface forged a lasting community of interest between the papacy and the Frankish monarchy, securing the papal anointing of Pippin in 754 and Frankish military involvement in the plight of the holy see. The extent to which Boniface knew his labours to be utterly dependent upon royal protection until the end of his life is evident in the plaintive letter he wrote in those years to Pippin's chief ecclesiastical adviser, Fulrad of St Denis.[20] In it he commends his fellow-missionaries to his protection, asking that Lullus become his successor.

As Boniface made headway in Thuringia and Hesse, he was able to found monasteries, colonised from England, to act as permanent centres of mission and education. When in 738 Charles Martel defeated the Saxons of

Westphalia, Boniface made a famous appeal to his church at home in England for active support and participation in what he hoped would be a new missionary opportunity.[21] He openly appealed to the historic kinship between the races: 'Have pity on them, because their repeated cry is "We are of one and the same blood and bone!"' Then he returned to Rome to seek the endorsement of pope Gregory III. This he received together with a carefully laid plan for Boniface to supervise the development and reform of the whole church in southern Germany. So Boniface returned as papal legate to achieve the division of Bavaria into four sees in 739 – at Passau, Regensburg, Salzburg and Freising. By 741 there were further dioceses created under Boniface's primacy in Hesse, Thuringia and Franconia, at least three of whose bishops were English: Witta of Fritzlar, Burchard of Wurzburg, and Willibald of Eichstatt.[22] The succession of Carloman to the eastern half of the Frankish empire in 741 gave great impetus to Boniface's attempts to strengthen and reform the Frankish church more widely. With the king's help, he became leader of the whole missionary enterprise, taking over Frisia upon the death of Willibrord in 739. His desire was that the established churches in the western lands should be reformed along the same canonical lines as those now governing the newer German churches. To this end a series of synods were held between 742 and 747 to which bishops and lay magnates came along English lines, whose decisions would affect both parts of the Frankish realm. The reiteration of basic canon law and its effective implementation influenced church life in England also at the council of Cloveshoe of 747.[23] Behind the whole movement lay Boniface's own unique authority, embodying he believed that of the pope himself as the successor of St Peter. In 745 he was given Mainz as his archiepiscopal see, and in the previous year he secured royal approval for his foundation of a monastery at Fulda, for which the pope gave a privilege of exemption in 751. Here he was buried after his final return to Frisia where his missionary career had begun: for in 754 he was martyred with his companions at Dokkum, refusing all resistance, having predicted his end to his friends.

His stature is best captured in the tribute paid to him after his death by Cuthbert, archbishop of Canterbury, in a letter to Lullus:[24] he records how:

> The race of the English . . . deserved to send out afar . . . so distinguished a searcher of scripture, so famous a soldier of Christ, with many well-trained and well-instructed disciples, to spiritual conflicts and to the salvation of souls. . . . We lovingly regard and venerate with praise this man among the foremost and best teachers of the orthodox faith.

The archbishop tells Lullus how a synod of the English church has ordered the day of the saint's martyrdom to be venerated annually, regarding him on a par with Gregory and Augustine as patron saints of the English church. The bishop of Worcester, lately returned from a visit to Boniface, similarly pays tribute in his letter to Lullus to the saint's 'pilgrimage accomplished with mighty effort' and to the example of 'the precepts of so eminent a teacher'.[25] Boniface had commanded the interest and loyalty of leaders in both church and state in England, and letters remain to him from kings of East Anglia and of Kent. By his actions he had exercised metropolitan authority to further mission by development of monastic life and reform of existing church structures. In so doing he had taken models derived from the examples of Augustine and Theodore in England and applied them consistently in a manner which in the end strengthened ties between the continental churches and the papacy in a potent and lasting way. The appeal of his missionary work gave also to the English church a sustained focus of interest, prayer and identity which persisted after his death. The longevity of his life and also that of Willibrord was an important factor here, as was the fearless, open and consistent approach that Boniface employed, evident in his correspondence.

These letters which remain, corroborated by Willibald's *Life* of the saint which was commissioned by Lullus within a decade of Boniface's death, give unique insight into conditions surrounding the mission and its impact upon church life in the eighth century.[26] Further light is shed by the lives of those who worked with him and succeeded him. He emerges as a credible, many-sided and attractive person from the tone of his letters.

The most striking feature of the correspondence is the support he received from friends in England. The prime mover behind the early years of his mission was undoubtedly bishop Daniel of Winchester. His commendation carried Boniface abroad, and to him he wrote on more than one occasion seeking advice. In 723-4 Daniel wrote with advice as to how to preach to the heathen, and a decade later there remains a letter from Boniface in which he outlines to his friend and mentor some of the problems he was encountering in the Frankish church.[27] Through Daniel he retained contact with Nursling, requesting a book of his old abbot Wibert, and probably also with Malmesbury whither the old bishop retired. There is a letter to Pechthelm another pupil of Aldhelm's and bishop of Whithorn.[28] Boniface sought advice and support also from the archbishops of Canterbury, Nothelm and Cuthbert, and also Egbert at York. From Nothelm he sought a copy of pope Gregory's replies to Augustine which he could not find in Rome, asking for a continuation of friendship such as that shown him by Nothelm's predecessor, Berhtwald. He wrote to Egbert in the context of a remonstrance he had sent to Aethelbald, king of Mercia, asking that it be checked first. He also thanked him for gifts of books and asked for copies of Bede's works, sending in return copies of further letters of Gregory the great not available in England. His letter to Cuthbert at Canterbury in 747 reported the progress of the Frankish synods in the reforms of the church in a manner which directly influenced the proceedings at Cloveshoe: they faced common problems, and Boniface reminds the archbishop of the peculiar duties laid upon primates.[29] His contacts extended north to Jarrow and in a letter to Hwaetbert the abbot of the double monastery there he asks for the prayers of the community and for copies of 'the treatises of the monk Bede, that profound student of the scriptures, who, as we have heard, lately shone in your midst like a light of the church'.[30]

Friendship within the common monastic life is very much in evidence throughout Boniface's letters, and one group of such friends was to be found in the royal nunneries. In this, spiritual affinity was built upon ties of natural kinship. Two minsters proved of lasting importance: Minster-in-Thanet and Wimborne. Early in his ministry, Boniface received a letter from the abbess of Minster, Eadburga, encouraging him to see the hand of Providence in his mission so far: in His protection of Boniface, in the seal of papal approval, and in the recent death of the pagan king of Frisia, Radbod. Her prayers for him have secured her spiritual peace and love.[31] Several letters between them remain, including one in which he cautions her against pilgrimage to Rome at that time on grounds of safety, another in which he thanks her for books, and another in which he requests a copy of I Peter 'in letters of gold' to impress the heathen with the source of his authority.[32] To her he also wrote recounting a vision of life after death received by a monk of Much Wenlock,[33] which was later translated and circulated in English. From under her wing sprang one of Boniface's closest friends and helpers, Leoba, who wrote him one of the most charming and moving letters. She was related to the saint by her mother and sought his friendship: 'I am my parent's only child and would like to regard you as my brother, for there is no other man in my family in whom I can put my trust as I can in you'.[34] She concludes with a little poem, very much in the style of Aldhelm, the art of which she learnt from 'my mistress Eadburga'. Two other letters between them remain, but it is in the *Life* of Leoba, written by Rudolf of Fulda and derived from her disciples, that the context and implications of these communications may be found. From Minster Leoba moved to Wimborne under the royal abbess, Tetta, a woman of character and holiness. To her Boniface wrote in 748 asking that Leoba be sent out to Germany to take charge of a convent he was intending to found, at Bischofsheim, for her 'reputation for learning and holiness had spread far and wide'.[35] She proved to be a second Hilda, steeped in learning and commanding the trust and respect of clergy and laity. Stories related by Rudolf indicate her qualities of leadership and her integrity, and soon her community was providing abbesses for other houses, like her friend Tecla, a nun also from Wimborne, who became abbess of Kitzingen. Her rapport with Boniface was so close that when he paid a last visit to her on the way to Frisia he asked that their remains be buried close together at Fulda. 'After these words he gave her his cowl and pleaded with her not to leave her adopted land.'[36] She retained the confidence of the royal family, had privileged access at Fulda, and died in 782 a saint. Venerated at Fulda, miracles occurred at her tomb.

Boniface could not have persevered and prevailed without the moral support of the papacy, to which he attached great importance and from which he derived real strength. He saw himself as the pope's surrogate and emissary, and to judge from the tone of papal letters to him throughout his mission this perception was just. For the papacy proved the backbone to both Willibrord's and Boniface's missions, and by this means, though perhaps inadvertently, the Frankish church was drawn closer into the orbit of Rome. In this expectation of papal involvement in mission, these English church-men were influenced by their contemporaries' understanding of how Gregory had sent Augustine, a vision carefully captured and promoted by Bede in his *History* and elsewhere. To receive the 'pallium', the mark of primacy, meant partnership with the successor of St Peter in the apostolic work of evangelisation.

The foundation laid by pope Sergius in consecrating Willibrord as mission-ary archbishop to the Frisians in 695 was followed up by the very active involvement of his successors in the support and supervision of Boniface's mission. The first of these was Gregory II, a protégé of Sergius who ruled from 715-731 with great determination and skill. His initial charge to Boniface remains, as does the oath taken by the saint binding him to complete obedi-ence to the holy see and its practices. In return for this Boniface went to Germany armed with a strong letter of commendation and direction to the German bishops. In it the pope expresses concern at heterodox sects of sub-Christian origin 'serving idols under the guise of the Christian religion'. Paganism is perceived as blindness to the Creator.[37] There is similar concern for orthodoxy in belief and morals in his formal charge to Boniface as bishop, warning him against accepting unworthy or corrupt priests or repre-sentatives of heretical sects, and laying upon him the standard Roman fourfold division of ecclesiastical revenue, for himself, his clergy, the poor and pilgrims, and for fabric. In everything he is to march in step with Roman custom, in which the pope claims Boniface is well-grounded. His sphere of mission is to be the eastern bank of the Rhine, for which the pope seeks the protection of Charles Martel, the Frankish ruler.[38] This was in 722. The next year Gregory sent a letter of encouragement to Boniface in response to early reports of his successes, and in 724 he followed this up by a further letter of commendation to the Christians in Thuringia, reminding them of the fundamental missionary duty of the church. He urges them to accept baptism at Boniface's hands, charging the new converts 'not to adore idols nor make bloody sacrifices, because God does not accept them'.[39] In the course of his activities, Boniface referred matters about which he was uncertain to Rome, like Augustine before him. These include degrees of consanguinity in marriage; circumstances permitting remarriage; the protection of priests upon oath and the proper celebration of the mass; eating of food sacrificed to idols, the obedience due from those dedicated since childhood to monastic life, and the inviolability of baptism in the name of the Trinity even at the hands of unworthy priests. The pope in reply deals with the place of lepers in church and the duty of monks to remain put even in times of plague, for 'no man can escape the hand of God.' He cautions the puritan Boniface against refusing to associate socially with errant priests: constant and gentle persuasion may succeed where correction has failed.[40] There are similar words of guidance in the letter by which the new pope invested Boniface with the pallium in 732: against the eating of horseflesh; justifying the commemoration of the Christian dead, though no others; permitting rebaptism in cases of doubt or when the priest sacrificed to Jupiter! The pope urges also against remarriage after death of a spouse, bars homicides from the eucharist except at the point of death, laying upon them a lifelong pattern of fasting, and condemning sale of slaves by Christians to pagans, 'for it is a crime against nature'.[41]

This next pope, Gregory III, was no less ardent a supporter of Boniface. He became pope in 731 and ruled for ten stormy years, during which both conviction and necessity caused him to look north to the interests and support of the Frankish realm. He was the first to seek military help from Charles Martel in 739 and 740 against the Lombards, though this was not forthcoming. He also took an active interest in the English church, receiving archbishop Tatwine of Canterbury in Rome, and in 735 sending the pallium to Egbert archbishop of York. In 738 Boniface revisited Rome and told his companions at home about his reception by the pope, and the letter sent in 739 outlining the reform of the Bavarian church at Boniface's hands also remains.[42] It endorses his creation of new sees and conformity wherever possible to Roman practice by clergy and bishops. Boniface is to attend a regional synod 'vested with Apostolic authority to act as our representative', but to serve as a peripatetic missionary bishop without a fixed see. He is not to shrink 'from difficult and protracted journeys in the service of the Christian faith': his missionary duty remains paramount.

Gregory's successor was his close disciple, Zacharias, a Greek with a devotion to the memory of Gregory the great. He ruled from 741-752, during which time he cultivated strong links between the papacy and the Frankish church and kingdom: his authority lay behind the succession of Frankish synods organised by Boniface, and in 750 he sanctioned the deposition of the last Merovingian king and consecration of Pippin in 751. The letters which remain between pope and archbishop reveal the growing strength of this connection.

In his letter greeting the new pope upon his accession, Boniface reveals a keen expectation of continued support in return for his loyalty. He reports the foundation of the sees of Wurzburg, Buraburg and Erfurt for which he seeks papal endorsement, and indicates how Carloman was urging the holding of synods to reform the Frankish church. His picture of the western part of that church is grim and he relates in some detail the proclivities of many of the clergy being corrupt and venal. Some of the bishops are no better, being 'shiftless drunkards, addicted to the chase who march armed into battle'. He requests the pope to nominate a successor to his position and challenges a reported papal decision in favour of an illegitimate marriage. Boniface appeals instead to the judgement of a synod at London held under Augustine and the Kentish missionaries. He warns also of how the ill repute of some of the clergy in Rome damages the credibility of Christianity among the pagans, as does purported papal leniency towards Frankish prelates who have appealed to Rome after being censured for their crimes. To all these matters the pope made reply, confirming the new sees and the forthcoming synod and entering into a long sermon of moral theology castigating corrupt clergy, but refusing on canonical grounds to name Boniface's successor at this stage.[43]

Perhaps the most interesting document records the meeting of a Roman synod in 745 at which Boniface requested help to deal with the claims of two heretics in the Frankish church, one a Gaul, the other an Irishman. These men worked miracles and exercised a charismatic leadership, becoming cult figures. One of them claimed veneration as a saint in his own lifetime! The Irishman was heterodox in his moral teaching, refusing all authority and proclaiming a universalist gospel. The synod read the so-called *Life* of the living saint, a letter claiming to come from Jesus himself, and also a prayer invoking demons as angels. The synod had little difficulty in condemning these conceits. Boniface's struggle with sub-Christian teaching and syncretism is illustrated also in a letter the pope sent him in response to a protest by Virgil of Salzburg cautioning him against being over-scrupulous in insisting that a man be re-baptized because the illiterate priest used the phrase: 'Baptizo te in nomine patria, et filia et spiritus sancti'(sic). In this case poor Latin could be given the benefit of the doubt.[44] Elsewhere Boniface had taken issue with Virgil over his gnostic cosmology. Papal authority lay behind the actions of synods in both the Frankish and English church in this decade to reform abuses and strengthen the integrity of church life and ministry. Pope Zacharias also played a key role in support of Boniface's foundation of Fulda as a centre of monastic and missionary life. His charter of privilege in response to Boniface's own letter of commendation gave complete exemption and protection to the place wherein the saint intended to be buried.[45]

Pope Zacharias died in 752 and was succeeded by Stephen to whom Boniface wrote a letter of greeting, delayed by heathen pillage and burning of more than thirty churches. The next year he reported on the background to Willibrord's mission in resistance to the claims of the see of Cologne to Utrecht.[46] In the same year, 753, the pope invited a military intervention by Pippin to rescue Rome from the Lombards, this time successfully. In 754 he went himself across the Alps to plead with the king and to anoint him and his family. Later that year the Franks came and defeated the Lombard king, returning again in 756 and creating despite Byzantine protest the foundations of the papal state.[47] Thus, at the very moment of his martyrdom, the connection which Boniface had laboured so hard to secure between the papacy and the Frankish kingdom and church became an alliance of portentous significance.

The double challenge of decay in the church and resistance from paganism emerges also in the theology of mission which may be discerned in the varied correspondence of Boniface. Because of the longer history of the Frankish church, both problems appear more complex and at time intractable than in England, although comparison between the acts of the Frankish synods and those at Cloveshoe in 747 reveal strong similarities in conditions, as do the strongly penitential preoccupations behind issues of moral theology. The most famous adumbration of missionary theology is found in the letter written by bishop Daniel of Winchester to Boniface early in his mission.[48] As his mentor, he was clearly in a strong position to offer the distilled wisdom of the English church in the matter of evangelising the heathen. The approach he recommends may be discerned throughout the theology remaining from this period. Instead of getting drawn into disputes about the genealogies of the gods, it is better to indicate that the fact of generation belies an eternal existence. He advances the classic argument for monotheism, the impossibility of an infinite regress. He challenges both the need for and the nature of heathen sacrifices, and mocks the poor reward of their gods, consigning them to the cold and barren lands of the north. Quite shamelessly, the bishop points out the prosperity of the Christians in the southern lands from which the faith emanated: 'The heathen are frequently to be reminded of the supremacy of the Christian world and of the fact that they who still cling to outworn beliefs are in a very small minority'. From such superstitions baptism and the rational belief in an almighty creator God liberate people. Such apologetic buttressed the unequivocal missionary vision with which Boniface was motivated: his hope was 'that the Word of the Lord may run its triumphant course and the gospel of Christ may be glorified among the heathen'.[49] He was confident that intercession secured the path of mission, and sure too that corruption in his mother church would undermine his labours.[50] He was not averse to spelling this out to the rulers and bishops of his own people. Bishop Daniel of Winchester remained a guide to the end of his life, and a final exchange of letters between these two friends remains in which Boniface seeks help and support in his dealings with the Frankish church.[51] In his letter to archbishop Cuthbert of Canterbury he gives a full review of his labours to date (747), and their rationale and consistency, indicating how purposeful reform of the church is the necessary concomitant of effective mission. In the light of his own long experience he does not baulk at pointing out to his younger colleague some of the particular weaknesses of the English church: the propensity of nuns to journey to Rome and fall into vice on the way; lay-appropriation of church lands and especially of monasteries; flamboyant fads in dress among clerics and monks; drunkenness, and 'the forced labour of monks upon royal buildings'.[52] In the end by his willing countenance of martyrdom, Boniface revealed the costly self-sacrifice which underlay his whole approach to mission: like St Paul, he was willing to spend and be spent in the service of the gospel.

Boniface considered his own commitment and role to be but the prelude to a sustained mission. In his letters the way in which he developed a reliable and devoted team around him, and worked to secure successors to his labours is everywhere apparent. This is most evident in the letter he wrote to Fulrad of St Denis at the very end of his life. Fulrad wielded great influence at court and went with the king to Italy in 754. Boniface openly asks him for consideration to be given to the future of the English missionaries: 'some are priests spending their lives in lonely places in the service of the church and the people. Some are monks in cloisters or children learning to read. Others are men of mature age who have been my companions and helpers for many years.' He fears their acute vulnerability being foreigners without a powerful patron after his death; so he asks that his coadjutor Lullus be nominated as his successor and their shepherd. Central to this future in Boniface's mind was his own foundation at Fulda. The manner of its foundation is told in the *Life of Sturm* by Eigil, abbot of Fulda. Sturm was the first abbot of Fulda, and Eigil his constant companion for twenty years and in due time his successor, dying in 822.

Sturm was from a noble Christian family in Germany who placed himself in the hands of Wigbert, one of Boniface's disciples at Fritzlar. After ordination to the priesthood he felt a vocation to become a hermit: 'this idea haunted him at every moment of the day, until on a divine impulse he opened his heart to his spiritual master, the archbishop Boniface'.[53] He encouraged this and in due course sent Sturm to search out a suitable site for a small monastery. Solitude and safety were their paramount concerns and it was only on the third reconnaissance that they were able to locate the place which became eventually the monastery of Fulda. The whole story of the search is told as an example of monastic obedience, being biblical in its prophetic character. Boniface for his part sought permission from the king to acquire the place though not without opposition from certain quarters. Carloman granted his request and induced the local nobility to co-operate. Boniface himself visited the place and ordered the construction of the first church and the clearing of the wooded site. It was to be a place of austerity, no wine was to be drunk and the Rule of St Benedict was to be adhered to. Boniface came annually for a time of retreat, praying on a hill which later became known as 'Mons Episcopi'. At about the time Lioba was summoned from England to lead the community at Bischofsheim, Sturm was sent with some of his brethren on a tour of other monasteries, mainly in Italy and Rome, to observe how the monastic life was lived. Upon his return he was bidden by the bishop to fashion life at Fulda according to the best practice he had witnessed. This he did, leading by example as the first abbot. The reputation of the place grew as did its influence under Boniface's patronage. In terms of spiritual strategy, Fulda proved counterpart to Leoba's community at Bischofsheim, and she and Sturm were regarded as the spiritual heirs of Boniface, and their houses the heart of his continuing mission. After his death it was to Fulda that his body was brought for burial, as he had wished, despite opposition by bishop Lullus and his people at Mainz. His tomb soon became a shrine and place of miracles.

After Boniface's death, conflict broke out between the two who could with good reason most claim to be his immediate spiritual successors – Sturm, abbot of Fulda, and Lullus, bishop of Mainz. According to the *Life of Sturm*, this was as a result of jealousy on the part of Lullus, who in the end secured Sturm's exile at Pippin's command to Jumièges for over two years.[54] Lullus intruded his own nominee as abbot who was never accepted by the monks; they finally persuaded the king to restore Sturm to favour. 'He released him from the jurisdiction of Bishop Lullus and commanded him to return with the privileges which blessed pope Zacharias had formerly granted to Boniface.[55] Under Sturm's renewed rule the monastery was steadily developed and endowed and a shrine created over the tomb of St Boniface. He played an active part also in the evangelisation of the Saxons which followed the victorious armies of Charlemagne after 773. This proved no easy matter and the conflict against them lasted for thirty years, with periods of apostasy from Christianity and invasion which on one occasion threatened Fulda itself. Sturm was himself a great preacher and tireless missionary: 'he seized every opportunity to impress on them in his preaching that they should forsake idols and images, accept the Christian faith, destroy the temples of the gods, cut down the groves and build sacred churches in their stead'.[56] Like Boniface before him he favoured at times direct action against pagan shrines. He died as the king was returning for his second major assault on the Saxons, with words of forgiveness on his lips, even towards his old rival, Lullus, 'who always took sides against me'.

The advance against the pagan Saxons elicited steady interest and support from England. Lullus received many letters from churchmen and rulers there, and was himself an active correspondent, seeking resources from home. In this way the writings of Bede became steadily of increasing value to the English missionaries and reformers on the continent.[57] The mission to the Frisians continued with Northumbrian help for many years. Utrecht was given after Boniface's death to his Frankish disciple, the priest and abbot Gregory, and in 767 a bishop Aluberht was consecrated at York to work among the Old Saxons.[58] With him went a Frisian pupil of Gregory's called Liudger for instruction by Alcuin, then master of the school there.[59] He returned after a second visit 'well educated and having with him a supply of books' to Gregory at Utrecht. Later he became the first bishop of Munster ruling over both Frisians and Saxons. His *Life* mentions also Leofwine who came from England as a 'holy and learned missionary priest, 'saying that he had been commanded in fearful fashion by the Lord with a threefold admonition that he must render service in teaching the people on the borders of the Franks and the Saxons by the river Yssel'. With Gregory's support he established a mission church and base at Deventer, but this was destroyed by the Saxons who feared his progress. After a setback he eventually returned, and the story of his activities is recorded in the *Life* written in the ninth century by Hucbald of St Amand.[60] It amplifies somewhat the account in the *Life of Liudger* and indicates the impact of his missions into Saxon lands. The reasons for pagan antagonism are vividly related as is the sympathy of his noble supporter, Folcbert, who tried to protect him from his enemies. Not at all deterred Leofwine went directly to the local annual gathering of the Saxons. He appeared in their midst 'clothed in his priestly garments, bearing a cross in his hands and a copy of the gospels in the crook of his arm'. He proclaimed himself an ambassador of Almighty God to the Saxons, with a divine command to become converted or to fall under the sway of an alien king. This caused them embarrassment, and upon reflection they granted Leofwine safe passage amongst them. After his death and burial at Deventer, the Saxons again attacked and destroyed the church, but in 775 Liudger was sent by the successor to Gregory to rescue the relics and to rebuild the church.

About that time a Northumbrian synod despatched Willehad, another friend of Alcuin's, to Frisia.[61] At Charlemagne's command he went on to evangelise the Saxons until their insurrection in 782. He then went to Rome before settling at Echternach, until in 785 conditions permitted him to resume his work among the Saxons whose leader had submitted to Charlemagne. In 787 he became first bishop of Bremen, and died in 789 having just consecrated its cathedral. A letter of Alcuin's in which he mentions Willehad with great fondness indicates also that the vision of these missionaries extended to include the Slavs and the Huns with whom the king was engaged in warfare. But the ruthless manner of the king's military operations, and his forcible attitude towards conversion created difficulties for the English missionaries as well as deep resentment among the Saxons and others. In a letter of 796 to the king, Alcuin did not flinch from setting out the spirit of mission as it had been practised by his fellow-countrymen. He questions the wisdom of imposing the tithe on newly converted people, a custom which established Christian populations were at this time finding hard to accept. He criticises the indiscriminate use of baptism: 'the body cannot receive the sacrament of baptism if the soul has not first received the truth of faith'. The words he cites are from St Jerome.[62] He reiterates the order of Christian instruction laid down by St Augustine, and in a related letter to one of Charlemagne's magnates, he quite trenchantly asserts his position:

Faith, as St Augustine says, is a matter of will, not necessity. A man can be attracted into faith, not forced. He can be forced to be baptised, but that is useless for faith, except in infancy. . . . A grown man should answer for himself about his beliefs and desires. If he professes faith falsely, he will not have true salvation. . . . If the light yoke and easy load of Christ were preached to the hard Saxon race as keenly as tithes were levied and the penalty of the law imposed for the smallest faults, perhaps they would not react against the rite of baptism. The teachers of the faith should be schooled in the examples of the apostles. They should be preachers, not predators, trusting in the goodness of Him who said, 'Do not take purse or wallet'.[63]

Under Charlemagne, conversion by force had become state policy. But he seems not to have resented the remonstrances of Alcuin which were persistent: he was heard, but perhaps in this matter, seldom heeded. Behind him lay the long years of effective English missionary work rooted in the memory and theology of their mother church. In these sharp words, Alcuin articulated unequivocally the principles of the disciples of St Gregory the great.

In the tenth century, the memory and example of this missionary tradition inspired English missions in Norway and Sweden which created lasting links between England and Scandinavia for many years.[64] From their reading of Bede, and their cognizance of the nature of the Carolingian reforms of the church which owed so much to the influence of Alcuin and before him Boniface, English churchmen learnt again that monasticism and mission flourished or waned together. Practical and consistent reform was indispensable to their progress and credibility, but at the heart of both lay the miracle of sanctity to mediate the reality of the gospel to both Christians and pagans.

ABBREVIATIONS

ASE   *Anglo-Saxon England*, ed P. Clemoes et al (Cambridge 1972 onwards)

APW   *Aldhelm, the Prose Works*, ed M. Lapidge & M. Herren (Ipswich 1979)

C   Confession of St Patrick, tr. R P C Hanson in *The Life & Writings of the historical St Patrick* (New York 1983)

CS   Camden Society publications

D   *Dialogues of Sulpicius Severus*, tr. A. Roberts, ed Schaff & Wace in select library of Nicene & post-Nicene Fathers, 2nd series, vol. XI (Michigan 1964 & 1973)

DT   *Bede on the Temple*, tr. S. Connolly (Liverpool 1995)

E   *Epistle to Coroticus by St Patrick*, tr. R. P. C. Hanson (New York 1983)

EETS   Early English Text Society

EHD   *English Historical Documents*, vol. I, ed D. Whitelock (London 1979)

EHR   *English Historical Review*

ep.   epistle

Hab   Bede *Lives of the Abbots*, tr. D. H. Farmer in *Age of Bede* (London 1983)

H&S   *Councils & Ecclesiastical Documents*, ed Haddan & Stubbs (Oxford 1869)

HE   Bede *Historia Ecclesiastica* tr. B. Colgrave & R. Mynors (Oxford 1969)

HF   Gregory of Tours *History of the Franks*, tr. L. Thorpe (London 1974)

inst   institutes

JTS   *Journal of Theological Studies*

MGH   *Monumenta Germaniae Historica*, ed G Pertz et al SS Scriptores, vols I-XXXII; Epp: Epistolae, vols I-VII (Hanover 1926, Berlin 1887)

ODCC   *Oxford Dictionary of the Christian Church*, F. L. Cross (Oxford 1974)

ODP   *Oxford Dictionary of Popes*, J. N. D. Kelly (Oxford 1986)

ODS   *Oxford Dictionary of Saints*, D. H. Farmer (Oxford 1976)

PL   *Patrologiae Cursus Completus*, Series Latina, ed J P Migne (Paris 1844)

reg   regula

RHS   Royal Historical Society

s.a   sub anno

SCH   *Studies in Church History*

T   C H Talbot, *The Anglo-Saxon Missionaries in Germany* (London 1954)

TRHS   *Transactions of the Royal Historical Society*

VC   *Adomnan's Life of Columba*, ed Anderson (Oxford 1991) & ed Sharpe (London 1995)

VCA   Anonymous *Life of Cuthbert*, ed Colgrave (Cambridge, 1985)

VCF   Anonymous *Life of Ceolfrith*, tr. Whitelock = *EHD* 155

VCL   *Life of Columbanus*, tr. D. C. Munro (Philadelphia 1895)

VCP   Bede *Prose Life of Cuthbert*, ed Colgrave (Cambridge 1985)

VG   *Earliest life of Gregory the Great*, ed Colgrave (Cambridge 1985)

Vg   *Vulgate*

VM   Sulpicius Severus *Life of Martin* (cf 'D')

VS   *Life of Samson*, tr. T. Taylor (London 1925)

VW   Eddius *Life of Wilfrid*, ed Colgrave (Cambridge 1985)

WMDA William of Malmesbury *De Antiquitate Glastonie Ecclesie*, ed J. Scott (Ipswich 1981)

REFERENCES

PROLOGUE: I. MARTIN – pages 13-26

1 Gregory of Tours' *History of the Franks* 10.31 (tr.Lewis Thorpe; London 1974) (hereafter HF)
2 The problems of Martin's chronology are well discussed by C. E. Stancliffe in *St Martin and his hagiographer*, pp111ff
3 For the early life of St Martin by Sulpicius Severus, see *Life of St Martin* in edition of his *Works*, 2-4 (hereafter VM)
4 ibid. *Dialogues* 3.15 (hereafter D)
5 There are some chronological difficulties here: cf Stancliffe op.cit. p134f
6 Cf references to Hilary in Stancliffe op.cit. passim, especially pp65-6
7 Discussed in Stancliffe op.cit. p71f
8 Cited ibid p31
9 Well discussed in Stancliffe op.cit p328f
10 HF 8.15
11 VM 5-6
12 ibid 14
13 ibid 15 & 17
14 D 2.4
15 VM 22; cf. D 3.6
16 D 2.13
17 D 3.8-9
18 VM 7
19 Stancliffe op.cit. pp23f
20 D 1.24
21 VM 17
22 D 3.6
23 VM 18
24 VM 22
25 VM 24
26 There is a useful analysis of these in Stancliffe's appendix op.cit. pp363f
27 D 3.9
28 VM 18
29 VM 3
30 D 2.1-2
31 cf P. Rousseau, *Ascetics, authority and the church in the age of Jerome and Cassian*; for an earlier period, see H.von Campenhausen, *Ecclesiastical authority and spiritual power in the church of the first three centuries.*
32 D 3.2
33 Stancliffe op.cit p143, 293
34 HF 2.13f
35 see W. E. Klingshirn, ed *Caesarius of Arles: Life, Testament & Letters.*
36 well-discussed in Stancliffe op.cit. 265f; cf also H. Chadwick, *Priscillian of Avila.*
37 VM 26 end
38 D 3.15

39 HF 2.1
40 Sulpicius Severus' *Sacred History* 2.50
41 D 3.11-13
42 VM 20 and D 2.5
43 D 3.4 and 8
44 VM 8 and 17
45 VM 19 and 25
46 VM 23
47 D 2.2; 3.7 and 14
48 VM 2, 5, 6, 9; and Sulpicius' Third Letter
49 D 2.10-13
50 Stancliffe op.cit p65-6
51 D 2.13 and 14

PART 1: II. PATRICK – Pages 27-37

1 cited in A W Haddan & W Stubbs ed *Councils and Ecclesiastical Documents relating to Great Britain and Ireland*, 3 vols (hereafter H&S + vol): volume 1. 3-5
2 *Historia ecclesiastica* (hereafter HE) 1.7; his authority here is Gildas.
3 Life 'B' of St Dunstan in W. Stubbs, ed *Memorials of St Dunstan*, cap3.
4 A. Hamilton Thompson, ed *Bede: his life, times and writings*, p135 n.4 (Levison); cf J. M. Wallace-Hadrill, *Bede's Historia ecclesiastica: a historical commentary*, pp12f
5 P. Salway, *Roman Britain*, p714f
6 H&S 1.7-10
7 cited ibid 10-12
8 ibid 9
9 Wallace-Hadrill op.cit 13-14 & 209;cf Bede HE 1.8
10 H&S 1.15-16
11 ibid 2.xxi (addenda): ex Sulpicius Severus *Hist. Sac.*, 2.51
12 *De laude sanctorum* cited in H&S 2 xxi cf Paulinus of Nola ep 28.4 tr. P G Walsh
13 Bede HE 1.17-21; cf Wallace-Hadrill op cit 216. This is fully discussed by E. A. Thompson in *St Germanus of Auxerre and the ending of Roman Britain*
14 Bede HE 1.13; see E. A. Thompson, *Who was St Patrick?* 57f & 170f; also H&S 1.25-6
15 Bede HE 1.4; H&S 2.290
16 Thompson op.cit p170-2; cf H&S 1.16; also O. Chadwick, *Cassian* p208-9
17 C. Thomas, *Christianity in Roman Britain* Chapter 11; HE 3.4
18 Summary and bibliography in D. Wilson, *The archaeology of Anglo-Saxon England* pp208-9
19 H&S 2.72-3
20 E. Gilson, *History of Christian Philosophy in the Middle Ages* p95; cf O. Chadwick op.cit. p149
21 R. P. C. Hanson, *The date of St Patrick*
22 R. P. C. Hanson *The Life and Writings of the Historical St Patrick*: hereafter "Confession" = C & "Epistle" = E; Chapters from Hanson's edition. Here – C.1 cf E.10
23 C.9-11
24 C.16
25 C.46
26 E.12
27 cf N. K. Chadwick, *The age of the Saints in the early Celtic Church* p23f; also Hanson op.cit. introduction p44-7
28 C.32-3; E.14
29 E.1, 6

30 E.10,
31 C.15
32 C.23; cf Chadwick op.cit p27
33 C.61
34 C.27-8
35 C.34
36 C.37
37 C.40
38 C.44, 55, 59
39 C.34; cf C.51
40 E.2; cf C.14
41 E.3 & C.50 cf C.38
42 E.3 cf E.17
43 E.6
44 E.16
45 C.4 cf 14; E.5
46 cf Chadwick op.cit 27-8
47 C.12 cf 23
48 C.17-21
49 C.24-5
50 C.20 & 29
51 E.12 & 13; cf C.41
52 C.41-3
53 C.44 & 47
54 C.49 & 55
55 C.51-3
56 C.55 & 59
57 E.9
58 cf C.8
59 C.41; 54-60

III. SAMSON AND GILDAS – pages 39-54

1 *Life of Columbanus* by Jonas, (ed B. Frusch MGH SRM 4 1902 p1-157 (part 2 1920) p822-7, ch 47; cf M. Redknap, *The Christian Celts*, p 13f; also D. Wilson, ed *Archaeology of Anglo-Saxon England*, p 209f

2 cf E. G. Bowen, *Saints, Seaways and settlements in celtic lands*

3 cf W. Davies, *An early Welsh microcosm: studies in the Llandaff charters*

4 cf *The Christian Celts*, op cit p50f

5 see entry for Fastidius in *ODCC*, and discussion in A. di Berardino, ed *Patrology* IV, p 468-9

6 cf O. Chadwick, *Cassian,* chapter 4 on Grace

7 cf C. Thomas, *The early Christian archaeology of North Britain*

8 cf N. K. Chadwick, *The age of the saints in the early Celtic church*, p49f

9 see introduction by D. Simon Evans to his edition of G. H. Doble's *Lives of the Welsh saints*; also E. G. Bowen, *The settlements of the Celtic saints in Wales*

10 cf relevant entries in ODS; also in G. H. Doble op cit

11 T. Taylor, tr. *Life of St Samson of Dol*, (hereafter VS) Prologue and Part II

12 VS Prologue 2

13 cf Taylor, op cit introduction 18; cf H&S 2 69f

14 Taylor ibid

15 V S 1.1

16 V S 1.3-5

17 V S 1.6
18 V S 1.29-30
19 V S 1.40
20 V S 1.42
21 V S 1.7
22 V S 1.12
23 V S 1.21, 11, 14
24 V S 1.36
25 V S 1.38
26 V S 1.40-1
27 V S 1.20
28 cf Taylor op.cit. introduction pxi, also V S 1.42
29 V S 1.44; n.b. Taylor's note on affinities to the Mozarabic Rite
30 cf Taylor's introduction pxii; cf V S 1.46
31 cf relevant entries in ODS
32 V S 1.48
33 V S 1.50; cf 58 & 32
34 V S 2.13; cf 1.26
35 V S 1.60
36 V S 2.9
37 V S 2.5
38 V S 2.3
39 V S 2.5
40 V S 2.11
41 V S 2.12
42 cf H&S 2.71f; also H F 4.20; cf V S 1.61 – 'In Brittany and Romania'
43 see D. Dumville, *Gildas: new approaches* p79-80
44 Gildas, *The Ruin of Britain* tr. M. Winterbottom p36
45 see the article by R. Sharpe, 'Gildas as a father of the church' in *Gildas: new approaches* p191f
46 cf Columbanus ep 1 in G. S. M. Walker, ed *Opera*
47 see D Dumville, 'Gildas and Uinniau' in *Gildas: new approaches* 1984 p207f
48 Adomnan's *Life of Columba* ed Anderson, p95
49 R. Sharpe art cit p199
50 see W. Davies *An early Welsh microcosm*, op cit
51 The *Fragmenta* and *Penitential* of Gildas are in H&S 1.108f and are also translated by Winterbottom op cit p80f
52 Gildas *De Excidio* preface p13f (Winterbottom's edition)
53 ibid p25-7
54 ibid p19
55 ibid p28
56 Bede HE 1.22
57 Gildas *De Excidio* p14
58 ibid p15
59 ibid p51-2 cf p69
60 ibid p28
61 ibid p33
62 ibid p54f; cf p70f and p76
63 ibid p79
64 cf Bede HE 2.2

IV. COLUMBA & COLUMBANUS – pages 55-74

1 Adomnan of Iona *Life of St Columba* tr. R Sharpe (cited hereafter as VC) p 11; VC3.2; 2.25; 2.1; 3.4; & note P317-8

2 VC Preface (p104-5) cf note p244

3 discussed in Sharpe 12-13; VC 3.3

4 ibid p19; cf p354

5 VC 3.5 (cf p355f) & 1.49 (cf p312f)

6 HE 3.4; cf Sharpe op cit 50f; also T. O. Clancy & G. Markus *Iona: the earliest poetry of a Celtic monastery'* p23-4 (cited hereafter as 'Iona')

7 VC 2.32-5

8 VC 2.9

9 cf Sharpe op cit p284; VC 1.25; 2.29; 3.15 & 23; 2.44-5; cf 'Iona' 120

10 cf H&S 2.10f & 137 for lists of abbots and dedications. The matter is well discussed in M. Herbert, *Iona, Kells and Derry*

11 cf Sharpe 34f; see VC 3.19

12 HE 3.2f; VC 1.1 cf Sharpe p252f

13 Herbert op cit 16-26; Sharpe of cit 245-7

14 VC 3.5; cf A. Anderson & M. O. Anderson *Adomnan's Life of Columba*, 111f; & Sharpe 357f

15 'Iona' 96f; citation from 3

16 discussed 'Iona' 39f

17 ibid 105-7:'Amra' stanzas 1 & 4

18 stanzas 6 & 8

19 discussed in 'Iona' 129f

20 ibid 149

21 ibid 164f; cf also 81-95; cf 'Culdee Rule' in H&S 2.119f

22 see 'Iona' 211f

23 HE 5.15

24 see Anderson op cit introduction p91; also Sharpe 51

25 printed in H&S 2.30f

26 cf 'Iona' 30f

27 HE 5.15

28 VC 2.46; cf HE 4.26; cf Sharpe 46

29 discussed in Sharpe 350

30 HE 5.21; cf also 5.15

31 HE 5.15; cf discussion in Sharpe 48f

32 HE 3.4: Sharpe p55f & p245f

33 VC preface 2

34 VC 1.1

35 ibid; cf HE 3.2f; discussed by Sharpe p250f

36 VC 1.36; cf Sharpe p296f

37 VC 3.5; cf Sharpe p355

38 VC 1.2;

39 VC 1.28

40 VC 1.37

41 VC 1.40

42 VC 1.44

43 VC 1.43; cf1.1 (Gregory's *Dialogues* 2.35 & 4.7; see Sharpe p305)

44 VC 2 1-2; 6f

45 VC 2.10 & 12-13; 11 & 17; cf 27 & 34

46 VC 2.41; earlier references are 2.5, 18, 30, 40

47 VC 2.20-1

48 VC 2.22-4
49 VC 2.25
50 VC 2.32-3
51 VC 3.1-4
52 VC 3.6-12
53 VC 3.16; cf 8 & 21
54 VC 3.17
55 VC 3.18
56 VC 3.19; cf 20-1
57 VC 3.22-3
58 HE 3.25
59 Eddius *Life of Wilfrid* ed B. Colgrave, Chapters 21-3 (hereafter VW)
60 HE 3.25
61 HE 5.9, 15, 21-2
62 HE 5.9 and 3.4
63 The Works of Columbanus are edited by G. S. M. Walker; the *Life* by Jonas, translated by D. C. Munro; cf also entry in *ODS*. (Hereafter VCL): ch 8
64 VCL 11
65 VCL 16
66 VCL 28
67 VCL 33
68 VCL 53
69 VCL 56
70 Entry in ODS for St Gall
71 Walker op cit ep 5, p39
72 ibid introduction p. lx & lxvii
73 An excellent summary in J. Leclercq, ed *A history of Christian spirituality* II p33f
74 Walker op cit ep 4 p34
75 ibid ep 5 p56
76 ibid inst 11 p106, and inst 12 & 13 p114f
77 ibid inst 12
78 ibid reg 8 p134f
79 VCL 11
80 VCL 15
81 cf H&S 1.139 for a 7th century view of Irish liturgical and spiritual tradition, including an endorsement of St Benedict on the authority of Gregory the Great.
82 HE 2.4
83 cf Levison, *England and the Continent in the Eighth Century* p458
84 cf J Campbell, 'The First Century of Christianity in England' in *Essays in Anglo-Saxon History* p53f; cf HE 1.33
85 Levison op cit p10
86 cf Campbell art cit p57-8
87 See entry in *ODS* for St Riquier; cf Campbell art cit p58
88 HE 2.15 and 3.18-9
89 HE 3.8; cf discussion in Wallace-Hadrill's commentary (1988) p101, 232. n.b. HE 4.23 for the intention of Hilda to go to Chelles also.

PART 2: V. AUGUSTINE AND PAULINUS – pages 75-92

1 Discussed in R A Markus, 'Gregory the Great's Europe': *J Eccl Hist* 36 (1981) p 24-5; and 'Gregory the Great and a papal missionary strategy' *SCH* 6 (1970) p 29-38.
2 HE 1.32
3 ed B Colgrave, *Earliest life of St Gregory* (hereafter VG)

4 HE 2.20
5 VG p45-54
6 Lapidge & Herren, ed *Aldhelm: the prose works* p70, 108, 125, 131. (Hereafter APW)
7 VG p91
8 EHD 161 = H&S 3.5; cf HE 3.5
9 VG p75 cf HE 2.1
10 HE 1.23
11 EHD 162 & 162
12 VG p79 & 142
13 VG p83-5
14 EHD 163; HE 1.31
15 VG p83
16 EHD 163
17 VG p85
18 VG p89
19 VG p83
20 VG p105f; here p117
21 VG p125
22 HE preface
23 H&S 3.6-12
24 HE 1.27: response 7, p87
25 H&S 3.33f cf Ian Wood, 'The mission of Augustine of Canterbury to the English', p6
26 H&S 3.13 cf Wood art cit p6-7; also HE 2.15
27 H&S 3.17 cf HE 1.32
28 HE 1.25
29 cf J. Campbell, ed *The Anglo-Saxons*, p44, 48-9
30 HE preface
31 HE 1.22
32 HE 1.25
33 HE 1.26 and 33
34 HE 1.26
35 HE 1.33
36 HE 1.32
37 HE 2.5
38 HE 1.27; 2.5; EHD 29; discussed in J M Wallace-Hadrill, *Early Germanic kingship in England and on the Continent* ch 2
39 HE 1.27 cf Acts 4.32
40 HE 1.33 and 1.29
41 HE 2.6; cf Levison op cit p34-5
42 HE 1.27-8
43 HE 1.29 and 2.4
44 HE 1.32
45 HE 2.3
46 HE 1.30
47 APW p161
48 HE 1.27 response 7
49 HE 2.2
50 HE 2.4
51 APW p155f
52 see R. Meens, *A background to Augustine's mission to Anglo-Saxon England* p5f
53 HE 2.5-6

54 HE 2.7-8
55 HE 2.4
56 EHD 2; cf HE 2.9
57 HE 2.12; cf Plummer's note to 2.93; cf VG p99-100
58 HE 2.15
59 HE 2.9
60 HE 2.10; discussion of difficulties of chronology here discussed by Plummer and Wallace-Hadrill in their commentaries (with articles cited in the latter).
61 HE 2.11
62 VG p97 and 101; cf HE 2.13
63 HE 2.14
64 HE 2.17 and 18
65 HE 2.19; see entry in ODP for Honorius
66 HE 2.15 and 3.18
67 HE 3.19
68 HE 3.18
69 HE 2.16
70 HE 2.10
71 ibid
72 HE 4.23
73 VG p 101-5

VI. AIDAN AND CUTHBERT – pages 93-112

1 HE 3.1-2; cf VC1.1
2 HE 3.5
3 HE 3.17
4 HE 3.3
5 HE 3.5
6 HE 3.6
7 HE 3.14
8 HE 3.15-17
9 HE 3.6; cf VC 1.1
10 see C. Stancliffe & E. Cambridge ed, *Oswald: Northumbrian king to European saint*
11 see P. Wormald, 'Bede, "Beowulf", and the conversion of the Anglo-Saxon aristocracy', in R. T. Farrell, ed *Bede and Anglo-Saxon England.*
12 HE 3.3
13 HE 3.7
14 HE 4.14
15 HE 3.12
16 HE 3.9-10
17 HE 3.13
18 HE 4.14
19 HE 3.11
20 HE 3.13; cf discussion in Plummer in HE ii p159-60
21 HE 3.14
22 HE 3.18
23 HE 4.11
24 HE 5.7; cf discussion in Levison, op cit p36f
25 HE 3.17
26 HE 4.13
27 HE 5.18; cf APW ep 6 and notes p6-7
28 see D. J. Dales, *Dunstan: saint and statesman*, p 10-11

29 HE 3.19
30 HE 3.21
31 HE 3.22
32 HE 3.23
33 HE 3.28
34 HE 3.30
35 HE 4.3
36 see Eddius, *Life of Wilfrid* ch 14 & 15 (hereafter VW)
37 HE 4.3
38 HE 3.25-6; cf VW 10
39 HE 3.26
40 HE 4.4
41 cf APW p154-5 and 160-3
42 HE 3.27
43 cf Colgrave's note in HE p225; ie HE 3.4, 27; 4.3, 26; 4.9, 10, 22, 24
44 HE 3.27
45 HE 4.26
46 cf Aethelwulf, *De Abbatibus* ed Campbell, p12
47 HE 5.9-10
48 HE 3.4
49 HE 5.22
50 ibid; nb in HE 5.24 he is referred to by Bede as *saint* Egbert s.a. 729
51 HE 3.8
52 cf M. Deanesly, 'The pre-conquest church in England' p 202f
53 HE 4.6
54 HE 4.7-9
55 HE 4.10
56 cf APW p59f
57 ibid p72
58 ibid p129 & 131
59 ibid p132
60 HE 4.19; cf VW 22; there are other early traditions in E. O. Blake, ed *Liber Eliensis*
61 HE 4.20
62 HE 4.23
63 HE 4.25
64 HE 4.24
65 for what follows see Bonner, ed *St Cuthbert, his cult and his community* ; the texts are edited by Colgrave in *Two Lives of St Cuthbert*, referred to as VCA and VCP
66 see M. Lapidge 'Bede's Metrical 'Vita S Cuthberti' in *St Cuthbert, cult and community* op cit p77f
67 HE preface and 4.27f
68 VCP 8
69 HE 4.28
70 see B. Ward, 'The spirituality of St Cuthbert' in *St Cuthbert, his cult and his community*, op cit p 65
71 VCP 36 and 37
72 VCA 4.9; cf VCP 28

VII. THEODORE AND WILFRID – pages 113-129

1 HE 3.14
2 HE 3.20
3 HE 3.29

4 see Bede's *Historia Abbatum* ed D. H. Farmer, *Age of Bede* (hereafter Hab) cited by chapter: here ch 3

5 APW p 5-10

6 see H. Mayr-Harting, *The coming of Christianity to Anglo-Saxon England* p192f; also M. Winterbottom, Aldhelm's prose style and its origins p39-76

7 APW ep 6

8 HE 4.2; cf APW ep 1

9 APW ep 5

10 APW ep ad Arcicium p 42

11 APW ep 5

12 HE 5.18

13 APW ep 9 & 10

14 APW ep 4 p160

15 HE 3.28

16 WMDA p6f; cf H. P. R. Finberg, 'Sherborne, Glastonbury, and the expansion of Wessex', in *Lucerna* p 95f

17 EHD 32

18 HE 5.7; cf J. M. Wallace-Hadrill, *Early Germanic Kingship in England and on the Continent* p90

19 HE 4.1; cf Hab 3

20 HE 4.18

21 cf VW 53; also H&S 3 140-1

22 The most recent study of the several aspects of Theodore's primacy is to be found in M. Lapidge, ed *Archbishop Theodore*

23 cf H&S 3 173f

24 HE 5.24

25 HE 4.2

26 see J. Stevenson, *The 'Laterculus Malalianus' and the school of Archbishop Theodore*

27 see B. Bischoff & M. Lapidge, ed *Biblical commentaries from the Canterbury school of Theodore and Hadrian*

28 cf Mayr-Harting op cit p204f;

29 H&S 3 173f; cf Levison op cit p98f

30 H&S 3 413f

31 HE 4.5

32 cf Stenton, *Anglo-Saxon England* p132f

33 HE 4.2

34 HE 4.3

35 HE 4.5

36 HE 4.12

37 ibid

38 HE 4.23, 5.28

39 HE 4.6, 28

40 VW 25

41 VW 29

42 HE 5.19 and passim: cf Plummer's note HE ii p315f

43 HE 5.20

44 cf Mayr-Harting op cit ch9

45 VW 2

46 VW 3

47 Hab 1-2

48 VW 5

49 VW 4 & 6 (nb there is some confusion over the identity of Dalfinus, his patron)

50 VW 12

51 VW 14
52 HE 4.12
53 VW 10, 16
54 VW 24
55 VW 43
56 VW 21
57 VW 24
58 HE 4.19
59 cf Mayr-Harting op cit p129f
60 APW ep 12, p168
61 VW 47
62 VW 13
63 VW 41; cf HE 4.13
64 HE 4.14
65 HE 4.15-16; cf VW 42
66 HE 5.7
67 HE 5.9
68 HE 5.10-1
69 HE 3.13
70 HE 4.23
71 Felix's *Life of Guthlac* ed Colgrave ch 17
72 see Colgrave's introduction to this text op cit
73 op cit ch 39
74 ibid ch 41
75 ibid ch 46
76 ibid ch 50

PART 3: VIII. BEDE – pages 131-144

 1 Hab 4-5; cf *Life of Ceolfrith,* anon:=EHD 155 (Whitelock) (hereafter VCF) ch 7
 2 ibid 6
 3 HE 4.18
 4 VCF 3-4
 5 VCF 12-13
 6 VCF 14; cf Hab 9
 7 Hab 15
 8 HE 5.21
 9 Hab 20
10 VCF 39
11 Hab 22
12 VCF 34
13 HE 5.24
14 see Bede's *Commentary on the Acts* tr. L. T. Martin
15 ibid p58
16 ibid p91
17 ibid p143
18 ibid p189
19 see Bede's *De Templo* tr. S Connolly (hereafter DT)
20 This was in 731: see HE p573
21 DT p1
22 DT p3
23 DT p28
24 DT p34

25 DT p52
26 DT p68
27 DT p80
28 DT p84
29 Bede's letter to Archbishop Egbert is in EHD 170 (Whitelock)
30 see E. O. Carragain, *The city of Rome and the world of Bede*
31 DT p91-2
32 DT p98
33 DT p112
34 DT p105-6
35 DT p116
36 see Cuthbert's letter on the death of Bede: HE p579f
37 EHD 170
38 H&S 3.412-3; cited by Mayr-Harting op cit p260
39 part of this may be found in *Alcuin of York* ed S. Allott
40 see P. Hunter Blair, 'Bede to Alcuin' in *Famulus Christi* ed G Bonner p254-5
41 see D. Whitelock, *After Bede*
42 A selection of these letters may be consulted in EHD 179, 185, 188

IX. WILLIBRORD AND BONIFACE – pages 145-160

1 VW 26-7; cf HE 5.19
2 HE 4.22
3 HE 3.13 and 5.11
4 HE 4.9
5 cf Levison op cit p48; also p56 note 2 – he is still the best authority
6 see J. M. Wallace-Hadrill, A background to St Boniface's mission' in *Early Medieval History*; also H. Lowe, *Pirmin, Willibrord und Bonifatius: ihre bedeutung fur die Missionsgeschichte ihrer Zeit*
7 Boniface ep 47, in C H Talbot, *The Anglo-Saxon missionaries in Germany* (hereafter =T)
8 Levison op cit p65
9 see discussion in G. Bonner, ed *St Cuthbert, his Cult and his Community* p175-212
10 VCA p135 & VCP p297 where Bede calls him Willibrord Clement
11 Aethelwulf, *De Abbatibus* ed Campbell p18; cf discussion in *St Cuthbert, his Cult and his Community* op cit p188
12 T p2f
13 cf Levison op cit ch 4; also N. Brooks, *The early history of the Church of Canterbury* p 83f
14 T p11
15 Levison op cit remains the best introduction to Boniface's career
16 T ep 3 (ep=letters of Boniface by number)
17 T ep 9-10
18 cf Wallace-Hadrill art cit
19 ibid p45
20 T ep 39
21 T ep 25
22 see Levison op cit p 80-1
23 ibid 85f
24 EHD 183
25 T p147
26 Willibald's 'Life of Boniface' is in Talbot op cit p 25f
27 T ep 11 and 30

28 H&S 3.310; cf HE 5.18 and 23
29 T ep 19, 33, 35; cf H&S 3.346f
30 T ep 34; cf EHD 180
31 T ep 4
32 T ep 15, 18, 21
33 see K. Sisam, 'An Old English translation of a letter from Wynfrith to Eadburga'
34 T ep 17; cf ep 41
35 T p 214f; cf EHD 159
36 T p 222
37 T ep 3, 5, 6
38 T ep 7, 8, 9
39 T ep 12-3
40 T ep 14
41 T ep 16
42 T ep 23-4
43 T ep 27-8
44 T ep 29 and 31; cf Levison op cit appendix 10 'Venus: a man'
45 T ep 36-7
46 T ep 46-7
47 see entry for Pope Stephen in ODP
48 T ep 11 = EHD 167
49 T ep 18
50 cf T ep 25; cf EHD 177
51 T ep 30 = EHD 175
52 T ep 35
53 T p 182
54 T p195
55 T p198
56 T p200
57 see D. Whitelock, *After Bede*; cf EHD 185 and 188
58 EHD 3 p 268; cf Levison op cit p108f
59 EHD 160
60 T p 228f; cf Levison op cit p109
61 ibid p110; cf H&S 3.433
62 see Allott, *Alcuin of York* p72f
63 ibid p74
64, see D. J. Dales *Dunstan: saint and statesman*, p120f

BIBLIOGRAPHY

Printed primary sources

The most convenient translation has been cited which will indicate editions of original texts

Adomnan, *Cain Adomnain*, tr. K. Meyer, Oxford, 1905
Adomnan, *Life of Columba*, ed A. O. Anderson & M. O. Anderson, 2nd ed, Oxford, 1991; also tr. R. Sharpe, London, 1995
Aethelwulf, *De Abbatibus*, ed A. Campbell, Oxford, 1962
Alcuin of York, ed S. Allott, York, 1974
Alcuin, *Bishops, Kings and saints of York*, ed P. Godman, Oxford 1983
Aldhelm, *Prose Works*, ed M. Lapidge & M. Herren, Ipswich, 1979
Anglo-Saxon Chronicle, ed C. Plummer & J. Earle, Oxford, 1952
Bede, *Venerabilis Baedae Opera Historica*, ed C. Plummer, (2 vols), Oxford, 1896
Bede, *Historia Ecclesiastica*, ed B. Colgrave & R. A. B. Mynors, Oxford, 1969
Bede, *Two lives of St Cuthbert*, ed B. Colgrave, Cambridge, 1940
Bede, *Greater Chronicle* ed J. McClure & R Collins, Oxford, 1994
Bede, *Lives of the Abbots* ed D. H. Farmer, (in *Age of Bede*) London 1983
Bede, Letter to Egbert in *English Historical Documents*, vol. 1, ed D. Whitelock, London, 1979
Bede, *Commentary on Acts*, tr. L. T. Martin, Michigan 1989
Bede, *On the Tabernacle*, tr. A. G. Holder, Liverpool, 1994
Bede, *On the Temple*, tr. S. Connolly, Liverpool, 1995
Benedict, *Rule of St Benedict*, tr. B. Bolton, London, 1969
Caesarius of Arles, *Life, Testament & Letters*, tr. W. E. Klingshirn, Liverpool, 1994
Cassian, *Institutes & Conferences*, tr. E. Gibson, Michigan, 1973
Ceolfrith, Anonymous life of in *EHD* 155
Columbanus, *Opera* ed G. S. M. Walker, Dublin 1957
Councils & Ecclesiastical documents relating to Great Britain & Ireland, ed A. W. Haddan & W. Stubbs, Oxford, reprint 1964
Cuthbert, Two Lives of ed B. Colgrave, Cambridge 1985
De antiquitate Glastonie ecclesie by William of Malmesbury ed J. Scott, Ipswich 1981
Memorials of St Dunstan ed W. Stubbs, Rolls series 63 London 1874
Fastidius, works of ed R. S. T. Haslehurst, London 1927
Gildas, *The ruin of Britain* tr. M. Winterbottom, Chichester 1978
Gregory the Great, *Dialogues* ed A. de Vogue, Paris 1978-80
Gregory the Great, earliest life of ed B. Colgrave, Cambridge 1985
Gregory of Tours, *History of the Franks* tr. L. Thorpe, London 1974
Guthlac, Felix's *Life* ed B. Colgrave, Cambridge 1985
Iona – the earliest poetry of a celtic monastery ed T. O. Clancy & G. Markus, Edinburgh 1995
Jonas, *Life of Columbanus* tr. D. C. Munro, Philadelphia 1895 (ed B. Krusch MGH Script Rerum Merov iv 1902 p 1-156 & vii 1920 p 822-7)
Liber Eliensis ed E. O. Blake, CS third series xcii London 1962
Liber Pontificalis (to A.D. 715) tr. R. Davis, Liverpool 1989
Lives of the desert fathers tr. N. Russell, Oxford & Kalamazoo 1981

Liber Landavensis: the book of Llan Dav ed J. G. Evans & J. Rhys, Oxford 1893 repr
  Aberystwyth 1979
Nennius tr. J. Morris, Chichester 1980
Oldest English Texts ed H. Sweet, EETS old series 83 1889
St Patrick, the life and historical writings of tr. R. P. C. Hanson, New York 1983
Paulinus of Nola – letters tr. P. G. Walsh London, 1966-7
Prosper of Aquitaine, *Chronicon* ed T. Mommsen, Chronica minora MGH AA ix & xi
  (2 vols) Berlin 1891 & 1894
Prudentius, *opera* tr. M. Lavaronne, (3 vols) Paris 1943-8
Samson of Dol, life of tr. T. Taylor, London 1925
La vie de St Samson ed R. Fawtier, Paris 1912
Sulpicius Severus, *opera* tr. A. Roberts, Michigan 1973 (contains *Life of St Martin* etc)
The Anglo-Saxon missionaries in Germany (contains lives of Willibrord, Boniface,
  Sturm et al., and select letters of Boniface) tr. C. H. Talbot, London 1954
Victricius of Rouen – de laude sanctorum, PL 20 p 443f
Vitae sanctorum hiberniae ed C. Plummer, Oxford 1910
Irish Litanies ed C. Plummer, London 1925
Wilfrid, *Life* by Eddius Stephanus ed B. Colgrave, Cambridge 1985

SECONDARY SOURCES

Anderson, A. O., Ninian and the southern Picts *Scottish historical review* 27 1948 25-
  47
Anderson, M. O., *Kings & Kingship in early Scotland*, Edinburgh, 1980
Backhouse, J., *The Lindisfarne Gospels*, London, 1981
Barley, M. W. & Hanson R. P. C. ed, *Christianity in Britain: 300-700*, Leicester, 1968
Battiscombe, C. F., *The relics of St Cuthbert*, Oxford, 1956
Berardino, A. di ed, *Encyclopedia of the Early Church*, Cambridge 1991
Berardino, A. di ed, *Patrology iv: the golden age of Latin patristic literature*, Westminster,
  Maryland, 1986
Bethell, D. L. T., The originality of the early Irish church *Journal of the Royal Society of
  antiquaries in Ireland* 110 1981 36-49
Bieler, L., The Christianization of the insular celts during the sub-Roman period, and its
  repercussions on the continent *Celtica* 8 1968 112-25
Bieler, L., The mission of Palladius *Traditio* 6 1948 1-32
Bieler, L., *The Irish penitentials*, Dublin, 1975
Bieler, L., *The life & legends of St Patrick*, Dublin, 1949
Bieler, L., St Patrick & the British church in *Christianity in Britain: 300-700* ed Barley
  & Hanson 1968 123-130
Binchy, D. A., *Celtic and Anglo-Saxon kingship* Oxford 1970
Binchy, D. A., St Patrick & his biographers *Studia Hibernica* 2 1962 7-173
Bischoff, B. & Lapidge, M. ed, *Biblical commentaries from the Canterbury school of
  Theodore & Hadrian*, Cambridge, 1994
Blair, J. & Sharpe, R. ed, *Pastoral Care before the parish*, Leicester. 1992
Bonner, G., *St Bede in the tradition of western apocalyptic commentary* Jarrow 1966
Bonner, G. ed, *Famulus Christi: essays for the thirteenth centenary of the birth of Bede*,
  London, 1976
Bonner, G. et al ed, *St Cuthbert: his cult and his community*, Ipswich, 1989
Bowen, E. G., The travels of St Samson of Dol *Aberystwyth studies* 13 1934
Bowen, E. G., *The settlements of the Celtic saints in Wales*, Cardiff, 1956
Bowen, E.G., *Saints, seaways and settlements in Celtic lands*, Cardiff. 1969
Bright, W., *Chapters of early English church history*, Oxford, 1897,

Brooks, N., *The early history of the church of Canterbury*, Leicester, 1984

Brown, P. R. L., Sorcery, demons & the rise of Christianity from late antiquity into the middle ages *Religion & Society* 1972 119f

Brown, P. R. L., The rise & function of the holy man in late antiquity *Journal of Roman studies* 61 1971 80-101

Brown, P. R. L., Pelagius & his supporters: aims & environment *Religion & Society* 1972 183f

Brown, P. R. L., *Religion & society in the age of St Augustine*, London, 1972

Brown, P. R. L., *The cult of the saint: its rise & function in Latin Christianity*, Chicago & London, 1981

Bullough, D. A., Columba, Adomnan & the achievement of Iona *Scottish historical review* 43 1963/4 111-30 & 44 1964/5 17-33

Burkitt, F. C., St Samson of Dol *JTS* 27 1925-6 42-57

Burkitt, F. C., The Bible of Gildas *Revue Benedictine* 46 1934 206-15

Campbell, J., ed, *The Anglo-Saxons*, London, 1982

Campbell, J., *Essays in Anglo-Saxon history*, London, 1986

Campenhausen, H. von, *Ecclesiastical authority & spiritual power in the church of the first three centuries*, London, 1969

Carragain, E. O., *The city of Rome and the world of Bede* Jarrow 1994

Chadwick, H., Gregory the great and the mission to the Anglo-Saxons *Augustinianum* XXXIII (Rome, 1991) 199-212

Chadwick, H., *Priscillian of Avila*, Oxford, 1976

Chadwick, N. K., St Ninian: a preliminary study of the sources *Transactions of the Dumfriesshire & Galloway Natural History & Antiquarian society* 27 1950

Chadwick, N. K. ed, *Studies in the early British church*, Cambridge, 1958

Chadwick, N. K., *Poetry and letters in early Christian Gaul*, Cambridge, 1954

Chadwick, N. K., *The age of the saints in the early Celtic church*, Oxford, 1961

Chadwick, O., Gildas & the monastic order *JTS* 5 1954 78-80

Chadwick, O., *Cassian*, 2nd ed, Cambridge, 1968

Chadwick, O., *Western Asceticism*, London, 1958

Charles-Edwards, T. M., The social background to Irish 'peregrinatio' *Celtica* 11 1976 43-59

Chitty, D., *The desert a city*, London & Oxford, 1977

Clarke, H. B. & Brennan M. ed, *Columbanus & Merovingian monasticism*, Oxford, 1981

Cleary, A. S. E., *The ending of Roman Britain*, London, 1989

Colgrave, B., The earliest saints lives written in England *Proceedings of the British Academy* 44 1958, 35-60

Cramp, R., *Whithorn and the Northumbrian expansion westwards* Whithorn 1995

Cubitt, C., *Anglo-Saxon Church Councils c.650-850*, Leicester, 1995

Cross, F. L., *Oxford Dictionary of the Christian church*, Oxford, 1974

Dales, D. J., *Dunstan: saint and statesman*, Cambridge, 1988

Dales, D. J., *Living through dying*, Cambridge, 1994

Davies, O., *Celtic Christianity in early medieval Wales*, Cardiff, 1996

Davies, W. The Celtic church *Journal of religious history* 8 1974/5 406-11

Davies, W., *An early Welsh microcosm – studies in the Llandaff charters*, London, 1978

Davies, W., *Patterns of power in early Wales*, Oxford, 1990

Davies, W., *Wales in the early middle ages*, Leicester, 1982

Davis, R. H. C. ed, *The writing of history in the middle ages*, Oxford, 1981

Deanesly, M. The Canterbury edition of the answers of pope Gregory to St Augustine *Journal of ecclesiastical history* 10 1959 1-49

Deanesly, M. Early English and Gallic minsters *TRHS* 23 1941 25-70

Deanesly, M. *The pre-conquest church in England* London, 1963

Delehaye, H. *The legends of the saints*, London, 1962

Delehaye, H. St Martin et Sulpice Severe *Analecta Bollandiana* 38 1920 5-136

Doble, G. H., *Lives of the Welsh saints* (ed D. Simon Evans) Cardiff 1971

Doble, G. H., *The saints of Cornwall*, ed D. Attwater, Truro, 1962-70

Duckett, E. S., *The wandering saints*, London, 1959

Dumville, D. & M. Lapidge eds, *Gildas – new approaches*, Ipswich, 1984

Dumville, D. N., Gildas and Uinniau in *Gildas: new approaches* 1984 207f

Dumville, D. N., *Some British aspects of the earliest Irish Christianity in Irland und Europa* ed P. Chathain & M. Richter, Stuttgart 1984 16-24

Duncan, A. A. M., Bede, Iona & the Picts in *The writing of history in the middle ages* ed R. H. C. Davis & J. M. Wallace-Hadrill, Oxford 1981 1f

Enright, M. J., Iona, Tara and Soissons: The origin of the royal anointing ritual *Arbeiten fur Fruhmittelalterforschung* 17 Berlin 1985

Enright, M. J., Royal succession & abbatial prerogative in Adomnan's 'Vita Columbani' *Peritiae* 4 1985 83-103

Evans, R. F., Pelagius, Fastidius and the pseudo-Augustine 'de vita christiana', *JTS* 13 1962 72-98

Farmer, D. H. ed, *Benedict's disciples*, Leicester, 1980

Farmer, D. H., *Oxford dictionary of saints*, Oxford, 1978

Finberg, H. P. R., Sherborne, Glastonbury and the expansion of Wessex in *Lucerna* 1964 95f

Finberg, H. P. R., *Lucerna*, London, 1964

Finberg, H. P. R., *The formation of England*, London, 1976

Fletcher, E., *Benedict Biscop* Jarrow 1981

Fletcher, E., The influence of Merovingian Gaul on Northumbria in the seventh century *Medieval archaeology* 19 1980 69-86

Foot, S., The making of 'Angelcynn': English identity before the Norman conquest *TRHS*, sixth series, vol. VI, 1996

Frend, W. H. C., Ecclesia Britannica: prelude or dead end? *Journal of ecclesiastical history* 30 1979 129-44

Frend, W. H. C., Religion in Roman Britain in the fourth century *Journal of the British archaeological Association* 18 1955 1-18

Gibbs, M., The decrees of Agatho and the Gregorian plan for York *Speculum* 48 1973 213-46

Gilson, E., *History of Christian philosophy in the middle ages*, London, 1955

Gougaud, L., *Christianity in celtic lands*, London, 1932

Grosjean, P., Gloria postuma S Martini Turonensis apud Scottos et Britannos *Analecta Bollandiana* 55 1937 300-348

Hamilton Thompson, A., ed, *Bede: his life, times and writings*, Oxford, 1935

Hanson, R. P. C., The date of St Patrick *Bulletin of the John Rylands Library* Manchester 61 1978

Hanson, R. P. C., *St Patrick: his origins and career*, Oxford, 1968

Herbert, M., Iona, *Kells and Derry: the history & hagiography of the monastic familia of Columba*, Oxford, 1988

Holdsworth, C., An airier aristocracy *TRHS*, sixth series, vol. VI, 1996

Horden, J. N. P. H., Disease, dragons and saints: the management of epidemics in the dark ages in *Epidemics and Ideas: essays on the historical perception of pestilence* ed T. Ranger & P. Slack Cambridge 1992

Hughes, K., *Early Christianity in Pictland* Jarrow 1970

Hughes, K., *Celtic Britain in the early middle ages: studies in Scottish & Welsh sources*, Ipswich, 1980

Hughes, K., *Early Christian Ireland: an introduction to the sources*, London 1972

Hughes, K., *The church in early Irish society*, London, 1966

Hunter Blair P., From Bede to Alcuin in *Famulus Christi* ed G Bonner 1976 239f

Hunter Blair, P., *The world of Bede*, London, 1970

Jenkins, F., Preliminary report on the excavations at the church of St Pancras in Canterbury *Canterbury archaeology* 1975/6 4-5

Jenkins, F., St Martin's church at Canterbury: a survey of the earliest structural features *Medieval archaeology* 9 1965 11-5

Kelly, J. N. D., *Jerome: his life, writings & controversies*, London, 1975

Kelly, J. N. D., *Oxford dictionary of popes*, Oxford, 1986

Kenney, J., *Sources for the early history of Ireland*, ed L. Bieler, New York, 1966

Keynes, S. D., *The councils of Clovesho* Leicester 1994

Kirby, D. P., Bede and the Pictish church *Innes review* 24 1973 6-25

Kirby, D. P., Bede's native sources for the 'Historia ecclesiastica' *Bulletin of the John Rylands Library* Manchester 48 1966 341-71

Kirby, D. P., *Bede's 'Historia ecclesiastica' in its contemporary setting* Jarrow 1992

Klingshirn, W., Charity and power: Caesarius of Arles and the ransoming of captives in sub-Roman Gaul *Journal of Roman studies* 75 1985 183-203

Klingshirn, W. E., *Caesarius of Arles: the making of a Christian community in late antique Gaul*, Cambridge, 1993

Laistner, M. L. W., *Thought & letters in western Europe* A.D 500-900, London, 1957

Lapidge, M, *Archbishop Theodore*, Cambridge, 1995

Lapidge, M., Gildas' education and the Latin culture of sub-Roman Britain in *Gildas: new approaches* ed Dumville 1984 27f

Lapidge, M., The school of Theodore & Hadrian *ASE* 15 1986

Leclerq, J. ed, *A history of Christian spirituality*, London, 1968

Leonardi, C., Il venerabile Beda e la cultura del sec. VIII *Settimane di studio del centro italiano di studi sull'alto medioevo* Spoleto 20 1973 603f

Levison, W., St Alban and St Albans *Antiquity* 15 1941

Levison, W., *Relations between England & the continent in the eighth century*, Oxford, 1946

Lienhard, J. T., Paulinus of Nola & early western monasticism *Theophaneia* 28 Cologne/Bonn 1977

Lowe, H., Pirmin, Willibrord und Bonifatius – ihre Bedeutung fur die Missionsgeschichte ihrere Zeit *Settimane di studio del centro italiano di studi sull'alto medioevo* Spoleto 14 1967 217f

MacQueen, J., *St Nynia*, Edinburgh, 1990

Macdonald, A. D. S., Aspects of the monastery and monastic life in Adomnan's 'Life of Columba' *Peritia* 3 1984 271-302

Mackey, J. P., ed, *An introduction to Celtic Christianity*, Edinburgh, 1989

Malone, E. E., The monk and the martyr *Studia anselmiana* 38 1956

Markus, R., *Bede and the tradition of ecclesiastical hagiography* Jarrow 1975

Markus, R., Gregory the great's Europe *Journal of ecclesiastical history* 36 1981 21f

Markus, R., Gregory the great and a papal missionary strategy *Studies in church history* 6 1970 29-38

Markus, R., The legacy of Pelagius: orthodoxy, heresy, and conciliation in *The making of orthodoxy* ed R. Williams Cambridge 1989 214-34

Markus, R., *From Augustine to Gregory the great*, London 1983

Mayr-Harting, H., *The venerable Bede, the Rule of St Benedict and social class* Jarrow 1976

Mayr-Harting, H., *The coming of Christianity to Anglo-Saxon England* (3rd ed), London, 1991

McCready, W. D., *Miracles and the venerable Bede*, Toronto, 1994

McKitterick, R., *The Frankish kingdoms under the Carolingians*, London, 1983

McNiell, J. T., The Celtic penitentials *Revue Celtique* 39/40 1922/3

Meens, R. A background to St Augustine's mission to Anglo-Saxon England *ASE* 23 Cambridge 1994 5f

Meyvaert, P. *Bede and Gregory the great* Jarrow 1964

Miller, M. Bede's use of Gildas *EHR* 90 1975 241-61

Mohrman, C., *The Latin of St Patrick*, Dublin, 1961

Moisl, H., The Bernician royal dynasty & the Irish in the seventh century *Peritia* 2 1983 103-26

Momigliano, A., ed, *The conflict between paganism & Christianity in the fourth century*, Oxford, 1963

Moule, C. F. D., ed, *Miracles: Cambridge studies in their philosophy & history*, London, 1965

Myres, J. N. L., Pelagius & the end of Roman rule Britain *Journal of Roman studies* 50 1960 21-36

Myres, J. N. L., *The English settlements*, Oxford, 1986

Nash-Williams, V. E., *The early Christian monuments of Wales*, Cardiff, 1950

Netzer, N., Willibrord's scriptorium at Echternach and its relationship to Ireland & Lindisfarne in *St Cuthbert, cult & Community* ed G. Bonner 1989 203f

Oakley, T. P., *English penitential discipline and Anglo-Saxon law*, New York, 1923

Oulton, J. E. L., *The credal statements of St Patrick*, London, 1940

Padberg, L. von, *Mission und christianisierung: formen und folgen bei Angelsachsen und franken in 7. und 8. jahrhundert*, Stuttgart 1995

Painter, K. S., *The Mildenhall treasure and the Water Newton early Christian silver* London 1977

Paor, L. de, *St Patrick's world: the Christian culture of Ireland's apostolic age*, Dublin, 1993

Picard, J. M., Bede, Adomnan and the writing of history *Peritia* 2 1983/4 50-70

Picard, J. M., The purpose of Adomnan's 'Vita Columbi' *Peritia* 1 1982 160-77

Poole, R. L., St Wilfrid and the see of Ripon *EHR* 34 1919

Radford, C. A. R., Christian origins in Britain *Medieval Archaeology* 15 1971 1-12

Redknap, M., *The Christian Celts: treasures of late Celtic Wales*, Cardiff, 1991

Rousseau, P., The spiritual authority of the 'monk-bishop' *JTS* 22 1971 380f

Rousseau, P., *Ascetics, authority & the church in the age of Jerome & Cassian*, Oxford, 1978

Salway, P., *Roman Britain*, Oxford, 1981

Sawyer, P. H. & Wood, I. N. ed, *Early medieval kingship*, Leeds, 1977

Sawyer, P. H., *Anglo-Saxon charters: an annotated list & bibliography*, London, 1968

Sharpe, R., Gildas as a father of the church in *Gildas: new approaches* ed D. Dumville 1984 191f

Sharpe, R., St Mauchteus, discipulus Patricii in *Britain 400-600: language & history* ed A. Bammesberger & A. Wollman Heidelberg 1990 85-93

Sims-Williams, P., Continental influence at Bath monastery in the seventh century *ASE* 4 1975 1-10

Sisam, K., An old English translation of a letter from Wynfrith to Eadburga *Modern Language review* 18 1923 253-72

Stancliffe, C. E. & Cambridge, E. ed, *Oswald: Northumbrian king to European saint*, Stamford, 1995

Stancliffe, C. E., *St Martin and his hagiographer*, Oxford, 1983

Stenton, F. M., *Anglo-Saxon England*, Oxford, 1971

Stevens, C. E., Gildas sapiens *EHR* 56 1941 353-373

Stevenson, J., *The 'Laterculus Malalianus' and the school of archbishop Theodore*, Cambridge, 1995

Thomas, C., *Bede, archaeology and the cult of relics* Jarrow 1973

Thomas, C., Hermits on islands or priests in a landscape *Cornish studies* 6 1979 28-44

Thomas, C., *Whithorn's Christian beginnings* Whithorn 1992

Thomas, C., *Celtic Britain*, London, 1986

Thomas, C., *Christianity in Roman Britain to A.D. 500*, London, 1981

Thomas, C., *The early Christian archaeology of north Britain*, Oxford, 1971

Thompson, E. A., Christianity and the northern barbarians *Nottingham medieval studies* 1 1957 3f

Thompson, E. A., St Patrick and Coroticus *JTS* 31 1980 12-27

Thompson, E. A., The origins of Christianity in Scotland *Scottish historical review* 37 1958 17-22

Thompson, E. A., *St Germanus of Auxerre & the end of Roman Britain*, Ipswich, 1984

Thompson, E. A., *Who was St Patrick?* Ipswich, 1985

Tolkien, J. R. R., Beowulf: the monsters and the critics *Proceedings of the British academy* London 22 1958

Wade-Evans, A. W. *Welsh Christian origins*, Oxford, 1934

Walker, G. S. M., St Columbanus: monk or missionary? *Studies in church history* ed G Cuming 6 1970 39-44

Wallace-Hadrill, J. M. A background to St Boniface's mission in *Early Medieval History* Oxford 1975

Wallace-Hadrill, J. M. Bede's Europe in *Early Medieval History* Oxford 1975

Wallace-Hadrill, J. M. Gregory of Tours and Bede: their views on the personal qualities of kings in *Early Medieval History* Oxford 1975

Wallace-Hadrill, J. M. Rome and the early English church: some questions of transmission in *Early Medieval History* Oxford 1975

Wallace-Hadrill, J. M., *Bede's 'Historia ecclesiastica': an historical commentary*, Oxford, 1988

Wallace-Hadrill, J. M., *Early Germanic Kingship in England & the Continent*, Oxford, 1971

Ward, B., *Bede and the psalter* Jarrow 1991

Ward, B., The spirituality of St Cuthbert in *St Cuthbert, cult & community* ed G Bonner 1989 65f

Ward, B., Theodore of Tarsus: a Greek archbishop of Canterbury *Signs & wonders*, London 1992 41-53

Ward, B., *Miracles and the medieval mind*, London, 1982

Ward, B., *The venerable Bede*, London, 1990

Warren, F. E., *The liturgy & ritual of the celtic church*, Oxford, 1881, (repr ed J Stevenson, Ipswich, 1987)

Webster, L. & Backhouse, J. ed, *The making of England: Anglo-Saxon art & culture 600-900*, London, 1991

Whitelock, D., *After Bede* Jarrow 1960

Whitelock, D., Anglo-Saxon poetry and the historian *TRHS* 31 1949 75f

Whitelock, D., *The audience of Beowulf*, Oxford, 1951

Whitelock, D. ed, *Ireland in early medieval Europe*, Cambridge, 1982

Wilson, D. M. ed, *The archaeology of Anglo-Saxon England*, Cambridge, 1981

Wilson, P. A., Romano-British and Welsh Christianity: continuity or discontinuity? *Welsh historical review* 3 1966 5-21 & 103-20

Wilson, P. A., St Ninian & Candida Casa: literary evidence from Ireland *Transactions of the Dumfriesshire & Galloway Natural history and antiquarian society* 41 1964 156-85

Wilson, P. A., St Patrick and Irish Christian origins *Studia Celtica* 14/15 1979/80 344-80

Winterbottom, M. Aldhelm's prose style and its origins *ASE* 6 1977 39-76

Winterbottom, M. Columbanus and Gildas *Vigiliae Christianae* 30 1976 310-7

Wood, I. N., Gregory of Tours and Clovis *Revue belge de philologie et d'histoire* 63 1985 249-272

Wood, I. N., *The Merovingian North Sea*, Alingsas, 1983

Wood, I. N., The mission of St Augustine to the English' *Speculum* 69 1994 1f

Wood, I. N., *The most holy abbot Ceolfrid* Jarrow 1995

Wormald, P., *Bede and the conversion of England: the charter evidence*, Jarrow, 1984

Wormald, P., Bede, the bretwaldas and the origins of the 'gens anglorum' Ideal and reality in *Frankish and Anglo-Saxon society* ed P. Wormald et al Oxford 1983 99-129

Wormald, P., Bede, 'Beowulf' and the conversion of the Anglo-Saxon aristocracy *Bede and Anglo-Saxon England* ed R. T. Farrell British Archaeological report 46 London 1978 32-95

Yorke, B., *Wessex in the early middle ages*, Leicester, 1995

Yorke, B., Sisters under the skin? Anglo-Saxon nuns and nunneries in Southern England, *Reading medieval studies* 15, 1989 95f

INDEX